SPEAK INTO THE MIRROR

A Story of Linguistic Anthropology

John Doe

UNIVERSITY
PRESS OF
AMERICA

Library of Congress Cataloging-in-Publication Data

Doe, John.
Speak into the mirror.

Bibliography: p.
Includes index.
1. Anthropological linguistics. 2. Structural
linguistics. 3. Linguistics—History. I. Title.
P35.D6   1988   408.9   88–236
ISBN 0–8191–6943–9 (alk. paper)
ISBN 0–1891–6944–7 (pbk. : alk. paper)

All University Press of America books are produced on acid-free
paper which exceeds the minimum standards set by the National
Historical Publications and Records Commission.

SPEAK INTO THE MIRROR:
A STORY OF LINGUISTIC ANTHROPOLOGY

CONTENTS

Preface

"Mirror, mirror on the wall..." Lines from the classic story of the wicked queen who speaks into her mirror. She peers searchingly into the glass and queries it. We are told that she regularly asks questions about herself: Is she still the fairest in all the land? If not she, then who?

The mirror responds with mechanical consistency and unfailing accuracy. It tells the truth. And so it goes in the magical world of fantasy and fairytale.

Merely a fantasy? Just a story? Perhaps. But this queen-and-mirror story spins out a thread which also runs through this book: humans can discover who they are by reflecting on the words they speak.

Like the queen, humans have a penchant for asking questions about themselves. Modern humans, in particular, are obsesssed with such questions. Every bit as narcissistic as the queen, we moderns repeatedly ask questions about ourselves: Who are we? How are we different from other animals? What is a human mind? What does having a mind entail?

We have no magical mirror to speak into. But we can avail ourselves of a reflection which responds to our questions as truthfully as the queen's mirror and with a good bit more detail. That reflection is our own reflective consideration of the words we speak and of the manner in which we speak them.

The point of departure in this book is that studies of language and speech are like the queen's mirror. If done skillfully and patiently, they can tell us who we are. One purpose of this book is to provide you, the reader, with the tools for accomplishing the skillful and patient reflection on the words you speak.

The queen, I imagine, posed questions to her magical mirror in the privacy of her boudoir and in dead of night when no one and no thing would distract her. Unfortunately, students of language and speech have no similar privilege. Linguistic reflections on language and speech are always subject to the forces of social life. Linguistic discourses bubble up in the huge cauldron of Western scholarship, and they respond to the economic and political fires that keep that cauldron boiling. This book aims to confront these political and economic entanglements of linguistic scholarship straight on.

The boiling cauldron of Western scholarship produces a steamy brew of competing viewpoints. Being part of this brew, language study is predictably complex. As a field of study, it is awash with struggling perspectives. The major task facing anyone who wants to understand linguistic anthropology is to appreciate these struggling perspectives by understanding the logic and reasoning on which they are based. This book plays up the disagreements in the field rather than hides them. And it aims to comprehend those disagreements by discovering the goals and objectives of different perspectives and by recognizing the political forces behind those goals and objectives.

The discussions here of the goals and practices of linguists and anthropologists will proceed at a general level. Complicating details are avoided if they would generate more clouds than light. At times, the distinguishing characteristics of different traditions of writings about language and communication are exaggerated so as to make those traditions stand out. The tripartite division of those writings into structuralist, ethnographic, and translinguistic writings is itself an idealization. However, this idealization, along with sometimes hyperbolic, sometimes simplified, aspects of this book, are warranted by the understanding which they promise of the complex whys and hows of linguistic anthropology.

I have tried to write in a style that is straightforward, free of unnecessary jargon, and picturesque; but, most importantly, I have tried to write in a way that is meant to serve as *half a conversation*. Yours must be the other half. This is not a book that aims to answer all your questions and leave you silent. It is a talk-talk where my talk is to be followed by your talk. I write with the hope that the words encourage you to take the floor and speak with those around you, if not with me. The writing is designed to provoke questions, sometimes to raise hackles, but always to elicit a response.

On the matter of my pen name, I have chosen to call myself John Doe for specific reasons. As I suggest above, linguistic anthropologists work at describing the speaking practices of humans so as to reveal answers to their self-questioning. But in addition to describing language and speech, anthropologists must shoulder the responsibility of altering their own languages and speaking practices in the light of those descriptions. Many of my own speaking and writing practices need revision, but I lack the requisite power or imagination to accomplish those revisions. But one practice I can change here and now and that is the practice of backing up scholarly discourses with a name.

The name "Mercedez Benz" has sold a lot of cars and garnered a great deal of prestige. In like fashion, the names "Franz Boas" and "Ferdinand de Saussure" have sold a lot of anthropological and linguistic ideas, and earned sizable reputations. And there is something unfortunate in that.

Cars contain hidden workings that sellers know about and that buyers want to know about. Has the odometer been turned back? Does the engine burn oil? With questions like these, buyers need to be able to trust the word of sellers. It follows that a car dealer's good and trustworthy name is a matter of top priority.

But anthropological ideas should not contain hidden workings unavailable to readers. There should be nothing between--or outside the lines--that readers cannot become aware of. In the realm of ideas, unlike the realm of cars, you should be able to see what you get.

It follows that a good and trustworthy name in the realm of ideas should have no bearing on whether ideas are accepted or rejected. In fact, to use a powerful name to sell ideas is to risk distracting readers from the ideas themselves; it risks having ideas accepted or rejected because of the name of the writer rather than because of the ideas themselves. Better not to advertise ideas with names.

Besides the risk of distracting readers from ideas, using names to sell ideas inflates the significances of the named authors. Let me explain it this way: Individuals have the right to talk for themselves. "Bill" can and should talk for Bill. But it is another thing for "Bill" to talk for John and Jane. In this latter case Bill should only be talking for the others because those others have in some way granted him the privilege of talking in their steads. In other words, a discourse about other human beings is not the right of an author, but a privilege given to an author by those for whom the author talks. Unfortunately, presenting such a discourse under one's own name obscures that privilege. It implies instead that the author by dint of his or her own effort has earned some right to speak for others. And it is implied that the awesome knowledge of such a writer-- any knowledge of another is, in a sense, awesome--is his or her personal achievement. Such an effect is unfortunate but pre- dictable given our culture with its common sense about the free- dom and dignity of individuals.

In sum, authorly names should be suppressed for reasons on two fronts: First, names should be suppressed for fear that ideas will be accepted or rejected because of the names of those who write; and, second, names should be suppressed because those who write about others ought not be celebrated for themselves (For more on names, naming, and John Doe, see pp. 207 and 236.).

I have opted to go by "John Doe" here because it seems to handle matters on both fronts. If you accept any of John Doe's proposals, you will probably do so in spite of the "John Doe." And I doubt that anyone will credit a faceless fellow named Doe with any venerable knowledge.

One final matter. I want to thank Goeff, Erik, and Fred for their careful readings of the whole of this manuscript, and I thank Pat, Ashley, and a number of students of anthropology for their readings of segments. Their comments have been invaluable. Kathleen deserves thanks for providing, in her research center, the atmosphere in which the ideas presented here were first drafted. This book is dedicated with love to Catherine, my wife. We talked through this book together, conversing long into many nights. If ever there were a one who taught me translinguistics, it was she.

Chapter One

Talking about Talk

Linguistic anthropology is an odd sort of study. It turns familiar communication into something strange. It asks questions like: How does a child learn a language? How do meanings differ from society to society? How do the uses of speech differ cross culturally?

Practical-minded folks in everyday life rarely ask such questions. They do, and probably should, take matters of communication and language for granted. After all, the answers to any of the questions above do very little to put bread on the table or wood in the stove. Neither practical nor particularly pleasing in an aesthetic sense, the inquiry into language and communication seems unrepentently and irredeemably strange. Who in their right mind would want to spend their life pursuing answers to such questions?

The only other folks that I know who ask questions about communication and languages are stand-up comics, people like George Carlin and Steven Wright. These folks spend the better part of their days searching for fractured phrases and stalking the rhetorical cul-de-sacs which elude the ears of common folks. Did you hear the one about the man who walked into a restaurant that advertized "Breakfast served anytime!". He ordered French toast in the late Renaissance. Jokes like this are evidence that the comic study of language rivals linguistic anthropology in strangeness.

For comedians, language and communication are a joke, nothing serious. But linguists and anthropologists *are* serious. Unlike comics, linguistic anthropologists reckon that their discourses on human discourses do make a difference. The major goal of this book is to explain why and how the serious study of languages and communication can make a difference.

Here in this first chapter, I will consider why it is that scholars study languages so seriously. Specifically, I will describe three viewpoints on language and speech. First will come the structuralist perspective. I will try to convey something of the excitement which structuralists feel at revealing the organization of the human mind. And in the chapters of this Part I, I will spin out a tale of how and why structuralist linguistics came to acquire the status of a gospel of language study.

It will become apparent in these discussions that I am not a disciple of the gospel of structuralism. However, I will be presenting the story as if I were. I will be trying to construct a sympathetic portrayal so as to make you feel the power and

1

attractiveness of the goals and methods of structuralists.

Successful gospels invite heresies. And in language study, Boasian ethnographic linguistics grew into a significant heretical departure from structuralism. I will introduce this ethnographic perspective here in the first chapter. Then in the chapters of Part II I will elaborate on this ethnographic approach, focussing especially on the goal of social reform which drives this search for an understanding of human practices of speaking. My aim will be to portray, in a sympathetic way, the complex feelings of these Jeremiah-like ethnographers whose descriptions of exotic talk cause us to discover the strangeness, if not the inadequacy, of our own talk.

Finally, I will present the reflexive, self-critical perspective of translinguistics. This first chapter will introduce this perspective; the chapters of Part III will present this perspective in greater detail.

The translinguistic perspective, like the ethnographic perspective introduced above, struggles towards a reform of talk and social life in the modern world. But unlike the ethnographers, and even more unlike the structuralists, translinguists recognize that their own discourses on language and talk are fraught with the very problems of modern talk with which they are struggling. No reform of modern talk is possible unless it starts with a reform of the selfsame academic and scholarly talk with which translinguists talk about talk. My aim in Part II will be to convey something of the translinguist's enthusiastic talk about the dangers of enthusiastic talk--sounds more and more like French toast in the late Renaissance, doesn't it?

We will examine three distinct perspectives on language and communication, all of which have been claimed to be anthropological. One lesson to be learned from this study is that the anthropological study of language and communication is a house divided. There is dissension in the ranks. Debates break out, not only over what linguistic phenomena to study, but also over why one should study them. The anthropological study of languages and of communication is full of disagreement and debate over fundamental issues.

As your reading of this work advances into Parts II and III, you will begin to appreciate the depth of the rifts in the area of anthropological study. At that point you will also recognize that my own sympathies lie with the ethnographers and translinguists, rather than with the structuralists. At that point you may find yourself wondering why I have devoted so much space in Part I to the perspective of the structuralists, and why more space isn't devoted to describing and promoting the ethnographic and translinguistic approaches to linguistic anthropology.

2

I offer two answers to this question. First, a good deal of research that goes under the label of anthropology is structuralist in its method and objective. And if that research were not presented here, you would be missing out on what many people regard as the substance of the field.

Second, a deep appreciation of the significance of both the ethnographic and translinguistic perspectives must begin with a recognition that they are a David confronting a Goliath. The ethnographers' objectives and methods are no match, in most peoples' eyes, for the objectives and methods of the structuralists. In terms of scientific rigor, definition, focus, and results, the structuralist's Goliath is far more powerful than the ethnographer's David. Ethnographers fight an up-hill battle wherever their descriptions run against the grain of the structuralists' descriptions. Hence, one cannot really appreciate the objectives and the style of translinguistic and ethnographic linguistic anthropology without understanding that these approaches are contending with a formidable theoretical adversary.

Saussurean/Chomskyan Structuralism

Anthropologists and linguists think that it is important to talk about talk and to discourse about discourse for a number of different reasons. The first, and currently the most popular, reason for studying languages is that linguistic description is a high road to an understanding of human nature. Understanding human nature is a philosophical undertaking. Hence linguistics should be understood as a handmaiden to the discipline of philosophy.

The Seventeenth Century In the past--the past, that is, of state-level societies--peoples invoked God to make sense of the human condition. True, scholars studied languages, but then, language studies were important only as contributions to theologies of one sort or another.

Since roughly 1625, however, theologies have grown increasingly less credible and reliable as foundations for making sense of the human condition. The fifteenth and sixteenth centuries saw the pot begin to simmer: the printing press and the Reformation rocked Europe. Where Reformation-thinking did not arise, popular and magical religious beliefs did (Ginzburg 1980). New lands, new peoples, and, with the fall of Constantinople, new classical texts were discovered. And suddenly it became apparent that non-Christians had traveled, done, and thought far more than had been supposed.

Glass mirrors were invented and produced in volume in the early thirteenth century. Soon artists were introducing visual perspective into painting. And astronomers were advancing a helio-centric theory of the universe. All these developments are

3

signs of a growing awareness of humans as part of the environment rather than divinely positioned over it. Politicians used methods (Machiavelli) and struggled towards goals (More) that were measured in terms of man's needs and capabilities rather than by the standard of God's will.

In the seventeenth century, the pot boiled. The new scientific method (Bacon) was wedded to a new human politics, a grand alliance which led directly to the age of absolutism. But that grand alliance was soon rocked by the thirty years war, the first in a series of "world wars." The new human politics persisted, but in precarious balance.

The new human knowledge was equally tentative. The pillars that supported science needed to be sunk deep into the ground to assure the credibility of the whole edifice. Accordingly, Descartes's philosophical writings cleared away the old doctrines and dug deep for the foundation of a knowledge which was based on reason rather than on belief, a knowledge which flowed from the human mind rather than from God.

Hard Science and Soft Ground

I am reminded here of Karl Popper's (1963) marvelous image of knowledge as a building constructed on swampy land. A building on swampy land can stand only if it rests on pillars sunk into the mud. Similarly, knowledge can stand only if it rests on well-founded, deep-seated assumptions about the nature of knowing and the knowing faculties of the mind. The enlightening feature of Popper's image is this: the heavier the superstructure of the building, the deeper the pillars must be driven. In like fashion, as scientific theories become broader and more complex, more work is needed on the founding assumptions so as to make the whole edifice secure. Thus as scientific knowledge grows, there must be a corresponding growth in philosophy, that discipline charged now with the responsibility of building confidence in the assumptions that support science.

Having been set in swampy land, the pillars of knowledge regularly need to be sunk deeper. Descartes and his followers began this process by digging into questions about rationality and mind. But through the centuries philosophers have had to continue the foundation-tending task. Science needs philosophers to pursue questions about the attributes of rationality, about the possibility of separate minds arriving at the same rational conceptions of reality, about the mental faculty that makes rational thought possible, and about the relationship between rational thought and rational discourse.

The pursuit of such a knowledge led directly to language study. Rationality, it was found, is a characteristic of speech. That is, a rational person is someone who can *say* "Socrates is mortal" after *saying* that all men are mortal and that Socrates is a man. Evidence about rational thought starts as a description of rational talk. This link between rationality and talk drove philosophers to inquire into the foundations of human speech. Thus, linguistics lies at the heart of philosophy for it tells us who we are, what our rationality consists of, and what it means to say that *homo* is *sapiens*. Linguistics is a discipline without which the whole edifice of science would quickly sink into the mud.

The structure of reason is mirrored in the structure of language. If you want to know what reason is, you must examine language structure through grammatical analysis. Accordingly, Enlightenment thinkers enthusiastically shouldered the task of grammatical analysis with a clear recognition of its philosophical importance.

Curiously, this philosophical linguistics is a case of a disease that became its own best medicine. Some of the very discoveries which had created the cultural confusion during the long century between 1450 and 1600 pointed the way in later centuries to the new cultural order. The classical texts which came to light in the 15th century were an invaluable resource for the construction of the 17th century understanding of the rational structure of scientific language. In a similar way, the 18th century discovery of links between Sanskrit and European languages paved the way for yet more giant steps in the comparative study of languages and their rational organization.

The Nineteenth Century Nineteenth century linguists transmogrified this linguistic/philosophical program, advancing it in some respects, but also re-directing it. Linguistics, like a number of other scientific disciplines, came into its own in this century. In fact, linguistics along with biology and economics came to dominate the sciences of the nineteenth century. These disciplines fed off each other and in turn contributed to numerous other budding disciplines like sociology, anthropology, and psychology.

Linguistics in the nineteenth century came into its own. That is, it developed a set of goals for description which were independent of the philosophical goals which gave it birth in earlier centuries. The nineteenth century goals included the description of the units of languages and their changes through time. Nineteenth century linguists did for languages what nineteenth century biologists did for organisms. They explained their nature by describing the evolution of their constituent parts.

5

In addition, nineteenth century linguistics, along with the other major sciences of the age, developed a manner of operating, or as television detectives say, an M.O. (*modus operandi*) that we now call empirical. As an ideal, the empirical M.O. means that the scientist describes just the individual and particular experiences which his or her senses can grasp.

The compulsion for the empirical in nineteenth century linguistics virtually dissolved the mentalistic goals of the philosophical linguistics of the previous century--you can't see reason; you can't measure mind. It drove linguistics apart from philosophy and left linguistics with the relatively simple task of describing the systems and processes of languages, understood now as systems of sounds and words. As a result, nineteenth century linguistics became an empirical science devoted to the description of laws of sound change and to the classification of languages according to form and parentage.

The focus on empirical description of language change and of language types altered the field of linguistics substantially. The century-long research effort of linguists, especially linguists in Germany, led to the view that languages are machines on rails. What they are now and what they will be in the future is determined by universal and inexorable laws. This image of languages as highly determined machines is hardly what Enlightenment philosophers had in mind when they advocated linguistic description. Their goal was the description of the free and rational human mind, not the description of a highly regulated machine.

The Twentieth Century Radical adjustments in all the human sciences--a term which includes anthropology, sociology, economics, linguistics, political philosophy, ethics, and psychology--between 1890 and 1920 led to a second major re-shaping of the science of linguistics. Curiously, this second re-shaping brought continental linguistics back into line with Enlightenment objectives for the study of languages. Note though, that while continental linguistics was greatly altered by the turn-of-the-century turmoil, British and American linguists generally went their own ways with their own concerns. These matters will be discussed later. The following paragraphs will describe the turn-of-the-century transformation of continental linguistics.

The first symptom of dissatisfaction with mechanistic linguistics in the late nineteenth century was a movement called "descriptivism." Mechanistic linguists, true to the empirical M.O., had focussed on individual elements of languages. Descriptivists emphasized relations between elements of a system (Koerner 1972).

This nineteenth century linguistic descriptivism was strongly influenced by biology, not Darwinian biology, but the older biology which was superceded by Darwin's. The specific biological principle that shaped descriptivism was what Cuvier at the turn of the nineteenth century called "the mysterious law of correlation." That principle stated that every morphological characteristic of an organism is accomodated to all other morphological characteristics. As a result of these mutual accomodations, the total morphology of the organism is a bundle of interrelated morphological characteristics. If given but a feather, Cuvier claimed, one could reconstruct the whole bird by following out morphological interrelations.

Both Darwin and the linguists whose mechanistic studies of sound change were based on Darwin's biology, ignored this "mysterious law of correlation." But descriptivists attended to it very closely. Just as Cuvier's biology required one to explain the form of a finch's beak by describing the relations of beak, legs, wings and tail; so, the descriptivists tried to account for the form of one sound in a language by describing the relations of sounds to one another.

In linguistics, Baudoin de Courtenay, Mikolaij Kruszewski, and Hermann Paul pioneered this sort of description of sound systems. Ferdinand de Saussure pushed this notion even further, arguing in effect, that linguistics is really two quite different disciplines, an historical one devoted to the documentation of mechanical changes in units, and a "descriptive" one, devoted to the analysis of relations of language units:

> We have been fostering for some years now the conviction that linguistics is a double science, so profoundly double that one might well ask if there is any real justification for continuing to maintain the name linguistics for this artificial unity (Saussure 1974: 23).

Saussure himself contributed a great deal to both halves of the double discipline, but he is remembered as the champion of "descriptive"--now known as "structural"--linguistics.

The descriptivist's argument is that a language is an abstract system of interrelated units. It is not a loose ensemble of words and sounds which are thrown together by historical accident. A language is not like a geologic moraine full of the debris of different geologic levels of different ages. Rather, despite the unique origin and history of each language unit, the units together form an integrated ensemble. A language is like an orchestra. Each piece is different, but all the pieces fit beautifully together in the playing of the music.

Metaphors can help to express the abstract integration of language systems. Saussure's favorite metaphor was the chess

7

game. A chess game, he argued, consists of units or pieces. Each piece may have its own story. Some pieces are made of ivory, some of onyx and others of plastic with magnetic inserts in the bases. And one could, if one wished, describe chess in terms of the materials and shape of the chess pieces. Perhaps these descriptions would be interesting. You would find out for example that the plastic pieces with magnetic inserts are used in travel sets, that ivory pieces are the first choices of the wealthy and that onyx pieces are quite popular in Latin America. But none of these descriptions would tell you anything about *the game of chess.*

If you would understand the game of chess you must forget about the histories and materials of chess pieces and focus instead on the relations between different pieces on a chess board. The relative positions of knights, bishops, rooks, pawns, queens, etc. on the board at any one moment is what the game is all about. And if you do not comprehend those relative positions, then you do not know chess.

When you do know chess, you can approach a game in progress, and, without knowing the histories of pieces or what they are made of, without even knowing what moves had been made in the past, you can comprehend the game in terms of the relations between pieces as they stand at this one moment in time. Systematic relations at one moment in time--we will call them synchronic relations--make the game of chess. All other matters are incidental.

The importance of Saussure's example is clear. Systematic relations constitute languages. The historical origins of words and sounds are incidental.

Saussure's Struggle

Saussure was struggling with the double task of making linguistics an empirical science while also achieving the Enlightenment objective of studying languages to reveal the nature of the human mind.

This double task was accomplished by a focus on *relations* between language units. Linguistic relations like relations between chessmen, are mental phenomena which can be approached empirically. Insofar as his linguistics focussed on mental relations, his science was consistent with the seventeenth century struggle to understand the mind. Insofar as his linguistics proceeded by an empirical M.O., it was consistent with nineteenth century views of science.

The movement of a single chess piece changes a whole game because it changes the relations between pieces on the board. In the same way, an alteration of one unit, say a vowel, in a language system alters the whole language by establishing a new configuration of relations between vowels. If you were to wake up one morning to find that, by some stroke of sorcery, the vowel in your word *wide* sounded the same as the vowel in your word *weed*, you could be sure that all the other vowels in your speech also underwent an adjustment. The new vowel system resulting from such a change would need to be described in its own right and independently of the previous day's vowel system.

> In a game of chess any particular position has the unique characteristic of being freed from all antecedent positions; the route used in arriving there makes absolutely no difference; one who has followed the entire match has no advantage over the curious party who comes up at a critical moment to inspect the state of the game; to describe this arrangement, it is perfectly useless to recall what had happened just a few minutes previously (Saussure 1959: 19).

The elegance of "descriptive" analyses is indisputable. And the chess game analogy renders that descriptive program convincing. But a serious problem remains to be discussed. What does it mean to say that there is a relationship between the vowels of a language system? What is that relationship? Is it a physiological relationship? Is it is psychological relationship of simple association? Is it a cognitive relationship of a more complex sort?

Saussure answered this question by proposing that relations between language units are abstractions housed in the minds of speakers of a language. They are something like the relationship between cases of Latin nouns:

Nominative	(subjective)	agricola	-a
Genitive	(possessive)	agricolae	-ae
Dative	(beneficiary)	agricolae	-ae
Accusative	(objective)	agricolam	-am
Ablative	(agency)	agricola	-a
Vocative	(address)	agricola	-a

Latin speakers are conscious and aware of the word meaning "farmer" (*agricola*) as it used in its various nominal cases. But in addition, Latin speakers have a sense that the universe of nouns is exhausted by six non-overlapping categories, each of which has its distinct part to play in the construction of a meaningful sentence. The abstract relationship between such noun categories exemplifies the structuralist notion of linguistic relations.

Such abstract relationships are housed in the minds of speakers of a language. Only human minds can manage algebraic equations and geometric equivalences. Managing Latin noun categories is a similar operation which only human minds have the capacity to perform.

Only minds can *know* language systems. And this is a special kind of knowing, because speakers, unlike chess players or mathematicians, are unaware of the systematic relations which they manipulate. The mental capabilities of language users can be summarized by saying that speakers have the cognitive ability to manipulate systems of abstract language relations which are beyond their own awareness.

Not everyone who labored in the "descriptive" sciences at the close of the nineteenth century was inclined to accept this mentalistic account offered by Saussure. Durkheim, for example, proposed that social systems--being, like languages, systems of relations--are located in groups, not in individuals. For Durkheim the group is prior to the individual in all respects:

> The objection may be raised that a phenomenon is collective only if it is common to all members of a society, if it is truly general. This may be true; but it is general because it is collective and certainly not collective because it is general (Durkheim 1895: 9).

Durkheim here contends that social facts, like a language or a society or a culture, are real over and above what individuals do, have, or know. In other words, a language is more than the sum of the linguistic knowledge of individuals in that society. Such a view often goes by the name *superorganic*.

Saussure rejected Durkheim's superorganicism, and preferred instead to argue that language systems were located in the individual minds of speaking subjects. His language theory implies that humans are creatures of extraordinary and distinctive mental potential, but also creatures who unlock that potential only in communicative interaction.

In this way, Saussure argued that language systems are individual mental realities, but he did not completely disregard the fact that they are also social. He saw a ray of truth in Durkheim's view that languages are fundamentally social phenomena. But he struggled to avoid Durkheim's excessive emphasis on their reality over and above the mind's unconscious grasp of linguistic relations. Following the lead of the American linguist W.D. Whitney, he characterized languages as social phenomena because they arise through the unconscious agreements of speakers and are maintained only by the continued use of a language in a community. If you should want to explain why languages are born or why they die, you must, according to Saussure and Whitney, consider the social relations between the speakers of that language.

Saussure's linguistics was, like a teeter-totter, in precarious balance. The emphasis on the mental nature of language systems on the one hand, was balanced by an emphasis on the social nature of all language phenomena on the other hand. Saussure's disciples have tried to elaborate and extend this precarious balance between the mental and the social, but they have almost always ended up tipping the balance to one side or the other. *Caveat lector*: Be suspicious of all interpretations of Saussure's linguistics, even this one. Disciples of a master almost always loose the subtleties of the master's thought in their struggle to clarify and systematize it.

Mental and Social Aspects of Language

It must be emphasized that Saussure struggled to describe both the mental and the social aspects of language. He tried to avoid outlining a linguistics that was overly psychological or overly social in its emphasis. He struggled toward a middle way.

This struggling is dramatically clear in his juggling of definitions for his central concepts of *langue* (roughly, grammar) and *parole* (roughly, speaking). At one point, during his three years of teaching a course on general linguistics, he described *langue* as a social fact and *parole* as an individual creation. But in another year he reversed himself and described *parole* as a social fact and *langue* as an individual creation.

Saussure's struggle to find a middle way between overemphasis on the mental and the social was a struggle that we shall see rocked all the human sciences at roughly the turn of the century. Certainly, the Boasian ethnographers, whose point of view we shall introduce momentarily, wrestled with this same problem. It is no accident that the emphasis on the mental over the social won out amongst most of the followers of both Saussure and Boas. Explaining why this should have happened is one objective behind Parts I and II of this book.

Saussure's work is a watershed in modern linguistics. He brought linguistics back to describing the mind. He helped to provoke a twentieth century controversy over language and human nature which has yet to be put to rest.

All through Europe in the twenties and thirties, this re-kindled philosophical/linguistic discipline gained strength. "Structuralisms," as we now call them, appeared all over the continent, in Geneva among Saussure's colleagues, in Prague a-round the work of Troubetskoy and Jakobson, in Copenhagen at the hand of Hjelmslev, in Paris with Meillet. Very much later, and from a different linguistic, but kindred philosophical, back-ground, Noam Chomsky sowed the seeds of this movement on American soil. Every one of these structuralist schools adopted Saussure as their father and proceeded to the task of describing mental language states for the ultimate purpose of making sense of the human mind.

At this point, I must confess that I have presented you with a linguist's history of modern linguistics. And it is perhaps marred by a little too much self-congratulation on the part of the linguists. Not that this story is not accurate. It is. But it is also incomplete.

Structuralism would not have swept Europe like a grass fire on a dry savanah if it were fed by nothing more than the rumina-tions of an obscure linguist from Geneva. In truth, Geneva was no hotbed of intellectual activity at the turn of the century. It could not hold a candle to Tubingen or Frankfurt when it came to linguistic prominence. So it is unlikely that Saussure, the Swiss linguist, was singlehandedly responsible for the intellect-ual transformation of twentieth century Europe.

There is another side to the history of modern European structuralisms. And that is a philosophical side, clearest in the work of Ludwig Wittgenstein, on the one hand, and of Edmund Husserl on the other.

In 1921, Wittgenstein, with his book <u>Tractatus Logico-Phil-osophicus</u> (1961) congealed a movement in philosophy that had been in the works since mid-nineteenth century applications of mathe-matics to logic. In his view, all statements are understood as products of rule-governed combinations of elementary meaningful units. Any analysis of the truth of a proposition must, he said, be directed not to the surface logic or obvious content of that proposition, but to the underlying meaningful units and to the rules for their combination. Thus, Wittgenstein, more than any-one, else gave credibility to the notion of mental language struc-ture.

In early twentieth century philosophy, the work of Edmund Husserl "had the effect of a great thunderstorm. It dispelled the clouds and clarified the whole intellectual atmosphere" (Cas-sirer 1945: 102). Specifically, Husserl's notion of the "tran-scendental ego," the speaking subject, defined that mental pre-sence in each individual which acquires and maintains structured protagonists of this movement (the structural trend in general linguistics) had close and effective connections with phenomenology in its Husserlian and Hegelian versions (Jakobson 1970: 13), and Coward and Ellis (1977: 129) argue that "Chomsky developed a notion which follows very closely the idea of the subject in Husserlian phenomenology. His explicit reference to this subject is symptomatic of the fact that Husserlian philosophy has been at the basis of signification theories in this century, and, consciously or not, at the basis of modern linguistics."

Plus Ça Change, Plus Ç'est La Même

Let me represent Husserl's philosophical enterprise in sinfully broad terms. Edmund Husserl's definition of the "transcendental ego" was prompted by the work of his teacher Franz Brentano, who was a priest as a matter of fact. Brentano's philosophical goal might be roughly described as that of demonstrating the nature of the human soul by scientific means. His goal was theological, but his M.O. was the empirical method of the day.

Brentano's inquiry into the soul was a search for a transcendent source of agency and action. He wanted to discover what made humans think and act the way they do. In this respect, his struggle resembled in a curious way the struggle of another scholar-priest seven hundred years his younger, Thomas Aquinas. Thomas had set his sights on *the* transcendental principle of agency and action, God. Like Brentano, he used the M.O. of the day, logic and systematic reason learned from the newly recovered classical texts of Aristotle.

Plus ça change, plus ç'est la même. Structuralists, whether they speak of the "transcendental ego" or "the consciousness of the speaking subject," are taking aim at roughly the same target that has been drawing the attention of scholars since the days of Thomas.

Let me summarize the preceding discussions of the goals of the structuralist linguistic program. For structuralists, describing languages is important because such descriptions offer insight into the operations of the human mind and into human rationality. For structuralists, to understand the mind is to understand human nature.

George Carlin studies language for laughs. He presents us with the oddities of our talk and invariably generates chuckles. People laugh, I think, because they are confounded by his revelations about behaviors they ordinarily give no thought to. Their

13

tions about behaviors they ordinarily give no thought to. Their only response to such confounding revelations is to laugh. Carlin's magic never fails to work because the fact of the matter is that people don't know themselves very well at all. He can avail himself of an endless supply of self-revelations for his routines.

Structural linguists have fashioned whole scholarly lives on this very same principle that people don't know themselves very well. As we have just seen, structuralists describe languages for the purpose of letting people know how their own minds operate. The key assumptions in this structuralist program are: 1) that the deepest workings of the mind are hidden; 2) that those deepest workings are central to human nature; 3) that a rational scientific method of description can reveal those deepest workings.

Boasian Linguistics-Ethnography

Franz Boas developed a linguistic-ethnographic program for some quite different reasons. He certainly was not an ancestral George Carlin, but neither was he a philosopher-linguist in quest of mind. Instead Boas threw himself into anthropology for the purpose of fostering respect among peoples, and most especially respect by modern metropolitan peoples for primitive peoples, who were, as they still are, being systematically exterminated. His objective was to foment a moral re-birth of modern societies by presenting to them the honorability and nobility of primitive peoples and primitive minds.

Boas's objectives may have been moral rather than philosophical, but his methods for achieving those objectives were scientific through and through. He demanded detailed empirical descriptions of primitive behaviors. He struggled to purge racist ethnocentric assumptions from his accounts. And, most importantly for our concerns, he reserved a very special place for language studies in his program of ethnography. In all these respects he pursued his moral objectives with the gait of a scientist.

At the core of his program for ethnography was the general assumption that repeated performances of an action create habits of "unconscious thought." The most frequently repeated actions of any people, and therefore their most firmly established habits, are those associated with using a language. Hence the acquisition and use of a distinctive language engenders in people a distinctive pattern of thinking. "Language," he said, "seems to be one of the most instructive fields of inquiry in an investigation of the formation of fundamental ethnic ideas" (Boas 1911: 59).

A language, for Boas, is a key to the "ethnic ideas" of its

again — it follow doesn't

Talking about Talk

and "ethnic ideas." But as much emphasis as Boas placed on languages as keys to human mental life, he placed an equally firm emphasis on language as a traditional, historical, and above all, social phenomenon. "Ethnic ideas," according to Boas, do not arise from any individual's cleverness or insight, but always from "man's irrational attachment to the (language) customs he has inherited from the past" (Hatch 1973: 56).

The Irrational in Language

Boas's celebration of the "irrational" in language is intended to underscore the complexity of human behavior. "Irrational," here, means complex. And if human behavior is complex, then it is probably not determined by any single factor. More likely, it is freely produced.

With the term "irrational," Boas is turning against that nineteenth century idea that human behavior is determined in its form and development by race and/or evolutionary destiny. When Boas writes of "irrational attachments to customs," he does not mean that such attachments are contrary to reason, but only that they are incompletely determined by laws of biology or psychology.

Boas's objectives for ethnographic-linguistic description were utopian objectives: he celebrated the "ethnic ideas" of primitive peoples and held them up as models to be emulated by us moderns. However, his methods of operation were scientific. With such a mixture of utopian objectives and scientific methods, it was almost inevitable that his linguistic program was compared to other scientific linguistics and, in the end, gravely misunderstood.

Boasian linguist-ethnographers operated with the rigor and precision of scientists. This scientific approach, together with their linguistic interests, brought Boasians into line with the then recent developments in European philosophy. As a result they won widespread acclaim for the scientific and linguistics aspects of their program. However, since they were motivated by utopian rather than philosophical objectives, they used their scientific-linguistic descriptions to describe and celebrate differences between peoples. This celebration of linguistic differences is called *linguistic relativity*. For this linguistic relativity, Boasians have been taken to task and accused of focussing on superficial aspects of cognition and personality. From the point of view of structuralists, Boasian description failed to dig to the deepest, almost always universal, workings of the mind.

15

of the mind.

Science, language, and linguistic relativity are the strange bedfellows whose tossing and turning pushed Boasian linguistics in a couple of different directions during the past fifty years. First, a penchant for the/scientific gave rise to American Structuralism under the strong hand of Leonard Bloomfield. Second, an emphasis on/linguistic relativity in the works of Sapir and Whorf gave rise to a heavily psychologial orientation which carried through the recent decades of interest in ethnoscience and the ethnography of speaking.

Leonard Bloomfield did more than anyone to transform Boasian linguistic ethnography into an exacting descriptive discipline. And in so doing, Bloomfield blunted the reformist objectives of Boasian ethnography.

Bloomfield shared with Boas a concern for the vanishing primitives of the Americas. But his response to this problem was, in a sense, less amibitious than Boas's. Bloomfield's aim was to describe the primitive languages before they vanished and to do so just as efficiently and reliably as possible. His concern was to develop systematic methods for linguistic description.

Bloomfield's concern for describing languages scientifically was prompted by an intense appreciation for nineteenth century linguistic scholarship. His methods of analysis may have leaned heavily on the then current European structuralist developments. However, his program for linguistic description was decidedly more mechanical and less focussed on the issues of mind and rationality which both Saussurean structuralism and Boasian ethnography were helping to bring back to life. He was not particularly fired up by Boas's interest in "ethnic ideas" which languages might foster in speakers. Nor was he interested in the philosophical concerns that were driving Saussurean structuralists to more abstract sorts of linguistic accounts. Bloomfield's primary concern was to develop clear reliable procedures for producing synchronic descriptions of languages.

The program of Bloomfieldian linguistics, often called American structuralism, persisted for many decades in American linguistic scholarship. But European interests in philosophy eventually took root in America when Noam Chomsky faced off against the anti-mentalism and anti-psychologism of American structuralism. Chomsky's program gained in popularity at the expense of American structuralism by wedding the scientific methods of the American structuralist school of thought to the philosophical objectives of European structuralisms.

American structuralism rode onto the scene on the coat tails of Bloomfield-the-scientist. A somewhat independent emphasis on

16

linguistic relativism rode in on the coat tails of Edward Sapir and Benjamin Lee Whorf. The research methods of Sapir and Whorf and their colleagues duplicated, in rigor, the methods of the Bloomfieldians. But these relativists stressed and emphasized cultural and linguistic diversity, and that stress led to ever more penetrating searches for cultural differences rooted in language structure and language use. In the forties, Whorf advanced the hypothesis of "linguistic determinism" according to which thought patterns are identical to language patterns. And in the sixties, ethnoscientists advanced the idea that the structure of a language's vocabulary holds the key to the organization of the thought processes of its speakers. This same unrelenting search for cultural differences leads contemporary "ethnographers of speaking" to play up varieties of language use and to play down the significance of structuralists' claims about universals of language form.

Bakhtinian Translinguistics

A third and rather unlikely perspective on language study in the twentieth century is translinguistics. Translinguistics is unlikely because it was born in the writing of a Russian, Mihail Bakhtin, in the twenties. And, no sooner was it born than it was buried by the Soviet state. Moreover, Bakhtin's translinguistics was a utopian theologically-rooted system of thought which was antagonistic to the abstracting methods of science that reign in contemporary practices of linguistics. That translinguistics should even see the light of day in the eighties is a wonder. That it should be embraced as a refreshing alternative to existing programs of language study borders on the miraculous.

Bakhtin's goals for language study were explicitly utopian. A young scholar at the time of the Revolution, Bakhtin was eager to help realize the promise of the Revolution by fashioning the best of all possible worlds. And for Bakhtin that meant doing away with oppressive centralized political powers bent on shaping behavior and molding minds according to a single standard. Bakhtin's utopia would be one that encouraged differences, cherished confusion, and celebrated the cacophany of heterogeneous voices.

The primary vehicle used by Bakhtin to outline his noisy utopia was literature. He wrote about the carnival in Rabelais' work and about the unruly characters of Dostoevsky. And at every turn he encouraged noisiness in the images of society that literature offered.

Bakhtin was also a linguist. And his linguistic work, when taken together with the psychology of Lev Vygotsky, a Russian contemporary of kindred spirit, offers a refreshing outlook on language and talk. With a subtlety reminiscent of Saussure's original proposals, the translinguistic perspective balances emphases on the individual and the social, and it finds a middle

17

way between synchronic and diachronic linguistic descriptions.

Let me briefly explain this translinguistic balancing act. In Bakhtin's scheme, talk is the utterance of individuals. Talk shares the uniqueness of individuals; it is specific to the times, places, and experiences of those individuals. The jabber of the members of a community is thus a cacophany of individual discourses. This stress on the individuality of talk and on the noisiness of social life is a sign of Bakhtin's focus on the individual.

However, there is a real danger that you might misunderstand the term "individual" here. Contrary to a common Romantic notion that the individual is self-grounded and that individuals are essentially alone in the world, Bakhtin's notion of individual is social through and through. Bakhtin notes that among the concrete forces that shape an individual, no force is stronger than the talk which that person has experienced through time. Indeed, the talk that individuals experience--their own talk as well as the talk of others--stays with individuals and fashions them through time. The words which individuals speak at any time are ghosts of words that those individuals have experienced in the past as they interacted with others.

The ghosts of past words breathe life into each individual's present words. Individuals experience the words of others. They collect those words through time in the course of inter-acting with others. They collect those words and compress them, forming a new sedimentary object, their individuality. Just as a new piece of slate is formed by the depositing and compressing of many older materials over time, the unique individual is formed out of experiences of talk collected and compressed through time.

Sedimentation is a psychological process. It occurs within individual minds. It transforms social experiences, particularly experiences of talking, into ghosts which live on in the indivi-duals, haunting them, leaping out whenever those individuals open their mouths. No spells can exorcize these word-ghosts. Their presence is part of the human condition. Word-ghosts are what make humans human.

Two facets of translinguistics are similar to the Boasian program of ethnography-linguistics described above: its initial utopian goals and its view that language use is the single most significant factor in shaping social habits. Perhaps that is why translinguistics is a revitalizing force in American anthropo-logy.

Summary and Prospect

We have covered three different perspectives on linguistic thought stretching over four centuries of modern intellectual life. We have seen that each perspective pivots around a distinct motivation or objective. And if you have appreciated these objectives, you have come a long way to understanding why linguistics and linguistic anthropology are important. Far from being the useless meanderings of scholars whose brains have been scrambled by over use, linguistic studies are eminently common sensical studies. And the linguists and anthropologists who have produced them are, for the most part, quite sane.

Structuralists spend their days spelunking in the deep caves of grammatical and mental structures. Theirs, they reckon, is the quickest route to discovering what it means to be a human. The motivation for their work is no more complicated than the motivation for looking into a mirror, only it is the face of the whole species that they seek in the glass.

Despite being plausible and laudible, linguistic studies can be frighteningly abstract. The reason I think, is that, in linguistic studies, discourse turns back upon itself. Everyone else, except stand-up comedians like George Carlin, takes talk for granted, and uses discourse to talk about something else as if discourse were a transparent tool. But linguists and linguistic anthropologists talk about talk itself. Theirs is a discourse on discourse, and for that reason and no other, linguistic studies are disturbing and confounding.

This book is designed to lead you to an appreciation of the practice of discoursing on discourse. Part I describes the principles of both structuralist linguistics and of American structuralism. Part II will address the objectives and principles of Boasian ethnography. And in Part III, we will consider the perspective of the translinguists.

PART I

STRUCTURALIST LINGUISTICS

Chapter Two

Mickey Mouse, Washoe, and Linguistics

The structuralist is interested in unlocking the secrets of the human mind. In this enterprise, language is the golden key; it reveals quasi-mathematical language capabilities of the mind that are surprizingly complex, but normally invisible. The capabilities that language analysis reveals are so complex that no computer can simulate them. But they are so invisible that they can be present in kids who cannot yet add two plus two. And no one, least of all the kids, is aware of them.

Structuralists approach these language capabilities in the same way that Alice approached the Cheshire cat. She focussed so intently on the cat's smile that soon the cat itself disappeared and only the smile remained. The smile, as if it had a life of its own, hung suspended in mid-air. Structuralists focus intently on the computational capabilities of the human mind. And under their gaze concrete human individuals and real human actions fade from view. Only those capabilities remain, as if they could exist in themselves.

The goal of Part I will be to describe in sympathetic but simple terms, those computational capabilities and how they are discovered. The sympathy in this description will consist in my conveying the enthusiasm and excitement which is generated in accomplishing the task of unlocking secrets of the mind. The simplicity in the description will be accomplished, starting in chapter three, by reducing structuralist discoveries to the elementary bipolar principles of figure/ground and token/type. Chapters four and five will build on those elementary notions so as to arrive at an appreciation of modern phonology and syntax. From there on, the selection of issues for discussion is directed by what anthropologists find most exciting about the structuralist perspective: chapter six deals with universals of language; chapter seven deals with variation in language systems; and chapter eight deals with the genesis of the language capability in the species as well as the genesis of languages in individuals.

But before we approach these issues, we will foray into one of the most hotly contended territories of modern language study, the territory of ape-language experiments. The value of such a beginning is that we will be able to see, in the heated exchanges of these ape-language experiments, the true colors of structur-

21

alist linguists. Here, structuralists reveal, as do others involved in these debates, their most deeply held assumptions about
the human mind and human nature. If we can appreciate the arguments about apes and language, we are well on the way to appreciating the central issues in structuralist approaches to human
languages.

Mickey Mouse and Language

Why Mickey Mouse? Did you a ever stop to wonder? Why
Donald Duck? Why Sylvester the Cat? Why any of the hundreds of
animals that waltz across our screens and through our picture
books? Have you never puzzled over our collective fascination
with such paradoxical creatures who are human and yet not? They
all have the forms of animals, but they behave like humans. Most
importantly for our concerns, they talk like humans. Why this
fascination with talking animals?

The fascination with talking animals is just the sort of
phenomenon that piques the structuralist's interest. Structuralists, including structuralist linguists, are philosophically
inclined scholars whose objective is to state as clearly as they
can what it means to be a human. Mickey Mouse toys with the problem of what it means to be a human. Therefore, structuralists
are excited by phenomena like Mickey Mouse.

Perhaps, we can arrive at a clearer appreciation of the
structuralist's objective by pursuing further the curious phenomenon of Mickey Mouse.

Mickey and all his talking kinsfolk serve us by smoothing
over our latent confusions about the boundaries of human nature.
They allow us to imagine, just for a moment, the utterly prepos-
terous scene of a mouse named Mickey asking another mouse named
Minnie for a date. And when we come back from that scene to
reality, we are, paradoxically, more settled on and contented
with the notion that animals are not human and that they raise no
threat to the uniqueness and power of the human species.

Claude Levi-Strauss argued that primitive myths work in this
fashion. Myths, he said, combine contrasting themes into sur-
realistic images. And in so doing, myths explore for people the
tensions of their cultural life. The story of the heroics of the
mythical figure Asdiwal serves the Tsimshian Indians of the North
West coast by wrestling through issues like life versus death and
patrilocal residence versus matrilineal descent. The tales of
Mickey Mouse's exploits serve us similarly by grappling with the
paradox of humanoid animals, and, more interestingly, with the
paradox of talking animals.

Children eat up Asdiwal and Mickey Mouse without even recognizing the profound significance of these stories. In fact, both

22

these stories are especially well packaged for consumption by children. And this fact is evidence enough these tales wrestle with culturally central problems. For the Tsimshin Indians the existence of matrilineal descent and patrilocal residence is a paradox that lies at the very heart of their culture. For us, talking animals is a similarly focal paradox.

Why talking animals should pose a special problem for us is hard to say. But for whatever reasons, this paradox is a big problem for us, big like the problem of life and death, and big enough to be brought straight to our children.

But our children are not the sole consumers of tales that grapple with talking animals. Adults in our society also follow the exploits of Mickey Mouse. And, as if that were not enough, adults fabricate stories which grapple with talking animals in a very explicit way. Some of our finest science fiction turns on just this issue. In Simak's City (1952), dogs are not only faithful companions to humans, they are also faithful conversationalists, thanks to some creative surgery and genetic engineering. In Bishop's Transfigurations (1979), the Asadi are Sasquatch-like creatures who communicate abstract thoughts and rich feelings, but not through words and sentences. Instead the Asadi communicate with spinning pinwheels of eye color. And it takes a talented linguist armed with an ancient Asadi decoder to reveal the eye color grammar. Finally, in a story based on more familiar experiences, Oh's Profit by Goulet (1975) presents us with a sagacious gorilla who relates to us the poignant tale of his own undoing at the hands of the paranoid linguists who taught him to sign.

These are just some of our adult tales about talking animals. But they do not nearly exhaust our repertoire of stories on this central cultural theme. Besides tales about Mickey Mouse and the Asadi, we have our stories of language experiments with chimps and gorillas.

It might seem strange to call these last accounts stories. They are hard, clear, dispassionate science. And most of us are reluctant to call a scientific account a story.

The Scientific and the Literary

At some point early in the modern era, written discourses were divided into scientific and literary. Science was understood to be the domain of truth; literature, the domain of stories, evaluations, beliefs, opinions, etc. And, rightly or not, literature came off as the weaker sister of the two.

This division of discourses into scientific and literary

has everything to do with the erosion of the old foundations and the construction of new foundations for modern society. All that was part of the old foundation has been relegated to the literary; all that is part of the new is called scientific.

Therefore, in calling scientific discourse a story, I am intentionally overturning the modern order of things. I am intentionally making that modern order strange to us so that we can examine it from a different standpoint and arrive at a deeper appreciation of it.

But these scientific accounts, which I am about to describe in this chapter, still serve as stories of a sort. They, no less than Mickey Mouse or the Asadi, grapple with the boundaries of our species of talkers. Though their method of presentation is rigorously scientific, they are, like our other stories, driven by the central cultural paradox of talking animals. They go by the name scientific accounts, but they function like our other myths/stories. How else to explain the acrimony of the debates over ape-language experiments except by saying that these experiments stir up very deep feelings? And how to explain the popularity of these accounts and debates except by saying that they speak to our collective restlessness over the boundaries of human nature?

Background

The background to ape-language experiments consists of two contrapuntal themes. The first is the conviction that language is an exclusively human property. The second is the suspicion that some non-human creatures possess rudimentary language-producing abilities.

For eons, scholars have considered language to be an exclusively human, indeed, a quintessentially human, ability. Quintillian told the Romans that "God...distinguished men (sic) from other living creatures...by nothing more than this, that he gave him the gift of speech." And in 1861, Max Müller responded to Darwin's evolutionism saying, "The one great barrier between the brute and man (sic) is Language. Man speaks and no brute has ever uttered a word. Language is our Rubicon, and no brute will dare to cross it."

On the other hand, another set of scholars have long nurtured the belief that some animals, specifically apes, possess language-like abilities. In 1661--at a time when philosophers were most deeply engaged with questions about what it is to be human--Samuel Pepys broached the issue of language in apes. After inspecting a baboon just imported from Guinea. He wrote, "I do believe it already understands much English; and I am of a mind

24

it might be taught to speak or make signs." Modern scholars have presented some evidence to confirm Pepys's belief: R.L. Garner reported in 1892 that some monkeys have a working vocabulary of about 40 words. W.H. Furness taught a young Orang to say two words, "cup" and "papa." But the bulk of modern research shows that apes cannot be taught an oral language. Kellog demonstrated that apes not only cannot produce many words, neither can they comprehend spoken words. Robert Yerkes concluded that apes have "no gift for the use of sounds ...Perhaps they can be taught to use their fingers somewhat as does the deaf and dumb person, and helped to acquire a simple, nonvocal 'sign language'." The research of Keith Hayes in the 1950's underscored the inability of chimps to produce sounds. For all his efforts with Vicki, she learned to produce only half a dozen English words.

The reasons for Vicki's failure are clear to us now. The ape's vocal tract is quite different from a human's, and its motor control over larynx, tongue, and lips is less well developed. As shown in the drawings below, the differences lie in the area above the larynx but behind and below the tongue. This area is called the pharynx. The human pharynx is larger than the chimp's and it meets the oral cavity at an angle. The epiglottis, a flap that covers the trachea during swallowing, is located at a position lower in the human pharynx than in the chimp's. And for all these reasons, together with inadequate motor control, chimps cannot produce anywhere near the variety of sounds managed by humans. They have particular difficulty with vowels and nasal consonants.

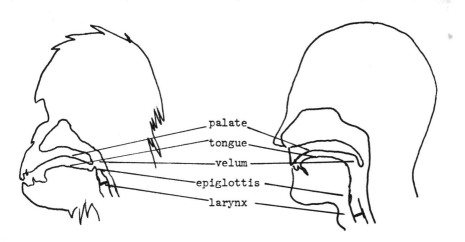

Ape-Language Experiments

The argument between the yea-sayers and the nay-sayers on language in apes is still raging. However, today all scholars admit that apes do not have the oral apparatus necessary for producing oral language expressions. Today, no one claims that chimps can speak, but the issue of their language abilities is not resolved by that fact.

Recognizing that apes could never talk as humans do, researchers in the late 1960's returned to Yerkes' suggestion. That is, they constructed experiments in which chimps were introduced to symbol systems in nonvocal media. The Gardners taught Washoe to produce manual gestures patterned after the signs of American Sign Language. Premack taught Sarah to manipulate plastic symbols on a magnetic board, and Rumbaugh introduced Lana to symbols on a computer keyboard.

Each of these experiments took advantage of the manual dexterity of chimpanzees. Apes may have limited vocal talents, but they are gifted with an ability to use their hands for precise manuevers. So the experimenters constructed language-like systems of expressions that could be manipulated manually.

The most interesting of the language-like systems used in these experiments was the system based on American Sign Language, the system taught to Washoe. American Sign Language (ASL) is a language of gestures used by many deaf people in the U.S. It is a natural language in the sense that it is acquired automatically by the deaf as they interact with other signing deaf people. And it is a real language with all the capabilities for abstract expression as any oral language.

ASL is a real language, but an unusual and unfamiliar language (See chapter six). The fact that signed expressions are visually rather than aurally perceived makes for distinctive characteristics in Sign languages. And we are just now coming to understand those distinctive characteristics. So, when the Gardners taught Washoe to produce ASL signs, they opened a Pandora's box of possibilities. Since the linguistic description of Sign languages of the deaf is still in its infancy, and since there is so much in a Sign language that is not yet well understood, the use of ASL signs with Washoe added a whole raft of new uncertainties to the investigation of the language abilities of apes.

Trading on the uncertainties in the linguistics of Sign, critics of these experiments argued that Washoe was faking it, that she never did learn to manage truly linguistic expressions. They argued that Washoe was just learning some of the picture-like signs of ASL, but never the syntax, i.e. the patterns of combining signs. And sometimes they argued that ASL was not

26

really a language at all--a conclusion which naturally upset many deaf people.

Neither the Gardners, nor Premack, nor Rumbaugh were aiming to see if their apes could acquire a human language. Their aims were simply to explore the cognitive capabilities of apes. They reckoned that mental powers vary in the world of creatures human and non. And, by any comparison, human mental powers rank at the top, especially considering the powers which humans use so blithely in constructing and interpreting language expressions. Apes, however, are first cousins to humans. Perhaps apes share with humans some of these extraordinary mental powers for language construction.

These experiments were not addressed to the question of whether an ape could handle a real human language. Experimenters were not even particularly interested in whether apes are clear and efficient communicators. For one thing, as soon as experimenters raise the issue of communication, they are forced to consider what apes might *mean*, that is, how they might feel, what they might think, etc. And, generally speaking, this is a can of worms that ape-language experimenters were reluctant to open. Once experimenters start asking about the thoughts and feelings of apes, they are very close to treating them as simple but amiable little chaps who need haircuts. Such an experimenter is close to becoming a Henry Higgins trying to transform a hirsute Lisa Doolittle into a civilized creature.

The main issue is not whether apes can think and feel and talk. The main issue is whether they can create and interpret syntactically structured symbolic expressions.

Their results of ape-language experiments along these lines has been nothing short of stunning, and therefore those results have been very unsettling. Washoe acquired a multiplicity of signed expressions. After four years of training, she controlled 132 signs. And now, at eighteen years of age, she commands 176 signs.

Not only does she command the signs, she also puts them together in creative ways. She learned the sign DIRTY to refer to feces and other soil, but then she began using that sign to create insults like DIRTY MONKEY and DIRTY ROGER. She fabricates such compounds as WATER BIRD for duck, CANDY FRUIT for watermelon, and CRY HURT FOOD for radishes. Interestingly, she has refashioned certain expressions, simplifying and relocating them as children often do with words they just learn. For example, she signs FLOWER with one finger rather than two.

The experiments of Premack and Rumbaugh left less room for such creativity; but, with tighter controls on the expressions to be used and on the situation in which those expression are pro-

27

duced, these latter experiments were able to pinpoint other talents of apes. Premack, for example, showed that Sarah could deal in abstractions. Of a triangular blue color chip which in this case meant apple, Sarah affirmed that it, i.e. an apple, was red and round. Rumbaugh's experiments were aimed at showing that Lana could be taught to respect the linear ordering of symbols as humans respect the order of words on a line. He showed, for example, that Lana could recognize the difference between a sentence like *Lana give machine apple* and *Machine give Lana apple* which differ only in regard to the order of words. It should be noted, however, that this simian ability to respect linear order is a far cry from the human command of syntax.

A second generation of ape language experiments has amplified and extended the conclusion that apes are cognitively gifted creatures. Fouts and Patterson have both continued the project of teaching apes to sign ASL. Patterson's gorilla Koko sports a vocabulary of 300 signed expressions. Koko has created such truly astounding compound expressions as EYE HAT for mask and ELEPHANT BABY for a Pinocchio doll.

Fouts has been working with groups of chimps, including Washoe, and he has shown that chimps can learn to sign from one another. Furthermore he has charted, for the first time, the sorts of occasions which elicit signing. He finds that chimps sign amongst themselves most often (39%) during social interactions like grooming and disciplining. They sign less often in situations of reassurance (29%) and play (20%). Finally, the chimps sign very seldom during eating (5%). This is understandable since when they eat, their hands are fully occupied.

The reaction of the scholarly audience to all these reports of experiments and observations has been mixed. And that is an understatement. Some scholars have gone far out on a limb, claiming that these experiments show that apes can acquire human languages. This conclusion, though a minority opinion, shakes the scientific and philosophical earth on which we all stand. Other scholars have adopted an equally extreme but contrary view, namely, that the chimps are faking it.

Mental Capabilities and Human Nature

The argument over whether apes do or do not exhibit language-like cognitive abilities is germane to the philosopher's enterprise of determining the limits of the human species.

Enlightenment philosophers supposed that the defining characteristics of the human species are mental. For that reason they examined human languages, looking for the logical, computational skills which are implied by those human languages. Con-

temporary researchers are continuing that same line of inquiry
with their ape-language experiments.

This last view, that the chimps are faking it, has been
strengthened by the gear-shifting of Herbert Terrace (1979).
Terrace began teaching a chimp ASL signs in 1973. After four
years of work, the chimp, Nim Chimpsky, had built a reliable
vocabulary of 125 signs and exhibited many of the same creative
behaviors described for Washoe and Koko. All seemed to be going
well in heaven and in ape-language experimentation.

But after Nim was returned to the Oklahoma Institute for
Primate Studies, Terrace had an opportunity to meditate on the
masses of data which had been accumulated during the project.
And, unexpectedly for many, his meditations led him to some
serious doubts about his experiment.

Nim, he said, certainly had a good memory, and an acute
ability for observing the people around him, especially his
observers, but he did not exhibit any behavior which could be
called language-like. When children learn to talk, they begin
with short utterances and build to longer ones. Nim never built
longer utterances. Children, even at the early stages of language acquisition, initiate many utterances. Nim almost never
did. As children grow, they imitate adult talk less and less
frequently, but as Nim developed, he imitated the utterances of
experimenters more frequently. Nim, Terrace concluded, was a
very shrewd chimp. He learned to produce the sorts of behaviors
that observers were looking for. And in return he was rewarded
with a pretty flashy life-style, chimp-wise. But he was not a
competent language user.

It is true, Nim learned a sign DIRTY for feces. And it is
also true that Nim, like Washoe, extended that sign beyond its
original context. But instead of interpreting this behavior as
an instance of linguistic creativity, Terrace is more cynical.
"Nim learned to sign DIRTY when he needed to use the toilet. He
also learned that this sign had a reliable effect on his teacher's behavior: the teacher interrupted whatever he or she was
doing and took him to the bathroom." Quickly Nim learned to use
DIRTY as an escape ploy. When he was confronted with a trying or
disagreeable situation, he would sign DIRTY to escape. Nim is
not so much a metaphor-maker as a shrewd operator. Washoe and
Koko were probably no different.

Terrace reviewed Nim's behavior with this sort of cynicism,
and then cast his jaundiced glance across the whole field of ape-
language experimentation. From other corners, similar suspicions
about these experiments were given voice. The Sebeoks of Indiana
University, for example, rehearsed the famous case of Clever

29

Hans, the turn-of-the-century "thinking horse." This horse seemed for all the world to be able to tap out answers to verbal and mathematical problems with its hooves, but not so. Hans's real talent consisted of observing his trainer closely. That is, Hans picked up unintentional cues from his trainer and discovered in those cues when to continue or stop his tapping. In the same way, said the Sebeoks, Washoe, Koko, Nim, Sarah, and Lana may be not gifted linguistically, but they are, like Hans, keen observers of the psychologists who wish they were.

The story continues. The critics of the ape language experiments have been met with cogent responses and then counter criticisms. And with each new level of criticism the edge on the debate gets sharper. Not only are the talents of the apes being investigated, now the talents of the experimenters are under scrutiny. However if I may say so, any dedicated student of Mickey Mouse would have expected such a bitterly fought contest over a such serious story about talking animals even if the story be called scientific. The issue is just too hot.

In a certain way, this scholarly debate is like a professional football game. It has two distinct groups of viewers who appreciate it in two quite different ways. The first groups of viewers of a football game is the general audience, the faithful, committed, often half-tanked, fans who cheer their home team forward. The game, from their perspective, is an event of gaining yards and scoring points. They may be able to distinguish a play action pass from a shot gun, but their attention is wholly focussed on pass completions, first downs, and points. The second group of viewers is the coaches and team mates on the side lines. For them the gross characteristics of a particular play are irrelevant compared to the fine points of execution.

These coaches and team mates really know what makes the game work. And that, of course, is the reason why networks invite the Giffords, the Simpsons, the Brodies, and the Tarkentons into the press boxes to comment on the play by play. These player-commentators bless the general audience with a view of the game through fine-tuned eyes. Who would know about soft hands, clothesline passes, and rapid lateral movement if Frank Gifford were not there to tell us about them? In short, it takes a player to know the game.

In a similar way, insiders appreciate the ape language experiments in ways that the general audience does not. General readers look for arguments to support the views they are rooting for or to negate opposing views. Hooray, apes are language-less brutes! Boo, apes can construct linguistic metaphors!

However, insiders are less concerned about rooting for or against apes. The linguist's objective is to clarify the term "a language" which is used in the debate and to distinguish the criteria used for rating the talents of apes.

For example, linguists are more interested in the specific talents of apes than in the gross issue of whether they can "talk." The linguist wants to know whether apes can manipulate symbols independently of their referents and if they can comprehend syntactically contrastive utterances as humans do. For linguists, the issue is not whether apes combine communicative skills with computational ability as humans do when they talk. Linguists want to know only if apes possess a computational ability.

In the same vein, the linguist is concerned with how the apes acquire their talents. Note that Terrace went to great lengths to compare Nim's linguistic development with child language acquisition. The motivation for this concern is the suspicion that linguistic knowledge is such a specialized kind of knowledge that it must be built up in a rigidly ordered step-wise fashion. A chimp might appear to sign without having acquired its "language" in such a step-wise fashion, but chances are, its talents would fall far short of human talents.

Finally Noam Chomsky has argued that the development of a mental grasp of sentence organization (syntactic structures) is especially critical in human language acquisition. Apes may show themselves to be extraordinary by their learning of a communication system. And they may even exhibit symbolic creativity by putting signs together in novel ways. But if apes cannot mark the relationships between constituents of a sentence, they cannot be said to have crossed Muller's Rubicon.

The rationale for Chomsky's emphasis on syntax is his belief that the syntactical core of any language is so complicated and so specific in its form that none but the specifically gifted human mind can acquire it. Communicative ability and symbolic representation are great talents that humans may share with other creatures, but only the human mind can manage the acquisition of syntax, and only the human person profits from the freedom and creativity that such syntactic knowledge affords.

Summary

As far as the man-in-the-street is concerned, ape-language experiments are like circus acts in which experimenters get chimps to talk with the hands. But the linguists on the inside see the matter this way: Ape-language experiments are inquiries into what a language is and into what mental powers are involved in the use of a language. By seeking answers to these questions in apes rather than in humans, the experimenters expect that they will get a clearer perspective on what it means to be human. Thus, as with Mickey Mouse stories, the story of ape-language experiments aims to unravel the culturally central paradox of talking animals so as to clarify our understanding of human nature.

In the forthcoming chapters we will enter into this linguistic project more fully. We will build on the elementary principles presented here in order to advance our understanding of human nature. First, we will reinforce the principle that the language ability is not synonymous with the ability to communicate. Communication, we will see again, has little or nothing to do with what linguists mean by language. Rather, the language ability involves mental powers for creating and comprehending symbolic expressions arranged in syntactically structured phrases. Second, we will move beyond Sarah's rudimentary symboling of APPLE, and beyond the primitive creativity of Washoe's WATER BIRD, and beyond Lana's simple phrase MACHINE GIVE LANA APPLE, and we will describe more precisely the mental powers that structuralist linguists identify as the core of human nature. We will begin this extended exploration of mental powers in the next chapter by considering the paired concepts of figure/ground and type/token.

Chapter Three

A Structuralist Primer

Four preface-like comments will set us on the right path towards understanding structuralist linguistics. A comment on the meaning of mind will clarify the purpose behind structuralist linguistic descriptions. Comments on two sets of oppositions, figure/ground and token/type, will describe the object of structuralist linguistic investigation. And a final comment on deduction will clarify the method used by structuralist linguists.

On Mind

Saussure, Chomsky, and a host of other structuralist linguists agree on a single central principle for their linguistic investigations: command of a language is made possible by a mind, and only humans are gifted with minds. However, this principle is enlightening only if we know what a mind is. And as the preceding discussion of apes and language has shown, it is sometimes difficult to determine what mind is and when it is operative.

For starters, we might consider the many meanings of the word "mind," and then settle on a single meaning for further discussion. The following common phrases all contain the word "mind," but the meaning of that word varies from phrase to phrase:

1. call to mind
2. something on my mind
3. change my mind
4. speak my mind
5. have a mind to...
6. mind reader
7. mind your own business
8. I don't mind...
9. the mind's eye.

In phrases 1 and 2, the word "mind" suggests a place or a location in which something can exist or to which something can be moved. Phrases 3-6 suggest a content rather than a place, a content of beliefs, attitudes, or concepts. All these phrases (1-6) may be commonplaces of everyday talk, but they do not figure prominently in structuralist discussions of mind. (Notable exceptions include the writings of Benjamin Lee Whorf and his followers, writings which associate languages and thought systems. Whorf's proposals will be examined more thoroughly in chapter ten.)

Phrases 7-8 require a more penetrating interpretation. People usually use these phrases without adverting to things mental.

33

I frequently heard West Indian women chiding their misbehaving children with a wagging finger and a sharp warning, "Mind!!!" These mothers were not referring to abstractions. Their intent was decidedly concrete. But despite their intentions, "Mind!!!," together with phrases 7 and 8, suggests a deeper meaning about mind. It suggests, not so much a place or a content, but a state, specifically a state of awareness or consciousness. To speak phrase 7 is to advise someone to be self-conscious rather than to be conscious of the doings of others. To say that one does not mind something, as in phrase 8, is to say that one has no particular feelings about something because one is not even conscious of it.

Psychologists have debated the issue of consciousness at great length. Some have argued that consciousness is a universal property of brains. Others, like Julian Jaynes (1976), have gone to the mat claiming that consciousness is a cultural trait which emerged during the course of human evolution. Phenomenological psychologists offer us methods for describing the contents of consciousness, and Freudians propose that human consciousness is paired with human unconsciousness, the latter being as rich with mental phenomena as the former.

Structuralist linguists deal in matter of consciousness and unconsciousness, but they generally stand clear of debates about the relationship between the two. For them, as we shall see, knowing a language involves an ability to manipulate abstract forms, an ability of which speakers are unaware. Such an ability, according to structuralists, is a kind of knowledge, but it is an unconscious knowledge. Their term "competence," which refers to this unconscious knowledge/ability, captures the subtlety of their notion of linguistic knowledge. Such a notion raises the hackles of some psychologists who cannot understand how a knowledge can be unconscious. But linguists leave the matter there. Their structuralist perspective does not prompt them to investigate the relationship of consciousness and un-consciousness in the mind.

Finally we come to the celebrated phrase 9, "the mind's eye." This phrase suggests a distinctive kind of vision, a capability of seeing what ordinary eyes cannot see. Such an extraordinary capability is just what Saussure, Chomsky, and most other linguists think of when they use the word "mind." Hence this phrase, "the mind's eye," deserves some lengthier discussion.

The mind's eye sees what bodily eyes cannot. The body's eyes see two mountain ranges running from north to south. The mind's eye sees parallel lines. The body's eyes see a palomino, a roan, an appaloosa, and a chestnut. The mind's eye sees "horse." In short the mind's eye sees abstract general form behind concrete particular substance.

Such a notion of mind's eye is as old as Plato. He argued that something like a "mind's eye" is what provides us with real knowledge. And for him, real knowledge meant a knowledge of ideal forms or essences which constitute the unchanging under-girders for the concrete but shifting realities that we can grasp with our senses.

Structuralists aim to reveal and describe such a mind's eye. But unlike Plato, the structuralists characterize the mind's eye as a specifically linguistic faculty, one which enables speakers to know the abstract forms which support the concrete but shifting realities of a language. Everyday and in many ways, speakers tap this mental faculty, this linguistic mind's eye. They call upon it in the course of interpreting the speech of others and in producing their own talk.

Does it surprise you to hear that a language user's genius consists in knowing the abstract forms that stand behind concrete expressions? I suspect that it does. We tend to associate languages closely with the activity of communicating. And consequently we expect that when linguists describe languages, they describe the process of communicating. However, structuralist linguists neither know very much nor care very much about the activity of communicating. Since the turn of the century, when Saussure returned the linguistic enterprise to its philosophical moorings, structuralist linguists have focussed their attention on languages as systems administered by something like a mind's eye. *Linguistic description is focussed not on communication, but on a speaker's ability to recognize as one, expressions which seem to be many.* A structuralist's grammar describes how a speaker knows to judge expressions invariant when in reality those expressions are quite variable. It describes how a speaker hears just a sound "k" in different productions of the word "kit" when, in reality, people are producing many varying "k"'s.

Figure and Ground

Languages in the structuralist view are systems of informative expressions. Being systems of informative expressions, languages are like distant galaxies which emit pulses of light. They are like aerial photographs of cities lit up for the night. They are like air traffic controllers' video screens, full of blips and flashes. They are simply presentations of information.

The light pulses of distant galaxies, the dots of light on the aerial photos, the blips on a video screen, and the expressions of a language are all information systems. Each is considered a system of information because each is a collection of contrasts, light against blackness, sound against silence. Information is contrast, and systems of information are collections of contrasts.

Perhaps you think this account mixes apples and oranges. The contrasting sounds of spoken English differ, you say, from the contrasting pulses of light from a distant galaxy. The contrasting sounds *mean* something; the contrasting pulses of light do not.

The structuralist response to such an observation is sharp and strong and unquavering: The meaning of spoken expressions is irrelevant. Meaning, after all, is a characteristic of communication; and, as has already been stated, structuralists ignore the fact that languages are used to communicate. Instead, structuralists focus on a language as if it were a system of meaningless pulses, a system of informative contrasts. In technical terms, they consider a language to be a "formal system."

The first thing to note about "formal systems" is that they can involve contrasts arranged temporally or atemporally. The light pulses of a distant galaxy constitute formal system of contrasts presented temporally or diachronically, i.e. through time. But the dots of light on an aerial photo constitute an atemporal system of information. The contrasts are presented all at one time on the photographic paper. Such a system can also be called a system of synchronic contrasts.

A language, understood as a formal system of contrasts, is really a diachronic system. Sounds, words, and sentences are rolled out one after the other through time. However, linguists always transcribe those expressions onto paper. And once on paper, the expressions constitute a synchronic system in which contrasts are presented all at once. On paper, the original diachronic contrasts of a language become like dots on an aerial photo.

Why such a transcription from a diachronic formal system to a synchronic one? One basic reason is ease of analysis. The analysis of a synchronic system does not rely on the photographic memory that would be required for doing an analysis of a complex diachronic system. It is for this reason that all scientists, and not just linguists, transcribe diachronic data into a printed form for analysis.

Now to the nature of contrasts in a formal system. A casual inspection of a synchronic formal system of visible contrasts, say, an aerial photo, suggests that information contrasts in such a system are contained in *figures* that stand out against a non-informative back*ground*. White dots draw our attention, not the black background on which they are displayed. The white dots, we suppose, present the information.

However, contrary to common sense, the ground can often be informative. Escher's drawing "Fish and Scales" on the next page

36

presents the case better than any words can. The black ground on which any white fish is defined is actually the figure of a black fish which stands out against its white ground. In this drawing, figure and ground both present informative contrasts. This drawing demonstrates that figures have no corner on information.

Generally, the simpler the figure and the more restricted and limited the possibilities for the ground, the greater is the likelihood that the ground carries information. Consider the drawing on the next page in which the black ground is as informative as the white figure MAIL BOX. Here the ground space is severely restricted and the white figure is relatively simply.

Both the size of ground and its manner of presentation have a bearing on our ability to recognize the information that the ground carries. Look carefully at the drawing and realize that the ground space is approximately one inch by four inches in size. Interestingly, the illustrator left off the frame for this ground space. The lack of a frame leads us to believe that the ground of the illustration is the white space of the page. Hence we fail to perceive the white figure MAIL BOX.

In the case of the formal systems of languages, similar ground conditions are realized, but to an extraordinary degree. That is, sound grounds are sufficiently restricted, and sound figures are presented in such a way, that the ground of language sounds becomes more informative than the sound figures. Though it flies in the face of common sense, linguists conclude that the human mind processes the elementary contrasts of language by perceiving and managing informative ground-silences rather than figure-sounds.

Silences, not sounds, are responsible for the elementary contrasts of human languages. Sound-figures present less information than silence-grounds. To ears trained according to the rules of common sense, the initial *sound* of "pat" seems to contrast with the initial sound of "bat." However, linguists tell us that our recognition of this "p/b" contrast is actually a recognition of the contrast between the silence-grounds that surround these figures. Specifically, the initial sound of "pat" is perceived as *lacking* the quality of voicing (vibration of vocal cords). Not just "p/b," but all contrasting human language sounds are recognized in terms of the sound qualities which are absent.

Actually, the perception of absent sound qualities is even more complex than the foregoing description suggests: Speech sounds do not differ by way of crisp clean absences of sound qualities. Rather, they are quite variable. If we were to think of sound systems as white dots on black paper, the edges of the dots would be varying shades of gray. Yet, amazingly, the human ear is able to sort through that variability and discern contrasts. It is as if the ear had a mind's eye of its own.

Experiments with synthetically produced speech sounds illustrate this process (Cutting and Eimas 1975). Machines that synthesize speech sounds are directed to produce unvoiced "p"'s

38

along with a continuum of other sounds with increasingly more voicing right up to the fully voiced "b"'s. Tests of sound-recognition show that speakers generally agree on the precise amount voicing which must be absent before that sound is considered a "p." Evidently humans are gifted with an almost uncanny ability for classifying speech sounds according to precise a-mounts of absence.

Some researchers doubt that such experiments demonstrate a unique human ability for perceiving speech sounds. Similar experiments with human speech sounds done with chinchillas and Japanese quail produce results like those above. Maybe the designs of all these perception experiments are faulty. Or maybe ground-based perception is not an exclusively human process.

A warning about this account of the perception of speech sounds. The linguists behind these experiments about ground-based perception do not claim to be proving that real people actually go through a psychological process like the ground-based perception described above. They are not describing actually operative human speech recognition or the manner in which the human brain processes speech sounds. Rather, the linguists are describing formal systems and how they *can be* known.

Structuralists are working with white dots on black pages, pulses on screens, blips of pure information. And, as they wrestle with the puzzle of information that such systems present, they try to explain how such information could be known if knowledge were maximally efficient and maximally simple. They hope that human brains operate with maximal efficiency and simplicity, and they hope that their descriptions accurately portray what happens in human brains. But only a direct inquiry into brain structure and function will say for sure. In the meantime, linguists work on languages as formal systems, hoping, but never directly documenting, that their descriptions of the formal systems of human languages are also descriptions of human cognitive operations.

A second comment on this same issue. It should not be particularly bothersome that the ground-based perception described for formal systems of speech sounds seems far too cumbersome ever to be an actual cognitive process. After all, the machine language of a word-processor seems far too abstract and cumbersome to ever serve as a vehicle for managing words. But in a word-processing computer, the operator works with a familiar language or a programming language which, at another level, controls the very abstract machine language which in turn controls the computer. Might not a human brain operate in the same way, with a sound recognition process that looks very simple but which controls that much more abstract ground-based perception at the core of cognition (see Hofstadter 1979)?

39

Cumbersome though it be, and based on analyses of formal systems rather than on brain processes, the conclusion that we have reached about elementary levels of information perception in languages is that they are ground-based rather than figure-based. The restricted grounds, i.e. absences of a limited number of sound qualities, make it possible for language contrasts to be perceived in terms of what is absent rather than in terms of sound that is present.

Such ground-based information processing clearly influences descriptions of languages as systems of sounds (chapter four). But, as chapters five, six, and ten will demonstrate, this same property figures into descriptions of syntax, language universals and semantics.

Tokens and Types

The letter "a" looks very little like any of the four letters below. Nor do the four letters below much resemble each other. Yet, without hesitation, all literate English speakers would agree that all five letters are identical. Any one of the five could occupy the slot in *p_t* and produce a single expression. But if *o* or *e* should fill that slot, the expression would be quite different. Thus, all five letters are different in appearance, but we treat them as one when they are doing the work of communicating.

The printed letters, so different in shape, are different *tokens* of a single letter *type*.

The tokens themselves can be described quite easily in terms of straight lines and curved. However, we cannot easily describe a shape for the type that stand behind the four tokens. Perhaps you want to argue that the letter type above is an "A" for that is how its token appears in most formal circumstances. But you might as well argue for "a" because that shape is the most frequently occurring. No one of these arguments prevails over others because what a letter type looks like is unknowable; it is abstract. Types are mental, not physical, realities.

Why are a diversity of tokens needed to stand in for a single letter type? Why not just one? Why four "a" tokens rather than just a single all-purpose "a"? The answer has a great deal to do with the positive qualities of letter tokens. Tokens, unlike types, are material objects and they always contribute some positive effect by reason of that materiality. Token (1) below, for example, in addition to summoning to mind a negatively defined letter type, unavoidably affects the eye by its great size and bold lines. It is an emphatic "a." Similarly, token (2) with its curving lines conveys a distinct fluidity and grace.

(1)   (2)   (3)

The contrast between the boldness of (1) and the grace of (2) is difficult to capture in words, but this contrast can be important for establishing associations between the token and external conditions. For example, the bold or graceful shape of the two tokens above effect two different emotional reactions. The illuminated letter (3) connects the token to a story, perhaps a sacred story. The physical characteristics of tokens bring certain experiences to mind quite apart from their function of standing in for letter types.

Letter tokens can remind us of situations and experiences. In this sense they point outside of themselves to other realities. But when they serve as stand-ins for letter types they point inward, that is, to aspects of a mental system of types. Most of the time, of course, they perform both kinds of communications simultaneously.

Searching out the external linkages of tokens is an especially complicated task. Such a search leads us back into a tangle of human needs for different sorts of communicative expressions. Different tokens have evolved to serve those needs, and, to the degree that the needs are complex, the tokens themselves defy all simple functional explanations. For example, imagine how complex would be the explanation for the diversity of alphabetic tokens, an explanation which would have to include an account of the flourished "c" of the Coca Cola trademark and the lightening bolt of a "z" in Zenith. Clearly the logic of tokens

41

is as tangled as the history of human expressive needs.

It is just this tangled logic of tokens, a logic bordering on silliness, that led George Bernard Shaw to ask why the letters "gh-o-ti" might not be used to spell the word "fish" instead of "f-i-s-h." After all, he argued with tongue firmly placed in cheek, "gh" can stand in for a sound like the one usually represented by the token "f", but only in a context like the word "trough". Similarly the token "o" can stand in for the sound usually represented by the letter token "i" but only in the context of the word "women". And the token "ti" can stand in for "sh," but only in a context like the word "nation."

Shaw's cynicism aside, he appreciated the double nature of alphabetic tokens. On the one hand, tokens stand in for types. On the other hand, tokens work together with surrounding tokens to create a rich and variable ambience in which the information of types can be presented.

The alphabetic token and types discussed above will help us to appreciate the objects described by structuralist linguists. Structuralist linguists struggle to identify abstract language types and to discern the relationship of those abstract types to concrete tokens. The different kinds or classes of language types that attract the attention of linguists are sound types or *phonemes* (chapter four), types of meaningful units or *morphemes* (chapter five), syntactic types or *phrase structures* (chapter five), and meaning types (chapter ten).

At each level, linguists aim to describe how it is that speakers of a language are able to recognize abstract types in the concrete tokens that are heard and spoken. Those descriptions take the form of *rules of grammar*. The purpose behind a rule of grammar is to describe type-token relations. (At this point it is customary for linguists to sound a claxon warning that structuralist rules of grammar *describe*; they do not *prescribe*. The linguistic assumption is that speakers are, from childhood, competent in their language; they don't need anyone setting down rules telling them how to put together units in a systematic fashion. Traditional school grammars prescribe rules for polite and literate talk; structuralist grammars describe rules that speakers use to construct strings of contrastive units.)

Rules of grammar are terse quasi-mathematical statements the core of which consists of three elements: Input --> Output. The input is the abstract type which makes up part of a speaker's competence or knowledge of his or her language. The output is the concrete token which realizes or makes concrete--"instantiate" is a helpful though cumbersome term for this realization/ concretization. The arrow (-->) expresses the relationship of instantiation. Linguists presume that the rules, as well as the inputs/types, are part of every speaker's competence. Speakers know language types/inputs and also how those types can be realized in tokens/outputs.

Rules of grammar are expressions of type/token relationships. Predictably there are phonological rules of grammar which relate phonological type (phonemes) to concrete sounds (phones). There are morphological rules of grammar which relate types of meaningful units (morphemes) to concrete words and word parts (morphs). Finally, there are syntactic rules which relate syntactic types (deep structures) to the concrete phrases and sentences of a language (surface structures).

A rule of grammar, whether at the phonological, morphological, or syntactic level, relates a type to a token. In terms of the preceding discussion, that means that rules relate abstract mental units which are ground-defined to concrete token-figures. Stating such a relationship is a tall order. And, because linguists operate only on formal language systems and have no direct access to brains or brain processes, the best they can do is to state the conditions of the relationship.

Rules of grammar state the conditions of type/token relationships by setting down the *linguistic environments* in which the relationship occurs. Setting down linguistic environments is the sort of thing G.B. Shaw did when he said that "o"-letter stands in for the "i"-sound in the word "women." "Women" is the linguistic environment in which the the "i" --> "o" is found in English spelling. Generally, the linguistic environments of a rule are the aspects or qualities (phonological, morphological, or syntactic) which precede or follow the type and which make possible the application of the rule. Linguistic environments are expressed in phonological and morphological rules--syntax marches to a different drummer--by a slash (/) following the output-token in the rule statement, together with a bar "___" which indicates the position of the type in its environment. For example:

$$I \rightarrow O \ / \ X \ \underline{\quad} \ Y$$

can be read as: I (Input) is realized as O (Output) in the environment in which I is preceded by X and followed by Y.

To nominate this as a rule of grammar is to say that a person who speaks O knows both that O realizes I and does so in the environment or circumstances where I is preceded by X and followed by Y. Once again, claiming that a speaker *knows* such a rule is not to say that the speaker is aware of such a rule. Nor is it to say that the speaker's brain operates in terms of such a rule. Claiming that a speaker knows such a rule or is competent in such a rule is just to say that such is the sort of knowledge which one would have to have in order to manage the instantiation

43

of I by O.

The M.O.

On the long car trips that we've taken with our kids, someone would always begin the "I'm going camping" game. The game would proceed like this:

Cathy: I'm going camping and I'm going to bring a kayak. Does anyone want to come along?

Bill: Sure. I'm going camping and I'm going to bring my knitting.

Cathy: Sorry, you can't go.

Fritz: I'm going camping and I'm going to bring a canteen.

Cathy: Sorry, you can't go.

Kate: I'm going camping and I'm going to bring a tent.

Cathy: Good, you can come along.

Just about now, Fritz and Bill would be scratching their heads. Then a face would brighten and one of them would say:

I'll bring some grog.

Cathy: Great, you can come too.

Friends who had come along for the ride jumped right in with an offer to go camping, but there was no plan behind their offerings. They shouted aimlessly, and got frustrated in the process. Fritz, Bill, and Kate, on the other hand, knew what they were driving at. They knew that before someone gets invited, they have to offer to bring along the right something, specifically the something that fits the unspoken rule which Cathy alone has in mind. In this case—have you figured it out?—the rule is that the word begins and ends with the same letter. So if someone wants to be invited, they have to figure out that rule. If someone should offer to bring a bib, they would be invited, or strawberries or a lentil.

The conditions of this game are analogous to the conditions of writing rules of grammar. The speaker has *in mind* some *rule*. But she never puts the rule into words. (In this case Cathy consciously knows the rule; in the case of speakers of a language, they are not aware that they know rules.) It is the task of linguist, just as it is the task of Bill, Kate, and Fritz, to

44

discern the mental rule.

In the game, as for the linguist, the speaker produces utterances that are in accord with the mental rule. But more importantly, the speaker can make judgments about whether some proposal is in accord with the rule. (Even though speakers are unaware of rules, they are able to distinguish proposed utterances that match those rules from utterances that do not. You perform just such a judgment of grammaticality when you say that *Boy the cookies chocolate baked.* is not a good English sentence--an asterisk conventionally notes a expression that is judged ungrammatical.)

Like Bill, Kate, and Fritz, linguists take advantage of the speaker's ability to make grammatical judgments. They make use of those judgments to ferret out grammatical rules. In the game, Bill started by proposing a likely utterance, an utterance which began with the same letter as Cathy's kayak. It was a guess. Nothing more. Further along, the kids ruled out the possibilities which Cathy's judgments excluded. By the time Fritz and Bill had heard the first right guess, tent, their minds were racing for a possible rule. When Fritz proposed grog, he thought he had it, but he couldn't be sure until he got Cathy's affirmation. Once his grog was affirmed, he could have continued all day long, applying the rule and having his proposals accepted.

The procedure followed by the kids in the game is precisely the sort of deductive procedure employed by linguists to discern rules of grammar. They start out by guessing. No shame in that. Karl Popper says that all of science begins with such guessing. Linguists subject their guesses to the tests of speaker judgments. Once they discover what sorts of phenomena are judged ungrammatical--and here wrong guesses can be every bit as enlightening as lucky right guesses--, they proceed by deduction to a likely rule of grammar. Once they have what they think is *the* rule, for a particular case, they test and retest their rule, trying it out on different speakers or using it in different ways.

This is linguist's M.O. Interestingly, it is also the M.O. which children seem to use as they go about acquiring their grammar of a language. Children, that is, are little linguists who deduce, without ever being aware of it, the structures of their languages.

The structuralists claim is that children are little linguists who acquire languages by deduction and hypothesis testing. Such a claim is altogether consistent with the structuralist imputation of power and significance to the human mind. Though a child's deductive activity proceeds at an unconscious level, it proceeds far more quickly and far more completely than can the conscious deductive activity of the linguists. After all, child-

45

ren on their own complete the task of grammar building in a couple of years, whereas linguists with all their heads together have not succeeded in accomplishing nearly as much in decades. The silent and natural operation of the human mind is a mysterious and uncanny force. Its full power is available to the naive and untutored, but out of reach of the conscious control of adults. (More will be said about the assumption that everyman is, as Kenneth Gergen says (1982), a "little scientist" in chapter fourteen.)

Summary

If you are to understand anthropological linguistics, you will need to understand the structuralist perspective. This is because the structuralist perspective is either the basis of anthropological linguistic descriptions or the foil against which alternative anthropological descriptions are raised.

If you are to understand the structuralist perspective, you must understand that it is, at its core, a deeply psychological perspective which presumes that the human mind is specially gifted to discern the abstract in the concrete, the general in the specific, the unitary in the diverse, and the universal in the particular. This capability is referred to by the expression "the mind's eye."

The mind's eye operates differently from the body's eye. First, the mind's eye perceives absences rather than presences, and grounds rather than figures. This ability to perceive absences and grounds is what makes it possible for the mind's eye to see categories and types whereas the body's eye can see only variable tokens.

A grammar of a language is a description of one portion of this grand human mental capability. A grammar of a language is a collection of descriptions of utterance tokens perceived as types.

The mind's eye and its amazing ability to see the abstract in the concrete is an abstract mental eye. Hence, linguistics is a science of the abstract, not a science of the concrete and physical world. It is therefore different from geology or astronomy. However, to say that linguistics is a science of the abstract is not to say that it is a voodoo. It is still an empirical science. It is empirical because linguists base their every description on the empirical evidence of utterances and judgments about utterances.

Chapter 4

Phonology

This chapter on phonology and the next chapter on morphology and syntax are the two most straightforwardly informative chapters in the book. Their aim is to walk you through structuralist approaches to the major classes of language types, phonemes, morphemes, and syntactic structures. A general knowledge of these approaches is a prerequisite for understanding the aspects of the structuralist perspective that appeal to anthropologists (chapters six, seven, and eight) and for appreciating alternatives to the structuralist perspective (Parts II and III).

First in line for discussion here is phonetics, the linguistic discipline devoted to the describing and transcribing of the physical sounds of languages. Then it is on to phonology where we will deal with the concept of the phoneme, the notion of distinctive feature, the characterization of a rule of grammar, and descriptions of phonological processes.

Phonetics

The physical sounds of speech are concrete acoustical expressions. They are, if you will, sound tokens, but are more commonly referred to as phones.

Phones are speech sounds. They are not the only sounds that humans make with their mouths. Humans also grunt and groan and uuh and aah. But only the phones are of interest to linguists.

Phones can be segmental, which means that they seem to consist of sound segments strung together. The word "cat," for example, seems to consist of three sounds, a [k], a [æ], and a [t] sound. Such segmental phones are either consonantal or vocalic. Consonantal phones, like the [k] and the [t] of "cat" are produced with an obstruction in the flow of air from the larnyx through the lips. Vocalic segmental phones, like [æ] of "cat" are produced with a relatively free flow of air through the vocal tract.

Segmental phones *seem* to be independent segments, but, in reality, when described in terms of their acoustic characteristics, they are actually continuous sounds that flow into one another like currents in a river. The [k] of "cat" actually flows right into the [æ]. A sound spectrograph, a machine which transcribes sounds into pictures, would show that these segments have no clear boundaries; they flow in continuous, unbroken sound currents.

Nonsegmental phones include tones which are qualities of pitch that range over a series of segmental phones. Probably the

47

majority of human languages, like many Oriental and West African languages, are tone languages; they make use of tones as part of the constitution of semantically contrasting words. The Indo-European languages which are most familiar to us are not tone languages. Speaking non-tone languages, we take for granted acts of whispering and singing which, in tone languages, can be challenging kinds of activities. Whispering, after all, is speaking without the vocal cord vibration that makes tones. And singing is speaking put to the consciously constructed tones of song. In either case, the non-segmental phones of a tone language are clouded or hidden.

Usually, linguists employ square brackets [ ] to designate the written version of phones, both segmental and non-segmental.

Considerable effort has been devoted over the years to working out notations for the phones of humans languages. Nineteenth century phoneticians, i.e. students of phones, devised a variety of symbolic and alphabetic systems for representing audible expressions on paper. By the turn of the century, general agreement was reached on an International Phonetic Alphabet (IPA) which made use of alphabetic letters modified by diacritics to represent speech sounds. The advantage of this IPA system is that it provides written symbols for each and every possible speech sound, for Hindi retroflections, for exotic Xhosa clicks and even for the breathy, creaky, and whispered voices that many peoples use for speaking in special circumstances.

Such is the discipline of phonetics. It involves the survey of human speech sounds and the accurate representation of those sounds in written forms.

Many people spend the whole of their days doing phonetic research. And that research can sometimes be inventive and exciting. Consider, for example, the recent study by Charles Hockett (1985) of the origin and distribution of the [f] and [v] phones in languages of the world. His painstaking comparisons of languages show that [f] and its kindred phones are curiously distributed. They tend to appear in the speech of agricultural peoples, but less often among hunters, fishers, etc.. Hockett explains this curious distribution by pointing out that the production of an [f] sound is facilitated by what dentists call an overbite. It is easier to make the bottom lip approach the upper incisors when the upper incisors bite down just in front of the lower incisors instead of end to end with them.

Much evidence, he argues, warrants a claim that dental overbite is a recent anatomical development among humans, and is associated with the agricultural revolution. The chewing of grains, he supposes, favors the overbite. If that evidence were to be borne out, then it would be reasonable to suppose that dental overbite and the [f] phone, which overbite makes possible,

48

are associated with the agricultural revolution. Other evidence, however, places the appearance of dental overbite in more nearly modern times and associates it with the use of eating utensils. When spoons and forks replaced the "stuff and cut" method of eating--the teeth grab onto a hunk of meat; the knife then slices off a mouthful--, the end-to-end bite gave way to the overbite. If the evidence supporting this latter version of the origin of the dental overbite were to be borne out, then Hockett's proposal on [f] would go down the tubes: The [f] phone, it happens, occurs widely among peoples who do not use eating utensils.

A phonetic study like this one has an interest all its own. The very possibility of a phone like [f] being linked to and explained by a central human activity like agriculture gets the scientist's juices flowing. Is the speech of non-agriculture humans hobbled by a lack of [f]? Are other speech sounds similarly motivated?

However exciting as these questions are, you should also recognize that they are all peripheral to the central concerns of structuralist linguists. For structuralist linguists, phonetics, that is, the scientific study of sound tokens, is a handmaiden to phonology. Phonology is the more significant of the two because it is the discipline devoted to describing type/token relationships and to describing how speakers' minds manage those relationships.

The phonetic work of Hockett provides me with an opportunity to point out again, as I have before, that not all linguists subscribe to the objectives of the structuralist program. Hockett stands in a line of language scientists which began with Leonard Bloomfield. And the tradition within that line is a tradition of New-York-Times linguistics. Just as the New York Times boasts "all the news that's fit to print," so Bloomfieldian linguists describe all the facts of languages that are fit to be described.

Linguists in the tradition of Bloomfield are not philosophically oriented, and do not intend their descriptions to reveal the nature of the human mind. Their only guiding principle is that law-like statements about languages should be produced with rigorously scientific methods. The law-like statements may be in the realm of phonetics or phonology or syntax. And a description of one sort of phenomenon is neither more or less valuable than a description of any other.

Linguistics: From Philosophy to Science

In the nineteenth century, language study was transformed from a philosophical enterprise into an empirical discipline, a science devoted to generating knowledge by a systematic use of observation and logic.

Nineteenth century scientists prided themselves on the purity of their work. Their descriptions were based solely on observation. No taint of philosophy nor stain of art entered their writings. They reckoned that they followed the directions pointed out by their pure scientific curiosity, and they proceeded down their paths of research with philosophy-free methods of scientific investigation.

It was there, in the nineteenth century, that the New-York-Times image of science became both popular and highly respected as a source of purity and surety that was lacking at every other turn. Hockett's work attests to the continued devotion of many linguists in the twentieth century to this image.

With that reminder that the discipline of linguistics is fractured by multiple traditions with distinctive objectives, we can return to a discussion of phonology as understood in the structuralist perspective.

Phonology

Every language has a finite number of phonemes just as every alphabet has a finite number of letter types. Moreover, the phonemes of all languages are ground-based units, units defined by the absence of qualities. The English phoneme /a/ can be said to be defined in terms of the absences of other phonemes, e.g. /a/ = -/d/, -/u/, -/e/, etc.. (Slashes (/ /) are used to distinguish phonemes from phones in square brackets ([ ]); minus signs indicate absences.)

Understood as ground-based, negatively defined units, the phonemes of a language can be said to form a self-defining system. The definitions of the /e/ and the /u/ that appear in the formula above which defines the English phoneme /a/ are themselves defined in terms of /a/. In general, the absence of phoneme /x/ defines phoneme /y/, but the absence of phoneme /y/ defines phoneme /x/. When you follow out these definitions you discover that the system is circular: neither /x/ nor /y/ has any substance. It is as if phonemic systems were systems that pulled themselves into existence by their bootstraps.

Linguists have sought to get a grip on the negative definitions of phonemes by postulating distinctive features. Distinctive features are minimal dimensions of contrast. They are the universally available parameters for phonemic difference. By describing phonemes as bundles of distinctive features linguists are able to ground what otherwise seems to be self-defining

50

phonemic systems.

Distinctive features are the primal types of sound qualities in terms of which phonemes contrast with one another. Structuralist linguists assume that distinctive features are wired into the human brain in some way. No one has to learn how types of speech sounds contrast. From birth the mind already organizes such types according to distinctive features. Newborns with no acquired knowledge of a language respond to contrasts in speech sounds in a way that suggests a command of distinctive features. This and other evidence suggests that such distinctive features are universal and innate, that is, part of the nature of the human mind. The existence of a dozen or so such universal mental distinctive features makes possible all the phonemic contrasts in all human languages.

Distinctive features are binary dimensions of phonemic contrast. In simpler terms that means that distinctive features specify the ways in which phonemes differ from one another. For example, /p/ and /b/ in English differ with respect to the feature [± voicing], a feature which refers to the vibration of the vocal cords. (Normally, a feature will be presented in square brackets ([ ]) accompanied by a + or a - sign to indicate the presence or absence of a feature.) /p/ is [- voicing], and /b/ is [+ voicing]. The difference in voicing accounts for their phonemic distinctiveness.

The phonemes /p/ and /t/ in English are identical with regard to the feature [voicing]. But they are distinguished by a another feature, [± labial], which refers to the role of the lips in sound production. /p/ is [+ labial] and /t/ is [- labial]. Thus /t/ is [- voicing; -labial] whereas /p/ is [- voicing; + labial].

Distinctive features look suspiciously like articulatory qualities of phones. They include the feature [voicing] which refers to the vibration of vocal cords, and [obstruent] which distinguishes stop, fricative, and affricated consonants from nasal and lateral consonants, glides, and vowels as shown on the chart on the next page. Features specifying manner of articulation distinguish consonant classes, e.g. nasals, stops, fricatives, affricates, glides, velarized, and retroflexed consonants and laterals. And features specifying place of articulation further distinguish consonants into those produced in the front, mid-portions, and rear of the mouth. Vowels are specified by features which describe the height of the tongue and the placement of the tongue in the front, mid-portion, and rear of the mouth.

All these distinctive features are phrased in terms of physical dimensions. But remember that as phonemic distinctive features, these features identify dimensions of abstract con-

51

trast. (Distinctive feature terminology is sometimes used to identify phonetic as well as phonemic contrast. One must be careful to distinguish these two uses.)

Not all languages make use of the entire set of universal distinctive features in defining their phonemes. The features may be universally available, but they are not uniformly employed across languages. Russian has two "l" sounds, a /l/ and velarized /ł/ distinguished by the phonemic feature [± velarization]. English speakers ignore that potential dimension of contrast. They recognize only one /l/. And they do so despite the fact that their phonetic [l]'s are distinguished into [+ velar] as in *look* and [- velar] as in *leak*. Russian has two phonemes, /l/ and /ł/ instantiated by [l] and [ł] respectively.

Feature differences in any set of phones may or may not be used by speakers to signal phonemic differences. That is, they may or may not mark semantically distinct words. When certain features do establish phonemic differences, you will know it because the two words that vary by way of the single phonemic contrast--they are called a *minimal pair*--mean different things. Such meaning differences are the sure test of phonemic contrast.

Minimal pairs locate phonemic contrasts. The English words "bus" and "buzz" are semantically different without a doubt. Since they contrast in meaning, and since they are virtually identical in sound except for the final phones we know the final phones must contrast phonemically.

The English word "tip" may be pronounced in two phonetically distinct ways, [t^{h}Ip] and [tIp]. But since these two expressions do not differ in meaning, the contrast between [t^h] and [t] is not phonemic. In this case a phonetic contrast does not instantiate a phonemic contrast. Here, the phonetic contrast responds to extraneous factors and not to an underlying phonemic contrast. Nothing in the subtle aspiration [h] prevents it from instantiating a phonemic contrast. Just because we don't hear it "making a difference" does not mean that speakers of other languages don't either. In fact, that same phonetic aspiration does instantiate phonemic contrasts in Hindi. The Hindi words [k^{h}iil] and [kiil] do contrast in meaning. The former means a parched grain, the latter means nail. So in Hindi the aspiration [h] signals a phonemic contrast, though it does not do so in English.

One way to get a bird's eye view of the features which a particular language utilizes in establishing its phonemic contrasts is to draw up a feature matrix. A feature matrix is simply a list of the features that underlie the phonemic inventory of a language. A glance down any column headed by a phoneme reveals the positive and negative values of features which dis-

Chart of Consonant Symbols

	labial	labio-dental	dental	alveopalatal	velar	uvular	glottal
Stops							
voiced	b		d		g	G	ʔ
voiceless	p		t		k	q	
Affricates							
voiced				ǰ			
voiceless				č			
Fricatives							
slit (vd.)		v	ɣ				
slit (vl.)		f	θ		x		h
grooved (vd.)			z	ž			
grooved (vl.)			s	š			
lateral (vl.)			ł	ł			
Resonants							
nasal	m				n	ŋ	
lateral			l	ł			
median	w		r		y		

Chart of Vowels

	front	*central*	*back*
High	i (ü)	ɨ	(ǐ) u
Lower High	I		U
Mid	e (ö)	ə	(ě) o
Lower Mid		ʌ	
Low	æ	a	ɔ

53

tinguish that phoneme from others. The advantage of a feature matrix is that it demonstrates the structural similarities of phonemes of a language.

Human languages pick and choose from among distinctive features for the creation of phonemic contrasts. The features are fixed in number, and probably do not exceed thirty. All forty-five English phonemes can be distinguished with little more than a dozen features.

A Partial Feature Matrix
For Selected English Vowels

vocalic features   **English Vocalic Phonemes**

	i	e	ü	ö	u	o	i	a
round	-	-	+	+	+	+	-	-
high	+	-	+	-	+	-	+	-
front	+	+	+	+	-	-	-	-

The same set of features is supposed to be available to all human speakers, at all times and in all places. Features need not be learned. They are part of the human language learning machinery, "the language faculty" as Chomsky calls it. Naturally, a description of the universal set of phonological distinctive features would go a long way towards characterizing the human language capacity. However, at the moment, all descriptions of phonological features are considered tentative.

Phonemes contrast in a certain language because they are constructed of features which are distinctive. But there is more to phonemic contrast than just features. The position of the phoneme relative to other phonemes, i.e. the linguistic environment of the phoneme, is crucial. Before we can say that two units which are built out of contrasting features are phonemically distinctive in a certain language, we must be assured that those two units can occupy the same position in a word.

In German, as in English, [voicing] can be responsible for creating phonemic contrasts. The difference between *but* [bət] and *bud* [bəd] is signaled by a voicing difference in the last phones. But consider that German *tag* [tak], meaning day, which is pronounced differently from the plural *tage* [tagə]. Here the [k] and [g] differ in voicing, but they do not signal a phonemic contrast. The reason is that they cannot occupy the same positions. The [k] lies in word-final position, which is a position that [g] in German can never take. In technical terms, [k] and [g] are in "complementary distribution" in German.

In German, all word-final obstruents are devoiced, or [-voicing]. So the phonetic differences between [tak] and [tag] are, in a way, superficial, non-phonemic differences. Phonemic contrasts involving voicing in word-final position just do not arise in German because phonemes which contrast in voicing cannot both occupy that position.

Different positions "condition" different versions of the same unit, different tokens for the same type, different phones for the same phoneme. In "complementary" positions, one phoneme is often realized as different phones. We say that such phones are "allophonic variants" of the phoneme. "Allophonic variation" is a term which describes single phonemes taking on different phonetic appearances in different positions.

Remember G.B. Shaws' spelling of fish as *ghoti*. You can see something like allophonic variation in his argument that the English sound "f" can sometimes be spelled with a *gh* as in the word "trough," and sometimes *f* as in the word "floor." The *gh* and the *f* are spelled variants that function like allophones. In proposing *ghoti* as a spelling for "fish," Shaw intentionally confused the environments in which the two alphabetic realizations of "f" are appropriate.

An economical way of representing allophonic variation in human languages is by way of a phonological rule. The notion of a phonological rule probably originated back in the nineteenth century when linguists described rules of historical sound change. In that historical linguistics, rules were descriptions of inexorable mechanical changes over time. Here, in the realm of tokens and types, phonological rules describe inexorable processes, but not processes of historical change. Phonological rules describe instead the inexorable processes of the shaping, filtering and constraining of phonemes to fit contextual conditions.

Who or what does the shaping, filtering, and constraining? It is the "mind's eye."

The statement of a phonological rule consists of an input, placed to the left of an operation arrow, and an output, placed to the right of the arrow. The input is usually the phoneme; the output is the reshaped token, the phone. Following the output and after a slash, / , appears the relevant environment of the input, a line being used to indicate the precise position of the input relative to other tokens. The phonological rule on the next page formalizes the process through which initial unvoiced stops are aspirated, e.g. /tIp/ --> [t^{h}Ip].

$$\begin{array}{l} \text{+stop} \\ \text{-voicing} \end{array} \quad \text{-->} \quad \begin{array}{l} \text{+stop} \\ \text{-voicing} \\ \text{+aspir.} \end{array} / \;\# \# \_ V$$

(Double cross hatches, ##, stand for word boundaries.)

Notice that this phonological rule, like most phonological rules, is stated in terms of features rather than in terms of phonemes.

We could have said that /t/ becomes [t^h] before the sounds a,i,o,u, etc.. However, the statement of the rule in terms of features allows for greater generality: Not just /t/ and not just certain vowels are involved in this rule, but all unvoiced stops and all vowels are involved. There is a lesson to be learned here. Phonemes are abstract units defined by way of relations to other phonemes. Being essentially relational units, phonemes behave, when subjected to the conditioning effects described in a phonological rule, not as isolated entities but as members of a class. Distinctive feature statements in phonological rules serve to identify the appropriate phonemic class. Phonemes which behave or operate alike in similar positions are phonemes which share features. And phonemes which share features are said to form a phonemic class.

An Empirical Science of Mental Realities

Linguistic descriptions are empirical descriptions, in that they are based on the tokens which are produced and interpreted by speaking subjects. But they also reveal the abstract processes of the human mind. They bring us ever closer to deep philosophical understanding of the human mind.

How can a description be both empirical and philosophical? For an answer to this question we can recall two points raised in chapter three. First, phonological description is a description of a formal system of contrasts; it is not a direct description of human phonological knowledge or processes. Second, the procedure followed in arriving at such a description is roughly the procedure followed in playing the game "I'm going camping..." (p. 44). In short, deduction of formal rules of phonology from speaker judgments is what makes the empirical and philosophical aspects of phonological description.

Stating phonological rules in terms of features enables one to discern clearly the phonological classes which a speaker controls. Consider for example the rule which describes the

56

allophonic variation presented in the words of columns A and B below.

$$
\begin{matrix}
& & & & p \\
+ \text{ vocalic} & & + \text{ vocalic} & / \quad C\_ & t \\
+ \text{ low} \quad \text{-->} & & - \text{ low} & & k \\
& & & & s
\end{matrix}
$$

A	B
bite	tie
rice	fire
type	ride
bike	file

The vowel in the words of column A is the centralized [ʌi] but the vowel of the words in B is a low [ai]. As you may have suspected, the [ʌi] vowel is an allophonic variant of the [ai]. The [ʌi] vowel differs from the [ai] vowel, but never in such a way as to constitute itself a meaning difference. The difference between [ʌi] and [ai] is like the difference between an aspirated and an unaspirated [t] in words like [tʰIp] and [pʰIt]. The [ʌi] vowels in A are centralized when the following segment is [p, t, k, s].

One could present the phonological rule that describes this allophonic variation as shown above. But such a rule suggests that the environment for the rule application is an unrelated bunch of phones. If, however, the list of conditioning consonants is replaced by a feature statement, then it becomes apparent that the phonological process here is a a general one, conditioned, not by an unrelated bunch of phones, but by a class of phones.

$$
\begin{matrix}
+\text{vocalic} \quad \text{-->} & +\text{vocalic} & / \quad C\_ & -\text{voicing} \\
+\text{low} & -\text{low} & & +\text{obstruent}
\end{matrix}
$$

The value of distinctive features is that they greatly simplify statements of phonological rules. And they do so by locating the general processes which drive specific phonological operations.

Besides discerning classes of features which condition phonological rules, phonologists are interested in discerning the range of relationships between rule inputs, rule outputs, and rule constraints. An example from Spanish will illustrate this point. Spanish speakers say [bola] as they pronounce the word for ball. But they say [la Bola] ([B] is a bilabial fricative) when the word is preceded by its appropriate article. Here [b] and [B] are allophones in complementary distribution, the latter variant being the one which appears after a vowel.

It is no accident that the allophone [B] and not, say, [p] instantiates /b/ after vowels. The post-vocalic position favors this "weakened" consonantal variant. Moreover, consonant weakening, e.g. from stop to fricative, does not just occur with /b/ in Spanish. The word for "where" [donde] and [de d̪onde] ([d̪] indicates an affricated [d]) shows that weakening applies to other stop consonants as well. Indeed, in all languages with this phonological process, consonants are weakened in roughly the same ways, e.g. from stop to fricative. Wherever the shape of a stop consonant is adjusted after a vowel, the resulting consonants always turns up a similarly weaker version of the input.

Much effort in linguistics is devoted to describing such processes because they enable linguists to test putative universals of sound systems. As more and more diverse phonological rules are brought to light, we begin to get a clearer and clearer sense of the sorts of features which *can* enter into the construction of contrasts, and of the classes of features which *can* govern the alternation of allophones. In other words, as more and more facts about phonology come to light, the outer limits to phonological possibilities become clearer, and the universe of human phonological possibilities becomes more definite. And making clear the universe of human linguistic possibilities as seen by "the mind's eye" is what linguistics is all about.

Summary

The discipline of phonetics has made possible the transformation of oral expressions into written expressions. The discipline of phonology has made possible the discovery of type-token regularities in those oral-become-written expressions. The sound types are called phonemes; the sound tokens are called phones.

In doing phonology we discover that the phonemes of a language constitute a formal system. That is, the phonemes are elementary units which, like the notes of a musical key, are nothing in isolation, but together they constitute themselves as a significant system of contrasts.

In phonological research, the highest priority is given to the description of language universal phonological features and of language universal constraints on phonological rules. Phonological universals of both sorts are the primary objective of phonological research. In the structuralist's house, these descriptions are to be understood as accounts of how the mind's eye manages the phones that stand in for phonemes.

The description of the sounds of particular languages is not important in and for itself. Structuralist linguists do not particularly care that Nootka has no nasal consonants whereas most other human languages do, or that agricultural peoples use

[f] more frequently than non-agricultural peoples. Rather phonological descriptions are valuable just to the degree that they move us closer to an understanding of how the mind's eye operates at the level of sound. With such an understanding, we are just a little bit closer to appreciating the capabilities of the human mind.

Chapter Five

Morphology and Syntax

Generative linguistics, the theory inaugurated by Noam Chomsky in 1957 with Syntactic Structures and refined in Aspects of the Theory of Syntax in 1965, differs from other post-Saussurean structuralisms in that it emphasizes syntax, the patternedness of sentences, above all other aspects of languages. The objective of this chapter is to sketch the studies of morphology that were central to pre-Chomskyan grammatical studies, and then to outline Chomsky's "standard theory" of generative syntax, which is most often associated with Aspects. Subsequently, I will comment on "government-binding theory," and on other developments in syntactic theory since 1965. Throughout this presentation I will continue to employ the type-token distinction as a fruitful heuristic device for understanding the relations between aspects of syntax.

Pre-Chomskyan Syntax

Syntax occupies a place of great significance in the house of Chomsky's generative linguistics. Grammatical descriptions include phonetics, phonology, morphology, syntax, and semantics, but the most important of these is syntax. W. Lehmann says "the syntactic component is the most distinctive of human language...(and) is central in language" (1978: 6).

The reason for according syntax a significant place over other aspects of a speaker's knowledge is that syntactic knowledge, more than any other, demonstrates the "creativity" of the speaking subject. Syntax is a door to the most inventive, insightful, creative, and logical aspects of the mind. It is the door to the most human side of the mind's eye.

In order to appreciate the heavy role played by syntactic competence in this theory, it is necessary to return for a moment to Saussurean linguistics, and to the understanding of linguistic knowledge that was developed there.

In Saussure's view, the central unit of a grammar is the morpheme. A morpheme is an abstract unit which is constituted of phonemes and which contrasts semantically (in meaning) with other morphemes. Being an abstract unit, a morpheme is a mental type which is made concrete in a morph-token. (In morphological studies, slashes / / will enclose morphemes; square brackets [ ] will enclose morphs.)

Morphemes may be single words that can stand on their own, /cat/, /talk/, etc.. In that case, we call them "free morphemes." Or morphemes can be attached to other morphemes, e.g. suffixes, prefixes, etc.. Such morphemes are called "bound morphemes" for

61

they cannot stand on their own. Saussure argued that morphemes, free and bound, constitute the fundamental units of a speaker's knowledge of a language.

Just as phonological rules describe the relationship between phonemes and phones, so morphological rules describe the relationship between morphemes-types and morphs-tokens. In such rules the input is a morpheme, the output is a morph, and the conditions of the variation are stated explicitly. A rule for accounting for one token of the past tense English suffix would be:

past --> /-ed/ / [regular verb root] # ___ ##

This rule says that the past tense is realized for regular verbs by the suffix <u>-ed</u>. (A single cross-hatch # indicates the seam between two morphemes; double cross-hatches ## indicates the seam between two words.)

Structural grammars as envisioned by Saussure should consist of all the rules needed to account for the appearance of morphs as they stand in for morphemes. Since morphemes were considered to be the fundamental units of a language, such a vast collection of morphological rules was considered the core of a grammar of a language.

Other aspects of grammatical description were secondary or tertiary relative to this core of morphological rules. Phonological description, for example, was significant primarily because it described the constitution of morphemes. And syntactic description of the patterns of morpheme combinations in phrases, clauses, and sentences, was considered to be a matter of accounting for morpheme groupings.

Look at almost any grammar of a language written in America in the 1940's and 1950's. You will find that the bulk of the work is a description of morpheme classes, that is, of the kinds of morpheme tokens which count, in that language, as morpheme types. The little rule above for past tense in English illustrates what is meant by a morpheme class in English when it states that *-ed* is bound to a "regular verb" root. Such a phrasing suggests that the grammar of English must include at least two morpheme classes of verbs, regular and irregular. The task of the linguist is to decide which morphs instantiate which morpheme classes.

Following a lengthy section of morphology, the typical grammar included a section on syntax and then a selection of texts which illustrate the syntax. The section on syntax consisting of morpheme sequences was usually little more than a list of the morpheme sequences that appear in the texts.

According to the Saussurean view of syntax, phonological-morphological processes are of quite a different order from syntactic processes. The realization of morphemes in morphs occurs in a synchronic, atemporal, vertical dimension. The combination of morphs to form phrases, clauses, and sentences occurs in a diachronic, temporal, horizontal dimension.

The vertical dimension, sometimes called the paradigmatic dimension of linguistic structures, constitutes the proper arena for the analysis of language systems. The horizontal dimension, also called the syntagmatic plane, is the dimension of history rather than of knowledge, and of change rather than of states.

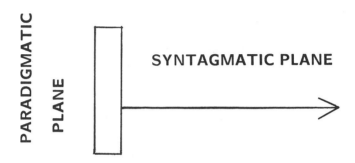

Consider, for example, the sentence, *The boy kissed the girl on the cheek.* For such a sentence, each morpheme is selected from numerous possibilities:

Article	Noun	Verb	Tense	Article	Noun
a	girl	kiss	ablaut	a	girl
the	spider	read	-s	0	dream
0	boy	write	-ed	the	nation

The short lists, or paradigms, presented here in columns give just a hint of the range of a speaker's knowledge of units and their classes.

The selection of morphemes from the vertical lists requires a consideration of the positions which those morpheme will take with respect to other morphemes. For example, the past tense morph that is appropriate for the verb *kiss* is -ed, and the past tense morph that is appropriate for the verb *write* is an ablaut (vowel change), i.e. *wrote.*

Describing the conditions for realizing morphemes as morphs is just what morphological rules are supposed to do. Operating in the same manner as the phonological rules described in the previous chapter, morphological rules describe the regularity of selecting morphs to instantiate morphemes in appropriate circumstances.

Morphological rules apply to the selection of morphs in the vertical dimension of the paradigms. Syntax, however, is handled in the horizontal dimension, and is a matter of the sequencing of morpheme classes. Supposedly one strings morphemes together in time as one speaks. Such sequencing is less a matter of paradigmatic knowledge, and more a matter of how the speaker decides at any moment to spin out the sentence. Hence, in this view, morphology involves the paradigmatic knowledge that linguists are most keenly interested in; syntax is a matter of speaker choices through time.

Standard Theory

Chomsky's generative syntactic theory starts from the structuralist views described above, but moves well beyond them. Specifically, Chomsky found and described regularities of syntax at the vertical, paradigmatic dimension of a speaker's linguistic knowledge. Syntactic regularities, Chomsky argued, ought not be understood as historical regularities. They are paradigmatic regularities that lie at the very heart of a speaker's knowledge of his/her language.

Syntactic patterns might be likened to architectural types, by which I mean the systematic assemblages of beams, joists, studs, and girders that give form to buildings. Syntactic patterns are not meaningful sentences any more than architectural types are livable buildings. Rather, syntactic patterns are the forms of sentences, just as architectural types are the forms of buildings. Moreover, each syntactic pattern involves interconnected parts which differ in their arrangement from other syntactic patterns in the same way that each architectural type differs from others.

Speakers have abstract knowledges of the syntactic patterns of their languages. Such abstract knowledges make themselves apparent in the judgments by speakers of the grammaticality of sentence patterns. Native speakers of English judge *The in the park bench is red* ungrammatical (though speakers of English whose native language is German might judge otherwise). But they judge *The bench in the park is red* to be grammatical. This ability to judge the grammaticality/ungrammaticality of sentence patterns is made possible by syntactic competence.

The syntactic patterns controlled by speakers are relatively independent of the morphemes that flesh out those patterns in any particular sentence. Syntactic competence enables speakers to recognize grammatical sentences regardless of their meaning. The famous example sentence, *Colorless green ideas sleep furiously,* is intended to demonstrate that speakers can affirm the grammaticality of even nonsense sentences.

64

Competence in syntactic patterns is independent of both meaning and of the morphemes that make up those sentences. Systematically ambiguous sentences provide evidence that speakers know the syntactic patterns as well as the morphological structure of sentences. Consider, for example, the sentence *The father of the girl and the boy got hit by a car.* Every morpheme in this sentence is unambiguous. Yet the sentence as a whole can be interpreted to mean that either one or two persons got hit by a car. The different interpretations rely on two syntactic patterns which are made clear here by grouping the constituents within brackets:

((The father (of the girl) and the boy) got hit by a car.)
((The father (of the girl and the boy)) got hit by a car.)

Both of the two groupings represent possible sentences in English and both can apply to the morphemes *the, father, of, the...* The groupings, and not the morphemes, are crucial for determining whether the sentence means that one or two people got hit by a car.

A syntactic pattern, or more precisely, a phrase structure, constitutes an aspect of linguistic competence independently of the morphemes that appear. Using our familiar terminology, abstract phrase structures can be considered syntactic types which are part of a speaker's competence in his/her language.

On Syntactic Types

Like phonological types, syntactic types form part of a system of relations. That proposition should bring to mind descriptivist linguistics founded on the principle of "the mysterious law of correlation."

The determination of the aspects of any syntactic type that can be correlated with each other is a matter of considerable debate. Some scholars suppose morphemic and semantic aspects are involved. Chomsky has always favored the opinion that only syntactic aspects are involved.

As with all other types and tokens, the relationships between the abstract phrase structure-types and the actually produced syntactic tokens is rule-governed. A definite, mechanical connection exists between abstract phrase structures and the actual sentences in which they are realized. Syntactic rules formalize that connection.

Let us explore the notion of syntactic rule more thoroughly. Recall that a rule in German phonology describes the devoicing of voiced obstruents in word final position, and by reason of that rule, linguists say that /tak/ and /tag / both involve an identical velar phoneme /g/. The rule of terminal devoicing describes what no one can hear, namely, that /tak/ contains the same phoneme as /tag /.

In the same way syntactic rules describe the alternations of syntactic phrase structures in different conditions. For example, English speakers regard *Hit yourself!* as a grammatical imperative sentence, (though not *Hit you!* or *Hit himself!*--asterisks indicate ungrammaticality). And they also know that *Hit yourself!*, is structured like the indicative sentence *You hit yourself*, though the nature of the relationship between the two is opaque to most speakers.

Syntacticians try to make explicit what speakers implicitly know about the relatedness of phrase structures. In regard to *Hit yourself!*, for example, they argue for an abstract imperative phrase structure in which *You* is the noun phrase subject of the imperative verb. The subject of the imperative must be able to be *you* otherwise the reflexive pronoun *yourself* could not be the direct object of the verb. (Independent evidence supports the claim that reflexive pronouns are formed by attaching a *-self* to a pronoun provided that that pronoun is identical in reference to a preceding pronoun.) And the subject of the imperative cannot be any pronoun other than *you* because other reflexive pronouns like *himself* always produce ungrammatical utterances.

So, it is argued, the phrase structure type underlying imperative sentences contains a *you* subject, and a syntactic rule deletes that subject. In this way, the similarity of imperative and indicative phrase structures is made clear and explicit.

Syntactic rules have a form quite like phonological rules. And that form is one which takes an input and reshapes it, for whatever purpose, into an output token of that type:

input (type) --> output (token) / conditions

Chomsky fitted this rule model to syntactic phenomena by proposing that in order to describe syntactic alternation, one needed to imagine a rule the input of which consists of a whole phrase structure.

In pre-Chomskyan structuralisms, such a rule was impossible. Syntax, you recall, was treated as a temporal process of stringing morphemes together. If the descriptions of such stringings together were to be put in any sort of rule format at all, the rules would consist of expansions of single morphemic categories at the left of an arrow into phrase structures at the right.

66

Pre-Chomskyan syntactic rules were expansion rules or re-write rules, and their configuration is as follows:

S   -->   NP + VP
NP -->   Article + (Adjective) + Noun + (Sentence)

(Here S represents "sentence," NP represents "noun phrase," VP represents "verb phrase.") Such descriptions specify the possibilities for stringing together morphemes in the construction of phrases, clauses, and sentences. Here all inputs are morphological categories and all outputs are combinations of morphemes.

The revolutionary character of Chomsky's rules of syntax is that they permit a whole phrase structure to stand to the left of the arrow. The implication of such a rule format is that the phrase structure-input to the left of the arrow is a kind of syntactic type, and that the phrase structure-output to the right of the arrow is a syntactic token which is reshaped or transformed in specified ways but which still instantiates the input type. Thus the following rule accounts for the reshaping of *The boat is hard to paddle* from the abstract phrase structure type *For someone to paddle the boat is hard*:

someone paddle boat   is   hard
NP (NP + V + NP) VP (V + Pred. Adj.)

1   2   3   4   5 ==>

3   4   5   2

(The order of the numbers in the input is altered in the output to indicate the structure of the sentence-token. A double arrow shaft identifies this rule as a transformational rule of syntax.)

This rule of syntax demonstrates what English speakers intuitively recognize, namely that two apparently different sentence tokens can instantiate the same syntactic type. Speakers usually just say that the two sentences above are synonymous. The syntactic rule says more. It says that, meaning aside, the fundamental relationships between the constituents of both sentences are identical despite their different positions.

The lesson taught by such a rule--if you can imagine rules with lessons--is the great lesson of all structuralisms. Types are not always evident in appearances. Often one must dig behind appearances before the underlying types can be revealed. The relationship between *For someone to paddle the boat is hard* and *The boat is hard to paddle* may elude casual inspection. But that relationship is made clear in the rule which describes the syntactic structures of these sentences.

Once it was established that syntactic configurations are

67

rooted in abstract types that can stand to the left of an arrow in a syntactic rule, the way was paved for charting the full shape of the syntactic component of linguistic competence.

The base subcomponent of syntax consists of rewrite or expansion rules, also called phrase structure rules of the base subcomponent of syntax. These phrase structure rules define the possible elementary strings or syntactic groups in a language. They are conventional rules in the sense that their input is always a single unit. The final outputs of the entire set of such rules are called the syntactic "deep structures" of a language. Deep structures are the fundamental but quite abstract syntactic types of a language.

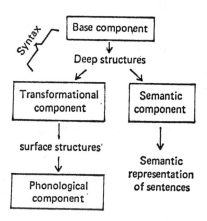

Phonological representation of sentences

These deep structures are the inputs for the transformational rules of a language. These transformational rules reshape deep structures to produce surface structures.

Transformational rules specify processes of movement, copying, addition, and deletion of constituents of deep structures. The transformational rule of imperative formation specifies the deletion of the subject pronoun *you* from the deep structure (*You hit you*). The transformational rule of reflexive formation describes the addition of a particle *-self* to a pronoun which in the deep structure refers to the subject of the immediately preceding verb, hence (*You hit yourself*) is derived from (*You hit you*). When both of these transformations are applied to the deep structure (*you hit you*), they generate the surface structure (*Hit yourself!*).

Two features of this derivation are worth special mention. First, the order in which transformational rules apply can be significant. If, for example, one were to apply the rule of imperative formation to (*You hit you*) before applying the rule of reflexive formation, one would generate the ungrammatical sentence **Hit you*. The reason for such a derivation is that the imperative formation would be deleting the subject *you* which is required if the rule of reflexive formation is to apply. Thus the application of these two transformational rules is strictly ordered: reflexive formation always applies before imperative formation in the syntax of English.

All of the rules which are ordered relative to one another form a "cycle" of rules. The notion of cycle implies the following condition: A rule which is ordered relative to other rules, can apply just once until all the other rules in the ordered set have a chance to apply. At that point, the round of rule applications can begin again.

This notion of cycle has been postulated to explain the fact that ordered rules seem to be able to apply to a subordinate clause at one point in the derivation of a sentence, and to the main clause at another point. For example, in a sentence like *Bring yourself over to the house tonight so you can cook for yourself in a real kitchen* the rule of reflexive formation must have applied once to the subordinate clause to generate *so you can cook for yourself* and again to the main clause to generate *bring yourself*. If reflexive formation were to have applied to the whole sentence only once, we would have a difficult time explaining why the "you" in (*...so you can cook...*) is not a reflexive pronoun. In short, transformational rules can be ordered relative to one another and can generate complex structures in the course of different cycles of application.

The transformational cycle and the knowledge of ordered rules of syntax have long been debated by generative syntacticians. Some argue that a knowledge of rule ordering and of a cycle of rules is part of a speaker's acquired competence. Others argue that such a knowledge is wired into the human language faculty, that it does not vary from language to language, and that it is not acquired during child language learning. Such debates about what is universal and what is acquired are to be expected among structuralist linguists whose goal is the description of the human mind. Such debates occur over phonological as well as over syntactic issues and will be reconsidered in both chapters six and seven.

The second feature to note is that transformational rules can be obligatory. Though speakers know the surface structure

69

Hit yourself! in terms of the abstract deep structure (*You hit you*), only the former and never the latter are acceptable in speech. The fact that **You hit you!* is ungrammatical suggests that some structures can be grammatical at the abstract deep level, but ungrammatical as surface structures. Such structures *must* be transformed if they are ever to be spoken. Here is an instance in which mental structures are said to exist despite the fact that they are never themselves realized concretely.

An Empirical Science of Mental Realities

Chomsky's generative linguistics is a "mentalistic" discipline insofar as it aims to describe cognitive processes, but it is no less empirically rigorous than any other science. Linguists always work from observations; they never simply make up the rules of a grammar.

The observations in syntactic research are the reports of judgments which native speakers make about the grammaticality of sentences. The syntactician's task is to construct rules that will make possible just the sentences that native speakers consider grammatical while ruling out all those sentences that native speakers consider ungrammatical.

Chomsky and his colleagues have invested a great deal of energy in the description of transformational rules because they have felt that such rules reveal the creativity of speaking subjects more clearly than either phonological or morphological rules. Transformational rules are complex and ordered to spectacular depths. And for these reasons, transformational rules reveal the quintessential precision and creativity of the mind's eye.

Government and Binding Theory

The publication by Chomsky of <u>Aspects of the Theory of Syntax</u> is a watershed in the history of generative linguistic theory. Following the publication of that work, the so-called standard theory of syntax, which is represented in that work, was subjected to a broadside of criticism. And in consequence of that criticism, the syntactic component of grammar was re-figured in a variety of ways by a variety of scholars.

A recent development out of this period of ferment is Chomsky's Government-Binding theory (GB theory). GB theory is worth considering briefly for the insight it provides into the fundamental axioms which have been assumed by generative linguists from its very inception.

70

A significant feature of generative syntax when it was presented in 1957 was the principle of autonomous syntax. According to this principle, syntactic types (deep structures) and their instantiation in syntactic tokens (surface structures) are independent of meaning and of morphology and phonology. Descriptions of syntax, on their own and without reference to descriptions of other knowledges, promised to reveal aspects of the structure and organization of the human mind.

GB theory holds forth that same promise, namely, to reveal the structure and operation of the mind. Only now, with more sophisticated descriptions of syntax than were available in 1957 or 1965, linguists are outlining a startlingly different picture of the human mind.

The standard theory view which prevailed in 1965 supposed a grammar to be a system of rules, phrase structure rules, and transformation rules, which are acquired by children under the guidance of a language faculty. The language faculty was understood to be a set of principles that leads child language learners to construct maximally simple, maximally general rules for generating sentences like those used by adults.

According to GB theory, the syntactic component of a grammar is not so much like a system of rules, but instead it consists of relatively independent modules. That is, underlying sentence forms are simultaneously generated in different grammatical components, one containing the structural representations of a sentence, another containing a representation specified for semantic operations, another containing a representation specified for phonological operations. Not all features of any one representation are available in other representations. Thus, the structure, meaning, and sound aspects of any sentence are "known" somewhat independently by the human mind.

In GB theory, the structural representation of sentences is not established by a set of phrase structures rules that generate syntactic types (deep structures) which in turn are operated on by transformational rules. Rather syntactic types are generated in a modular fashion. The lexicon, which lists word meanings, specifies the possible syntactic relations of its words, e.g. the lexical entries for *ask*, *wonder*, and *care* are specified as able to be followed by clauses as shown in (1-3). But only the entry for *ask* specifies that it can be followed also by an NP (4-6). Thus, basic syntactic relations are provided for by the lexical entries.

1. I asked what time it is.
2. I wonder what time it is.
3. I care what time it is.

71

4. I asked the time.
5. *I wondered the time.
6. *I cared the time.

A sentence type is generated when the structures allowed by the lexical entries of several words are combined in a sentence. At that point a variety of sentence types are provisionally generated. We can imagine, for example, that both (7) and (*8) are generated out of structures made available by the lexical entries for *student, hair, long, chemistry, old,* etc.. At that point, a set of universal principles regarding possible sentence types ranges over the provisionally generated strings and screens or filters out those which fail to meet up to their specifications. Here universal principles would filter out (*8) on the grounds that the phrase *the student* in *the student with long hair* is structurally different from the phrase *the student* in *the student of chemistry* and therefore the pronoun-like *one*, which implies an identity of the two noun phrases cannot be used in (*8).

(7)   The student with short hair is older than the one with long hair.

(8)   *The student of chemistry is older than the one with long hair.

This discussion leads us to understand that a syntactic surface structure (a token) does not instantiate a simple and unified syntactic type. Rather it instantiates a type which arises from the interaction of lexically dictated structures filtered by universal principles that govern possible structures.

Syntactic types are generated in roughly the same way that cars are produced. In the case of cars, a foundry produces sheet metal in large rolls for the stamping plant. The stamping plant cuts up the rolls, forms fenders, trunks, hoods, etc. and has inspectors cull out the poorly shaped pieces. In syntax, lexically specified structures are produced in one module of grammatical competence; in another module those structures are inspected and poorly formed versions are culled out by universal principles.

One of the advantages of this modular approach to syntax is that most rules of syntax are no longer needed. Phrase structure rules are virtually eliminated, and transformational rules are limited to just the statement that an element be moved, i.e. "move x." What elements can be subjected to this rule and where they can be moved are all matters that are handled by universal principles.

The characterization of the language faculty or Universal Grammar is also distinctive in GB theory. According to the GB "principles and parameters" model, children, in acquiring a language, make choices from a finite number of parameters for sentence structures, and those choices govern many of the lexically specified structural relations of the grammars they acquire. Different choices are like paths taken, or not taken, and give a definite shape to the core syntax of the emerging language. The consequences and ramifications of the parameter choices that are made in acquisition are monitored by principles of Universal Grammar, the very same principles described above as principles governing syntactic structures.

The grammatical parameter settings that occur during acquisition might be likened to the program settings in word processing software. The word processing program comes ready-made. It invites you to select options from menus for determining margin sizes, spacing, print style, etc., but the soft-ware producer has provided the program with default settings on many parameters. The default setting specifies a format if the user fails to. The user may make choices in each parameter, or the user may rely on default settings.

Similarly, a grammar comes already made in the form of universal principles for generating sentence structures. In language learning, as in word processing, one may select structural characteristics from a finite range of parameters. (In language learning, such selections are always unconscious, and dictated by the adult language model.) But, also as in word processing, there may be default settings on structural parameters. That is, language learners, for a variety of reasons, may fall back on the structures dictated by the language faculty. In this view the language faculty is more than just a guiding light which directs language acquisition, it is a Universal Grammar which contains specifications for a grammar under construction.

It is also helpful to liken a Universal Grammar and its operation to a biological system. In the process of generating an egg and a sperm, the genetic material of the parents's cells are selected and sometimes mutated; and, in consequence, a genetically distinct individual is formed. We can say that the individual, at his or her core, is a product of the selections and mutations (choices). The choices are neither completely independent of other genes nor completely variable. Rather they are subject to regulatory genes (constraints) which constrain phenomena like the speed of maturation, and they are restricted in their impact by the genetic organization that has arisen in the course of the biological history of the species. Finally, the genetic choices are not the sole determinants of the appearance of the individual. Conditions external to the biological core of genes, e.g. hormonal balance, environmental conditions, etc., can influence the appearance of the organism.

73

selected from humanly possible language parameters. The impact of those choices is mediated by universal principles. After this core grammar is determined, a variety of external forces can further impose themselves on the periphery of the grammar, and produce a variety of possible appearances.

Summary

How shall we interpret these theoretical developments within generative syntactic theory? First, we should recognize that GB theory is consistent with Chomsky's long-standing view that the syntactic organization of a language is autonomous and made possible by a very special faculty of the mind. Syntax is not just one among many aspects of the organization of a language. It is a specially developed characteristic which can reveal a special and distinctively human capability of the human mind.

"Man (sic), for Chomsky, is an essentially syntactical animal. The structure of his brain determines the structure of his syntax, and for this reason the study of syntax is one of the keys, perhaps the most important key, to the study of the human mind" (Searle 1974: 15). The more that descriptions of syntax are cluttered with phonological, morphological, and semantic phenomena, the muddier becomes the picture of the human mind. Autonomous syntax is a desideratum only because it promises a clear picture of the most sophisticated abilities of the mind's eye.

The mind's eye is what Chomsky aims to describe. And syntax is the primary vehicle for that description. No aspect of a language has more complex token-type relations than syntax. No linguistic description displays more clearly than syntactic description the powers of the mind's eye. That, in a word, is the substance and intention of generative syntactic research.

Chapter Six

Unity Out of Diversity: On Language Universals

Having peeked at the objectives, procedures, and findings of structuralist linguists, we need now to review the forces that spur structuralist linguists on in their work.   Such a review will lead us to recognize two tender and itchy spots on the otherwise firm body of structuralist linguistics.   Those two itchy spots are, first, the problem of language varieties, and second, the problem of the heterogeneity of language communities. The present chapter will address the former; chapter seven will address the latter.

An itch you love to scratch!   That is what these issues are, a theoretical itch linguists love to scratch.   And it is not just the structuralist linguists who love to scratch at the issues of the variety of languages and the heterogeneity of communites. Anthropologists have long felt these to be the most fascinating issues in modern linguistics.

How can we account for the curious attraction of these issues, the variety of languages and the heterogeneity of communities?   Let me suggest that these two issues are as itchy as they are because they both lie very close to the political forces that motivate and spur on modern linguistic theory.   Let us consider these forces here.

Theology, Politics, and Language Variety

In any era and in any tradition, the focus of intellectual discussion is usually directed to issues that are central in social life. With due respect for the curiosity and creativity which leads intellectuals into a grand variety of enterprises, and with respect, too, for the ability of intellectuals to avoid having their vision clouded by the swirls of events around them, I contend that intellectual life is always closely if invisibly tied to social life.   Those who claim that sciences are or can be "autonomous" are whistling in the dark (see p. 97).

In the seventeenth century, the focus of Western intellectual debate shifted to mind after having been fixed for many centuries on God.   Such a shift occurred because God, the keystone of social life of pre-fourteenth century Europe, was replaced by a new keystone for a new kind of social life in post-sixteenth century Europe. If God had been the single most significant political notion in medieval life, then mind has been the single most significant political notion in modern life.

The links between mind and modern political life are suggested by the title of B.F. Skinner's <u>Beyond</u> <u>Freedom</u> <u>and</u> <u>Dignity</u>. In post-sixteenth century Europe--and explicitly so since the era of the Enlightenment--the human condition has been described as *dignified* by the possession of rational abilities; and in view of that dignity, humans deserve to be *free* of the constraints that are placed on lesser creatures. Being gifted with reason, humans have the right to freely determine their own destinies.

This mind-based emphasis on essential human freedom and dignity forms the foundation of modern political systems--communist as well as democratic (See Berger 1976). But it also contributes to the perilous condition of modern political systems. That is, modern nation-states live politically precarious lives because of the very emphasis on freedom and dignity that forms their foundations.

In a word, modern nation-states are critically vulnerable to *disintegration*. First, they are as vulnerable as any other political unit to disintegration as a result of outside forces, e.g. foreign enemies. But secondly, they are critically vulnerable to threats of disintegration that arise from within.

Nation-states are vulnerable to disintegration from within for two reasons. First, they are heterogeneous units. They were formed out of federations of older city-states so that massive enterprises like the Crusades, the reconquest of Iberia, and the discovery of new trade routes to the east could be accomplished. No one city-state possessed the wherewithal to carry off such enterprises, but heterogeneous federations were able to undertake such projects. However, being heterogeneous, the integrity of these federations was cracked and flawed from the very beginning. The factions that form nation-states have always been potential loci for revolutionary movements. Look at Spain, one of the oldest of nation-states. It still struggles with Basque separatists and Catalan dissidents.

This problem of the heterogeneity of nation-states has been almost too sensitive for the leaders of nation-states to broach openly (Harrington 1983). However, just as primitive myth-makers tell stories to handle the insoluble conundrums of the human condition, language scholars have told stories which help to resolve the conundrum of the heterogenous but integrated nation-state. Most prominent among these stories are linguistic discourses on language purity. The storytellers include writers like Edwin Newman and William Safire who descant on the abominations of modern English usage. The effect of such stories is to promote uniformity of the national language by emphasizing virtues like clarity and logic in discourse.

The storytellers also include a whole raft of linguists whose research on second language acquisition and foreign language learning supports formal educational programs. On the surface their stories deal with what is logical, what is beautiful, what is acquisitionally possible, and what is pedagogically feasible. But below the surface, these stories of modern linguists are not substantially different from the story of Antonio de Nebrija who wrote the first grammar of a European vernacular in 1492. He wrote that grammar with the expressed intention of providing his monarch with a linguistic way to handle the heterogeneity of the Spanish state.

The second internal threat of disintegration in nation-states comes from the emphasis on freedom. If individuals in modern life possess, as the political philosophers claim that they possess, the gift of reason which confers dignity and authorizes their free self-determination, then why should an individual submit to the dictates of an authority? Specifically, why shouldn't the members of dissident factions of nation-states pursue secession and independence.

To this threat that arises from the philosophical emphasis on freedom, language scholars have been responding, since the late seventeenth century, with stories that suggest that the diverse paths that are open to free individuals actually lead to one unified goal, one Universal Grammar (Newmeyer 1986: 21). The diversity is really a unity, hence the individual who pursues diversity, will be returned to the unity from which he or she started. Languages may seem to differ from one another, but they are all ultimately formed in the same mold. Languages are variations on one theme, constructed with the guidance of one single universal gyroscopic mental faculty. In matters linguistic, as in matters political, "*e pluribus unum.*" The moral of such a story is that the pursuit of diverse languages, e.g. Basque, Catalan, etc., is a waste of energy since Basque and Catalan are at their roots the same as all other languages.

Different eras of modern linguistic scholarship have seen different versions of this same basic "*e pluribus unum*" story. The nineteenth century version involved three assumptions: First, nineteenth century linguists assumed that languages could be classified into species just like biological organisms. Secondly, they assumed that languages evolved just like biological species. Thirdly, they assumed evolution was unilinear, leading from simple primitive forms to complex sophisticated forms.

Nineteenth century scholars told the story of "language typology" (Lounsbury 1968) which was popularized early on by the work of W. von Humboldt. Following him, German linguists of the era thought in terms of simple "isolating" languages which encode separate meanings with separate words, not unlike modern Chinese, "agglutinating" languages which combine meaning components in words, and "inflecting" languages like Latin and Greek which make use of word-altering inflections. Languages, it was supposed, evolve from simple "isolating" varieties, progress through "agglutinating" varieties, and culminate in the development of "inflecting" varieties.

The statement about evolutionary development is the statement which resolves the diversity of language types into a unity. All languages are ultimately one because they all participate in a unitary evolution.

Edward Sapir (1921) reconsidered this whole body of nineteeth century assumptions and descriptions. It may be possible, he argued, to discern language types, though the descriptions of American Indian languages suggest that existing typologies were far from exhaustive. But it is not acceptable to suppose that those different types represent stalled stages of a single evolutionary process.

Sapir's critique of the nineteenth century "language typology" raises anew the theoretical problem of language varieties. His writings offer convincing evidence that language varieties are real, but do not explain how they are one.

Chomsky's universal language faculty fills the gap opened by Sapir's critique of "language typology." In Chomsky's account, it is not an historical process of evolution that unifies all, but a static mental faculty, a gyroscope of the mind which guides language acquisition. The structuralist's universal language faculty make it possible to again affirm that, in languages as in political life, "*e pluribus unum.*"

Neither the nineteenth century version of this "e pluribus unum" story that we have described, nor the twentieth century structuralist versions which we are about to describe, were *consciously* developed to handle threats to the integrity of nation-states. Linguists usually claim that their writings are independent of political affairs and that they are interested in hypotheses about universals in order to advance the theory of language, or because such hypotheses ignite their curiosity and are theoretically "interesting." But explanations for scientific discourse that appeal to what is "interesting," to what advances theory, or to what piques "curiosity," are surface explanations that hide a deeper latent motivation which is oftentimes political.

Structuralist Views on Language Universals

Keeping in mind the political significance of the questions we are pursuing, let us consider the various approaches of structuralist linguists for describing the "*unum*" behind the "*pluribus*" of languages. At center stage in all these approaches is the language faculty, a human mental gyroscope--gyroscopes being devices which maintain a steady balance and direction because of the force of a spinning wheel and which are therefore used as navigational devices. The language faculty is a mental, not a physical gyroscope. It is given to humans from birth through genes in the same way that eyes and brains are given. But though it is mental not physical, and though it is given, not made, the gyroscope for language acquisition functions like any other gyroscope. It holds movement to a single direction.

The movement which the linguistic gyroscope constrains is the movement of a child towards an adult competence in a language. More simply, the gyroscope establishes the paths which children can follow as they develop an adult competence in a language.

This talk of mental gyroscopes must sound fanciful to one not familiar with linguistic theory. But linguists are dead serious on the matter. The gyroscope actually exists as a mental entity. It is really available to each individual. And its sole function is to guide language acquisition. Calling it a language faculty or a Universal Grammar, linguists say that it must exist because without it children could never succeed in constructing an adult language competence.

Two conditions handicap child language acquisition. First, the adult model of speech, which provides children with a target for their language acquisition, is marred by errors and blunders. The adults who speak to children produce false starts and missteps in their talk. So, for a child to acquire a language just by listening to adult utterances would be like a person trying to learn how to play chess by watching chess games in which players occasionally made illegal moves. Second, many of the phonological and syntactic constructions in which children do acquire competence are constructions which children never experience during language acquisition. For example, it is highly unlikely that any child is ever taught to avoid a sentence like *Here is the snowball which I chased the boy who threw at our teacher.* Parents would never imagine such a sentence even long enough to tell their children not to say it. Yet with mechanical regularity speakers would recognize that such a sentence is ill-formed. (In fact, in any language, such a sentence would be judged ungrammatical.) Linguists cannot explain how English speakers recognize such ill-formedness except by way of a gyroscopic language faculty.

Structuralist linguists postulate a gyroscopic language faculty because the facts of language acquisition cannot be explained without it. But linguists go a bit further than simply postulating the language faculty. They embrace that postulation, and they hoist it aloft as the standard of their discipline. They suggest that linguistic research should be centered around the gyroscopic language faculty.

Why should explication of the language faculty be the central task of linguistics? Generative linguists justify their descriptions of the gyroscopic language faculty by saying that it is a component of the human mind. And describing mind is so very important in the modern era because mind is a central but hazy political principle. Because humans have minds, they have freedom and dignity. And as free and dignified citizens, they have certain rights and duties to perform vis-a-vis others in their society. The investigation of mind helps to clarify just what those rights and duties are.

Looking over the range of descriptions of the *unum* that undergirds the *pluribus* in human languages, one can see three major ways of using data to arrive at pictures of the human language faculty. Let me call these deduction, induction, and bridge building.

The last of these three is perhaps the only unfamiliar method. Partly because it is an unfamiliar method, and partly because it is a method dear to the hearts of anthropologists, I will spend more time discussing it than the other two.

Deduction

The linguistic deductivists that I have in mind are those like Chomsky himself who argue that "as analysts of language, we should restrict attention to familiar and everyday data" (Lightfoot 1982: 84). There is no need to go off and away from the data of, say, English in an effort to describe Universal Grammar. The data of one language alone are plenty rich enough to found theories of the human language faculty, provided that the linguist is clever enough to come up with hypotheses which can take advantage of those data.

A deductivist often begins by discovering some facts which existing theories cannot handle. Pondering the anomalous facts, the deductivist proposes a hypothesis which revises existing theory in such a way that the revision handles both the newly discovered facts and all the familiar facts which theories had previously handled. If s/he finds no counter evidence to the new hypothesis, then that hypothesis is tentatively accepted as true.

Chomsky's proposal of the notion of a transformational rule is a deductively developed description of the language faculty. It is a specific and detailed characterization of how the mind operates. However it is a deduced conclusion and not a generalization from particular observations.

First, Chomsky noted that speakers of all languages judge certain dissimilar sentences to be synonymous. For example, English speakers consider *The boat is hard to paddle* to be synonymous with *For someone to paddle the boat is hard*. Secondly he considered the fact that speakers can discern ambiguity in certain sentences like *Flying planes can be dangerous.* Judging a sentence ambiguous means finding two possible readings for that sentence such as *Flying planes endanger the pilots who fly them* and *Flying planes endanger bystanders who may stray into their paths.*

With these two considerations in hand, he drew the conclusion that just as phonemes can be instantiated by allophones and morphemes by allomorphs, distinctive syntactic structures can be instantiated by allo-structures or transformations. *The boat is hard to paddle* and *For someone to paddle the boat is hard* are two allo-structures with the same underlying structure. And *Flying planes can be dangerous* can be a surface realization of two quite different deep structures depending on how it is read.

The specific notion of a transformational rule is a formalization of these notions. That is, it is a way of displaying allo-structural relations on paper and of making them clear.

Though it is based on a relatively small amount of data this deductive proposal of transformational rules is universal in scope. It implies that the human mind, whether it be competent in English or Russian or Hindi, operates on sentences to discern transformational or allo-structural relations. Though this proposal is founded on a small bit of evidence from one language, it applies to all human languages of the past as well as the present and it claims a very specific capability for speakers of those languages.

Such is the power of deduction. It leads by rational argument from minimal facts to maximal conclusions.

Admittedly, deductions like this one tell us little about the different languages of the world. They tell us little about the unique features of languages despite their ability to reveal the common foundations of all languages. You might walk away from such a deduction with a feeling of emptiness. And a romantic impulse might tell you that we really should be ferreting out the details of linguistic diversity. But self-disciplined deductivists fend off this romantic impulse as irrational, if not politically unsettling.

Induction

Romantic impulses are not to be sneezed at. The human scientists of the nineteenth century--especially the linguists and anthropologsts--marched to the step of romantic impulses. The romantic supposition that "the principle of variation is alone vital and that one's genius and originality are in pretty direct ratio to one's eccentricity" (Babbitt 1919: 55) led many to assume that description of human nature is largely a matter of describing the eccentricities of human societies and human individuals. In the current era, this romantic impulse to study the eccentric still fuels inductivist approaches to the language faculty.

Inductivists may share with deductivists the desire to describe the contents of the language faculty, but they want to know more. They are unwilling to stop with an understanding of the common ground of languages, they want to know how, that is, along what lines, languages can differ from one another. To the inductivist, knowing the possible lines of language variation is a way of appreciating the outer limits of the universe of languages. And appreciating the outer limits of the universe of languages is tantamount to appreciating the structure of the human language faculty.

Deductivists understand this goal, but are skeptical. Chomsky argues that, "Linguistic principles of any real significance generally deal with properties of rule systems, not observed phenomena, and can thus be confirmed or refuted only indirectly through the construction of grammars, a task that goes well beyond even substantial accumulation and organization of observation" (Chomsky 1980a: 2).

Perhaps this skepticism is well-founded. Often linguists induce language generalizations from cross-language comparisons which say little or nothing about the precise constitution of the language faculty. For example, in his ground-breaking work on language universals, Joseph Greenberg (1966) concluded that almost all languages of the world make use of either a Subject-Verb-Object (SVO), or a Subject-Object-Verb (SOV) or a Verb-Subject-Object (VSO) order for simple declarative sentences. Certainly such a generalization is provocative. But such an observation does not tell us what to do with the 350 Hixkaryana speakers of Northern Brazil whose declarative sentences are characteristically OVS. What is there about the language faculty that permits such deviations from the norm?

In order to get inductive research to respond to such a question, the image of the language faculty had to be shifted from that of a treasure box to the image of an evolutionary tree.

The language faculty, which is the source of the grammatical principles of all languages, is frequently likened, in standard theory, to a treasure box filled with all the humanly possible linguistic principles and capabilities. Individual languages select their particular characteristics from this treasure box. (Ruth Benedict characterized cultural universals with a similar image of a "great arc on which are ranged the possible interests" of humans (1934: 24).) In this treasure box are found SVO, SOV, and VSO canonical structures, for example, but not a VOS structure.

The problem with the treasure box view of Universal Grammar is that it offers us no insight into how the principles and capabilities within the box related to each other and it offers no account of why they are there in the first place. Nor does it lead us to consider how principles and capabilities within the treasure box relate to the usually unrealized but still imaginable characteristics that lie outside of the box.

The metaphor of an evolutionary tree offers deeper insight into just these issues of Universal Grammar. Think of the Universal Grammar as a set of increasingly complex abilities that have been--and continue to be--built up from trunk to branches to leaves through time. The trunk is a set of basic and fundamental adaptive linguistic knowledges/abilities, and the branches and leaves are successively more complicated adjustments to and refinements of those basics which evolve in order to handle particularly complex conditions.

The conditions which stimulate the development of the branches and leaves may be external. That is, they may pertain to the expressive needs of speakers. Suppose, for example, that Caveman Trog is looking for a way to say, "I see the rabbit coming down the run" in such a way as to let Glog know about the rabbit right away. He happens on the structure "It's a rabbit I see coming down the run." Here Trog is taking the first step towards the development of a new linguistic ability, and it is the expressive need for focussing an object noun phrase that stimulates that development.

On the other hand, the pressures which stimulate the development of branches and leaves may be internal. Suppose, for example, that Trog has developed the characteristics of placing a negative particle after a verb, e.g. "Glog does not need to skin this rabbit." The process of developing a question with subject-verb inversion then needs to be worked out for such sentences with negative particles. Shall Trog say *Does Glog not need to skin this rabbit?* or *Does not Glog need to skin this rabbit?*. Here the stimulus for the development of new sentence types is some already acquired grammatical knowledge rather than external expressive needs.

As with a tree, the branching and leafing structures of the Universal Grammar are added onto the trunk of fundamental constructions. And any particular branch is a complication of the fundamental trunk structure. As a complication it establishes a condition for subsequent branches and leaves which adapt to that branch. Thus the structure of the Universal Grammar, when viewed from the leaves, is a series of adaptations which respond to and which therefore imply the existence of more fundamental structures even down to trunk structures.

According to such a view, the tree of the Universal Grammar

83

could theoretically embrace all logically possible characteristics, provided that they arose through plausible leaf to branch
to trunk relations. No possibility is ruled out in advance.
Even a penchant for VOS canonical word orders could arise if
conditions were extreme enough. However, the actually occurring
branches and leaves are limited by finite human memory and by
limited human calculation abilities. English speakers know that
*The boy that the girl that the dog that ran away belonged to
kissed is my brother* is unacceptable whether or not it be grammatical because it is too complicated for interpretation. In the
same way, some branching and leafing possibilities in Universal
Grammar are ruled out because they exceed human production and
interpretation abilities.

Structuralist linguists pursue descriptions of the tree of
possibilities in Universal Grammar from leaves to branches to
trunk. Accordingly, their research is framed in terms of questions like "What prior structures and conditions does structure X
imply?" Let me illustrate this type of research with some data
on the syntactic transformation of raising.

Raising is a transformational syntactic operation that accounts for the synonymy of sentences like *It is easy to like you*
and *You are easy to like.* A transformational rule moves a relevant NP, here *you*, from its position in a subordinate clause, to
a position in the main clause.

When we examine the facts of different languages, we find
that different sorts of raising operations are judged to be
grammatical depending on the position of the noun phrase in the
subordinate clause and the position to which it is moved. On the
basis of those judgments, we can distinguish three different
kinds of raising.

Type 1	I believe that he is rich. =>	
	I believe him to be rich.	(S to O)
Type 2	It is certain that he is rich. =>	
	He is certain to be rich.	(S to S)
Type 3	It is easy to like you. =>	
	You are easy to like.	(O to S)

In Type 1, the subject of the subordinate clause is raised into
the position of object of the main verb. In Type 2, the subject
of the subordinate clause is raised into the position of subject
of the main verb. And in Type 3, the object of the subordinate
clause is raised into the position of subject of the main verb.

The grammaticality or ungrammaticality of these different
kinds of raising operations in any language is not a random
matter (Eckman 1976). The judgments of speakers show the follow-

ing: If a language permits Type 3 raising, it also permits Type 2 and Type 1 raising. If a language permits Type 2, it also permits Type 1, but not necessarily Type 3. If a language permits Type 1, it does not necessarily permit Type 2 or Type 3. In other words, there is an implicational relationship between the three types of raising. English permits all three kinds of raising. Hungarian permits only Type 1 raising.

The discovery of this cross language implicational relationship between types of raising transformations leads us to conclude that raising transformations are made possible by particular branches and leaves of Universal Grammar. Type 1 raising is a most fundamental type of raising which all humans have access to. Types 2 and 3 are progressively more complicated kinds of raising which are grammatical in fewer and fewer languages and which are acquired later and later in life by children learning those languages.

Type 3 raising, which, of course, is available in English, is a most extreme form of raising. It is, if you will, a most distant leaf on the tree of Universal Grammar with respect of raising operations. But Type 3 raising is not *necessarily* the last word in raising. We can at least imagine raising a noun phrase out of a clause embedded within an embedded clause (*It is easy to like a person who eats chocolate* => *Chocolate is easy to like a person who eats*) though it seems likely that practical limitations on human computational abilities rule out such an imagined possibility. Indeed linguists have added constraints to Universal Grammar to reflect just such human limitations.

The Mysterious Law of Correlation

Studies such as this assume the truth of the linguistic version of the "mysterious law of correlation." Not only grammars of languages, but the grammar of grammars of languages, Universal Grammar, is a system all parts of which are related to one another. Thus, language differences, far from being willy-nilly, arbitrary differences, are systematic in the sense that they follow out the branches and leaves of possibilities which are given in the Universal Grammar.

Note that the "correlations" in Universal Grammar differ from those at the level of a grammar of a language in being universal and present in speakers from the beginning, from before those speakers acquire the grammars of their languages.

Implicational generalizations like those above give us a new appreciation of the language faculty. The language faculty is not so much a statement of what is and what is not possible in human languages, but a roadmap of routes to be followed in linguistic development. The language faculty is a gyroscope which steers children from the basic or unmarked features of their language to the more complicated, marked features. All these features are evolutionary adaptations that build upon each other to constitute highly structured marvelously specialized linguistic competences.

Bridge Building

Both the deductivists and the inductivists make use of relatively familiar and ordinary data to produce generalizations about the language faculty. Deductivists often use the data of just one very well described language; inductivists draw from many languages, but always their data are indisputably linguistic. Bridge builders go beyond indisputably linguistic data. They believe that the only way to reach breakthrough insights about the language faculty is to build bridges between the taken-for-granted facts about languages and facts about extraordinary, often marginal, linguistic phenomena. The extraordinary phenomena provoke new insights into the ordinary and the result is a new and more powerful theory.

Take as an example, Hans Selye's (1956) discovery of the extraordinary phenomenon which he calls the General Adaptation Syndrome. Prior to his discovery, diseases, familiar diseases that is, were distinguished by specific symptoms. Pneumonia is marked by breathing difficulties. Hepatitis is indicated by jaundice, etc.. But in addition to these characteristic symptoms, doctors recognized that these diseases were accompanied by highly variable non-specific disturbances, such as fever, enlarged spleen, inflammed tonsils, and skin rashes. The doctors never bothered to account for these variable phenomena in their epidemiology. But it was just these disturbances that Selye set out to study. And he hoped that by linking them to diseases, he might uncover some new insights into the nature of diseases and the body's response to them.

Selye's persistence paid off for he found that "disease is a fight to maintain the homeostatic balance of other tissues despite damage." The non-specific disturbances in diseases were evidence of this ubiquitous effort of organisms to maintain homeostasis. General Adaptation Syndrome is the name he gave to the body's own defensive reaction to disease. The postulation of the G.A.S. helped to advance the field of epidemiology by offering a "unified theory of disease."

Selye has described for us the method of building bridges from extraordinary phenomena to new insights: "It is not to see something (extraordinary) first, but to establish connections between the previously known and the hitherto unknown that con-

86

stitutes the essence of scientific discovery....The important difference between the discovery of America by the Indians, by the Norsemen, and by Columbus is that only Columbus succeeded in attaching the American continent to the rest of the world." The bridge building method is one in which a phenomenon, previously regarded as an inconsequential oddity, is related to the realm of familiar cases and thus requires a revision in the generalizations which had, until that time, been drawn from just those familiar cases.

Anthropologists should be most comfortable at bridge building. The discovery of the extraordinary cases and the revision of received generalizations about behavior in the light of those cases has always been central to the practice of anthropology. Who are primitive peoples if not extraordinary humans whose behavior fails to match our expectations? By comparing the extraordinary behavior of primitives to the ordinary taken-for-granted behavior of familiar peoples, anthropologists generate new insight about the roots and foundations of behavior in general.

The extraordinary cases have been no less important for linguistic anthropology than for anthropology as a whole. Franz Boas wrote in 1911 that "grammarians who have studied the languages of Europe and Western Asia have developed a system of categories which we are inclined to look for in every language. It seems desirable to show herein how far the system with which we are familiar is characteristic only of certain groups of languages." And from this remark he proceeded to point out that the category of gender "is on the whole rare in America." And again, "While according to the structure of our European languages we always tend to look for the expressions of singularity or plurality for the sake of clearness of expressions, there are other languages that are entirely indifferent towards this distinction (Kwakiutl)." Some familiar categories are not to be found in American languages. Some quite unfamiliar categories *are* found.

Anthropological linguists still embrace the practice of building bridges from the extraordinary to the ordinary. Instead of limiting their attention to the behavior of monolinguals, anthropologists consider bilinguals, and speakers who regularly switch between dialects or languages. Instead of focussing exclusively on speech which serves in the main to transfer information, anthropologists attend to playful speech, regulatory speech, and ritual speech, all with the aim of revising the generalizations about communicative behavior that are produced by describing more familiar facts.

To be sure, not all these descriptions build bridges towards a clearer understanding of the nature of the universal and innate language faculty. Often enough, as we have seen, the scholarly

87

efforts of anthropologists are motivated by objectives quite different from the philosophical-psychological objectives of structuralists.

However, some research within the Saussurean-Chomskyan structuralist tradition does proceed by bridge building. And such research is directly motivated by a desire to clarify the nature of the language faculty. It may not be called anthropological research, and it may not include primitive peoples, but such bridge building is carried on by linguists, and it feels like home to anthropologists.

Let me discuss two examples of linguistic bridge building both of which aim to clarify the nature of the language faculty. The two examples are almost subfields of research unto themselves: Creole languages studies and Sign language studies.

Creole Language Studies   The term Creole probably puts you in mind of French, of the people who ply the Louisiana bayous and who cook up dishes like jambalaya.

Linguists use the term for kindred phenomena, but the linguist's term is predictably more general in its application and precise in its definition.   To the linguist, Creole languages are mixed languages spoken by the descendants of slaves or indentured laborers in former European plantation colonies like Louisiana, Jamaica, Haiti, Surinam, South Africa, the Cape Verde's, Mauritius, New Guinea, Hawaii, etc..

Like the colonies themselves, the different Creole languages are influenced by different European stocks; French, English, and Portuguese predominate.   They are also shaped by different non-European languages;   West African linguistic influences prevail in the Atlantic region;   Bantu and Xhosa contribute to Afrikaans in South Africa;   New Guinea languages contribute to Tok Pisin; Japanese and Tagalog contribute to Hawaiian Creole.

Nineteenth century linguists generally disregarded Creole languages, considering them linguistic dirt that ought to be swept aside rather than studied.   Only linguist-mavericks like Hugo Schuchardt paid serious attention to Creoles.

In America, research into Creole languages remained undeveloped until the 1960's despite the efforts of scholars like John Reinecke and Robert Hall.   However, since the 1960's a considerable number of descriptions of Creole languages have surfaced, and have generated interest and debate.

The curious and provocative feature of Creole languages is that they are structurally similar despite their wide distribution and variegated parentage.   Whether they be French Creoles of the Indian Ocean or the Caribbean, or English Creoles of the

88

Pacific or the Caribbean, all exhibit the same general features. Creole language syntax is based on word order, not on affixing or inflecting principles. The Creole verb phrase has a distinctive organization, displays elaborate aspects (progressive aspect, habitual aspect, completive aspect) but few tenses. The Creole system of articles is distinctive. Negative concord, lack of passive voice, distinct copula forms for different functions, are all endemic to Creole languages.

Much of the discussion about Creole languages has consisted of attempts and counter-attempts to explain Creole similarities. These explanations are remarkably creative.

Some scholars have argued that Creole languages are similar because they have developed from a historically unitary source. Schuchardt, for one, suggested that a fourteenth century Mediterranean trade language called Lingua Franca or Sabir was the model for all existing Creoles. The English and the French simply substituted their own lexicon for the Spanish-Italian words in the original. This hypothesis is called monogenesis.

Other scholars, like Mervyn Alleyne (1980), contend that the common heritage of West African languages explains the similarities of French, English, and Portuguese Creoles of the Atlantic region. As they see it, Creole languages are only a problem to those who refuse to credit Africans with having made a significant cultural/linguistic contribution to New World cultures.

Still other historical hypotheses focus on the role of maritime jargons in the development of plantation languages. All Creole languages, it is suggested, are spoken by people whose lives were intimately influenced by maritime trade. And the merchant marine during the time of the formation and maintenance of the plantation colonies was distinguished by its curious dialects.

These historical hypotheses have an interest of their own, but in current debate, they are overshadowed by the arguments that invoke a universal language faculty to account for Creole similarities. Two such hypotheses come to mind: the universal pidginization hypothesis, and the universal creolization hypothesis.

Universal pidginization proposes that Creoles are similar in form because they are all recently sprung from a maximally simple universal base called a Pidgin language.

A Pidgin language is a structurally reduced language used by speakers as a second language for handling a restricted range of communicative activities. Its vocabulary is small; its morphology is sparse and its syntax is simple. The forerunners of Creole speakers took advantage of universal innate strategies for simplifying languages, and, in using those strategies, they produced Pidgin languages. The children of Pidgin speakers took over those Pidgin languages and expanded them so that their languages could serve as fully functional vernaculars, i.e. Creoles.

The bottom line of this universal pidginization hypothesis is that the language faculty not only directs the acquisition of linguistic complexities, it also directs the simplification of languages to their universal core.

Derek Bickerton has opposed this universal pidginization hypothesis. In his book <u>Roots</u> <u>of</u> <u>Language</u> (1981) he put forward the universal creolization hypothesis.

According to Bickerton's hypothesis, Creole language structures are the universal innate language structures that underly all languages. We all, in our roots, are native speakers of a Creole language. However, most of us, in the course of normal language acquisition, are drawn away from our Creole roots and pushed into learning the languages of our communities, e.g. English, German, Russian, etc..

In other words, Creole language structures form the trunk of all languages. The features which distinguish most languages from one another are at the level of branches and leaves. The parents of the first Creole speakers offered them no systematic language models with the drawing power to set them on a course of normal language acquisition. The parents refused to use their native languages in the new social situation, and the Pidgin languages that they did use were unsystematic. Having no models for language acquisition, these Creole children returned to their roots, to Universal Grammar. They constructed Creole languages.

Two sorts of evidence support Bickerton's hypothesis. First, he presents evidence that Creole language structures are maximally unmarked, which one would expect of a grammar drawn from the Universal Grammar, and they are uniformly distributed across Creole languages. On a second front, Bickerton presents evidence that so-called Pidgin languages are unsystematic congeries of words and structures. Pidgins, he says, are not really languages at all.

Bickerton's evidence on this latter front is strong. He shows that Hawaiian Pidgin varies in its form depending on the native languages of its speakers. For Filipino speakers, Pidgin is a VSO language after the fashion of Tagalog. For Japanese speakers, Pidgin is a SOV language after the fashion of Japanese. Pidgin itself does not exist except perhaps for its characteristic words and idioms. Its grammar is basically the grammar of the speaker's native tongue.

The evidence that Hawaiian Pidgin is unsystematic is convincing. But Bickerton leaps from this evidence to the conclusion that all Pidgins are equally unsystematic. Such a leap is not so well justified.

The debate about universal pidginization and universal creolization will be continued for some time, I suspect. And, at the moment, it is hard to predict whether scholarly approval will swing towards the one hypothesis or towards the other.

But what does seem clear is that in the current climate of opinion, a universal account is more heavily favored than an historical explanation. That is, hypotheses like universal creolization or universal pidginization which explain Creole data in terms of universal innate operations of the language faculty are generally regarded as "more interesting" and worth pursuing than historical explanations like monogenesis or African derivation. And without a doubt, Bickerton's hypothesis, with its claim that Creole languages emanate directly from a universal innate "linguistic bioprogram" is as strong as any innatist and universalist hypothesis presented to date.

In the current intellectual atmosphere, historical explanations are considered uninteresting and passé. They are disregarded because they fail to address the issue which is central to current linguistic concerns, namely the role of the mind in the constitution of languages. Universalist accounts like universal pidginization and universal creolization engender lively debate and command wide approval because they shed light on central issues in linguistic theory, building bridges from marginal linguistic phenomena to the core of the human mental language faculty.

Sign Language Studies Sign language studies is a second arena in which bridge building has served the linguist's objective of clarifying the nature of the language faculty.

Like Creole languages, Sign languages of the deaf were, for a very long time, considered non-languages. Some scholars considered them to be pantomimic systems which require a skill and creativity like that necessary for playing charades. But such creativity is of no interest to linguists.

Other scholars regarded Sign languages to be manual versions of spoken languages. According to this view, anything grammatical about deaf signing must be borrowed by the deaf from the hearing who surround them. Sign languages do not develop true grammatical characteristics of their own.

Still other scholars have suggested that Sign languages of the deaf are universal communication systems. The deaf from all parts of the world seem to be able to communicate with one an-

91

other, and that is because their language is a universal language.

Such a view, while seeming to attribute value and worth to deaf signing, is an implicit denial of the linguistic nature of deaf signing. Real languages differ from place to place and from people to people. A Russian cannot talk to a Bantu, and a Basque cannot talk to a Samoan. If Sign languages are not mutually unintelligible like oral languages, then they must not be real languages.

The research of contemporary Sign linguists runs against the grain of all these preceding views. Sign linguists contend that Sign languages of the deaf can be complete and independent languages. And the research shows that the organization of vernacular Sign languages (vernacular, meaning naturally acquired by children) of the deaf promises special insight into the human langage faculty.

William Stokoe (1961) pioneered the linguistic description of Sign languages when he demonstrated that deaf signs are doubly structured like words.

Double structuring, or duality of patterning as it is sometimes called, refers to the fact that words consist of phonemic units drawn from a finite set and combined in different ways. Stokoe demonstrated that deaf signs, even though they may seem to be pantomimic, are really doubly structured. They consist of four simultaneously presented dimensions in which a finite set of expression elements contrast. Variation in any one of the dimensions is sufficient to distinguish one sign from others.

The dimensions are handshape, orientation of hand, place of signing, and movement of sign. The signs COW and HORSE have identical places, orientation, and movements. But because they exhibit different handshapes, they are different signs. NAME and EGG have identical handshapes, but are distinguished by different movements.

In addition to these simultaneously presented dimensions of contrast, signs also contrast in the sequences of "movements" and "holds" that constitute them. Some signs involve continuous motion. Other signs contain stopped or held motion. The sequence of "movements" and "holds" for a certain sign helps distinguish it from other signs.

Klima and Bellugi demonstrated that the signs of the deaf operate in roughly the same fashion as words. That is, signers rely on the correlation of formational characteristics with semantic distinctions to interpret the meanings of signs. Those who argue that signs are pantomimic say that signs operate by reminding signers of experiences with which those signs are associated. They say that the sign COW reminds signers of the horns which they associate with cows and CAT reminds signers of the whiskers which they associate with cats.

Klima and Bellugi's experiments (1979) have demonstrated that American signers attend to the contrastive features of signs, not to their associations with experience. They asked a group of hearing persons to memorize a long list of simple words like "home," "bird," and "name." A group of deaf persons memorized an identical list of signs. After a period of time, the individuals in both groups were asked to reproduce the words-signs they had memorized. Due to the time lapse, both the hearing and the deaf persons mis-remembered many words/signs. But the way in which they mis-remembered them was identical. The hearers made a number of recollection errors and most of them involved phonological substitutions like "coat" for "coke" and "bother" for "father." The deaf made similar substitutions, only in Sign. They substituted YESTERDAY for HOME, which are identical in all respects except for handshape. They substituted PRINT for BIRD which are identical in all respects save place of articulation. And they substituted EGG for NAME which are identical except in motion.

Deaf errors on this test were identical in quality to hearing errors. That is, both deaf and hearing subjects erred by mis-remembering distinctive features of expressions. This identical type of error suggests that deaf persons process signs just as hearing persons process words, i.e. according to their linguistic structure and not according to their associations.

Through the efforts of scholars like Stokoe, Klima, and Bellugi, vernacular Sign languages of the deaf have been demonstrated to be authentic languages. And once vernacular Sign languages were confirmed authentic languages, scholars began looking at Sign languages to see whether they were constrained like oral language by the innate universals of the language faculty.

Some interesting results are surfacing from this research. Feldman, Goldin-Meadow, and Gleitman (1978), for example, have been investigating the acquisition of linguistic structures by deaf children who are deprived of access to language models. The parents of these deaf children are hearing persons who refuse to use any kind of signing. They have found that these deaf children develop the same sorts of linguistic characteristics as hearing children who are in similarly abnormal acquisition situations. That is, the deaf children, even though they lack access to adult language models, still construct lexical signs and put them together according to sign order rules. It is as if they are guided in their acquisition by an innate language faculty. They are beginning to construct a language despite the fact that they have no language model to follow.

93

Elissa Newport (1982) has shown that some characteristics which had previously been thought to be specific to oral languages are characteristic of Sign languages. For example, it is known that speakers perceive speech sounds in categories. Even though a sound is varied continuously, a listener hears it as a sound of either one category or another. And when such a continuum of variation stretches across two phonemic units like /pa/ and /ba/, listeners sharply contrast whole groups of sounds as /pa/ and other whole groups of sounds as /ba/.

Sign language receivers operate similarly in categorizing signed productions. Consider, for example, ONION and APPLE which differ only by way of place on the face where they are signed. When signers are presented with variants of ONION and APPLE such that those variants cover all the space between the typical locations of those signs, they sharply contrast one group of signs with another, considering one group to be ONION and another to be APPLE. Thus, categorical perception is not just characteristic of the aural processing of speech, it is also characteristic of the visual processing of signs.

The lesson to be learned from the researches of both Feldman et al. and Newport is that the language faculty works its ways on the acquisition of language in different media. The language faculty is a general faculty, and not specific to oral languages.

Bridge builders' contributions to the understanding of the language faculty have been considerable. They have described both the content and the role of the language faculty, saying that it is well fleshed out with specific syntactic features and constrains the acquisition of language in the visual as well as the aural mode. These conclusions expand on and extend the more modest claims which are generated through deductive and inductive analyses of more familiar data. Some deductivists and inductivists might balk at the validity of such extensions, but no one denies the significance of the story which those conclusions tell about the human mind.

Summary

Deductivists, inductivists and bridge builders all begin with certain assumptions about what is important in the universe of people and their speech. And in the preceding review it should be clear that two major common assumptions stand out, namely, that the language faculty is a uniform mental capability which guides all vernacular language acquisition, and that each and every individual is endowed with that language faculty and can take advantage of its guidance in language acquisition.

Nothing in the data tells linguists to construct hypotheses about the uniform language faculty of human individuals. Nothing

94

in the data tells them to search for mental constraints on language acquisition. They do it just because *common sense* tells them that it is worth doing. They do it because they *assume* that an understanding of language leads to an understanding of human nature, and that an understanding of human nature is worth while.

Common sense and *assumptions* about what kinds of questions are important and about what kind of explanations are desirable are obviously very powerful forces in scientific research. They, and not the data, direct and shape the research. Eyes and ears tell the researcher what is out there in the world, but common sense and assumptions tell him or her what to focus on and what to play up amongst the phenomena that are out there.

The common sense and the assumptions that figure into scientific research so strongly but so subtly are *not* politically innocent. It is not mere coincidence that *e pluribus unum* characterizes a major orientation in both structuralist linguistic research and in the development of modern nations.

Chapter Seven

The Glue of Social Life: Sociolinguistics

"T's all in peeces; all cohaerence gone..." With these words John Donne described modern social life in 1611 when modern life was but a stripling. In 1987, modern life has grown up, but it remains "in peeces."

Those who are in a position to wield power certainly have an interest in finding a way to glue the "peeces" together. They should like to have a glue thick enough to hide the seams between the different ethnic groups that form modern nation-states. But even more, they should like to have a glue strong enough to bind members of every group together so as to return society to the blissful state of unanimity wherein every person believed and behaved like every other person--was there ever such a state?

For centuries, language scholars have been providing just such a glue in the form of the notion of "shared language." The earliest of the modern grammarians, Antonio de Nebrija, was aware of the power of his grammar to bind people together. In his introductory comments to Queen Isabella he declared: "This Castilian language has been left by us loose and unruly...Greek and Latin...have kept their uniformity throughout two thousand years. Unless the like be done for our language, your labour will not outlast more than a few years." Likewise, our own Noah Webster was well enough aware that his dictionary served as a glue for our heterogeneous newborn nation. The spelling system which he left us is a marvel of political savvy; it affirms American independence from Britain, while borrowing on the antiquity and sacredness of British English.

Modern linguists are generally committed to the age-old principle that a shared language is the glue of a community (Gumperz 1968: 463; Romaine 1982: 23; Trudgill 1983: 13), though they seldom acknowledge the political significance of that commitment.

On the Autonomy of Science

Modern linguists generally operate with the attitude of scientists of the nineteenth century. That is, in their view science is, and should be, independent of the forces of social life. Some historians of linguistics (Newmeyer 1986) state this condition positively by saying that from the mid-nineteenth century to the present, there has developed an "autonomous linguistics" which aims to describe a language faculty that is fundamentally non-political and non-social. In Newmeyer's view, the

97

descriptions of the language faculty by linguists are no more political than the descriptions of elementary particles by physicists. Therefore, scholars who pursue this "autonomous linguistics" need not be sensitive to the political ramifications of their work because their objective of study is the non-political language faculty.

What Newmeyer does not make clear is that the nineteenth century devotion to autonomy in science is an extension and deepening of the rift between science and social life which appeared in the seventeenth century. Interestingly, that seventeenth century rift came about for patently political reasons and not because an autonomous science was inherently logical. That is, the English Puritan regime of the mid-seventeenth century found it desirable to emphasize the independence of scientific research from the past authorities and the past political circumstances which they were struggling to banish from the consciousness of the English citizenry. An "autonomous" science served their needs well in this regard (Bleier 1986: 5).

Thus, the autonomy of science itself is, in its historical roots, evidence that science is anything but autonomous and independent of social forces.

A shared language is supposedly the glue of a community. However, the close and careful observation of languages during the past one hundred years has shown that the closer you look, the less clear are the facts of language sharedness. The members of modern societies may continue to tell themselves that they are one and are bound together by a shared language, but the facts of the matter suggest otherwise. The facts suggest that no language is really shared. The facts suggest that individuals in every community possess slightly, and sometimes dramatically, different grammars. The political ramifications of such facts are unsettling to say the least.

The discussion that follows here is a discussion of how modern structuralist sociolinguists have struggled to save the principle of shared language, society's glue, by using the vintage structuralist argument that variation is a superficial complexity that hides an underlying unity.

First, I will consider Saussure's view on language sharedness. Second, I will rehearse the major advances in sociolinguistic description, the documentation of geographical, social, and stylistic language variation. Finally, I will review the efforts of William Labov and Derek Bickerton to account for that ubiquitous language variation.

Saussure and Sharedness

After he defined a language as a kind of mental state, Saussure was faced with the issue of how such a mental state could be called social. He was aware of Whitney's emphatic statements on the sharedness of language, and his own programmatic statements reflect a similar attitude:

> For the realization of language a community of speakers is necessary...Contrary to all appearances, language never exists apart from the social fact, for it is a semiological phenomenon. Its social nature is one of its inner characteristics (1959: 77).

But in detailing his doctrine that the mental states of a language are socially shared, Saussure found it necessary to do some fast and fancy explaining.

The problem was to describe how a language could be both a mental state and a shared state. His solution was to mention but play down the social dimension of language while playing up the psychological dimension. He accomplished this double task with his concept of sharedness. As Saussure saw it, language is represented in individual minds. And what makes language a social phenomenon is that the minds of all speakers in a group are identically formed: "Language exists in the form of a sum of impressions deposited in the brain of each member of a community, almost like a dictionary of which identical copies have been distributed to each individual. Language exists in each individual yet it is common to all" (Ibid., p. 19).

Even linguists of Saussure's day knew that such a description of sharedness as "identical distribution" could not be empirically supported. Anyone who listens carefully to speech as it is used in everyday life can hear that it varies from individual to individual.

First, all language communities exhibit geographical variation. People of one region speak differently from the people of other regions. Linguistic geography or dialectology is the discipline devoted to describing such geographical differences. The linguistic atlases which linguistic geographers compile present the boundaries, called "isoglosses," between areas where distinctive words or sounds are used. With such an atlas in hand, a linguist can locate the precise region to which a grammatical description applies.

But, as if the geographical variation in language communities were not enough of a scandal to Saussure's doctrine of identical distribution of mental states, linguists, beginning with Gauchat in 1905, demonstrated that the speech of any particular

99

geographical region is itself variable.

One source of this additional variation is social class. Speakers of different socio-economic classes produce different sounds, words, and syntactic structures. John Fischer (1964) was among the first in America to document the effect of social class on language. He observed that the suffix on words like *fighting* and *swimming* was pronounced [in] by members of lower classes and [iŋ] by members of upper classes. In addition he provided evidence that the variation between [in] and [iŋ] was correlated with factors beyond social class, like sex, personality and mood.

One of the most dramatic demonstrations of phonological variation across social classes is William Labov's ingenious department store study (1972). Aiming to record the variations in the pronunciation of post-vocalic [r], Labov sampled the speech of clerks in three department stores in New York City, the clientel of which were upper, middle, and lower classes respectively. Labov assumed that the clerks in these stores were of the same social classes as the patrons of these stores. In each store he inquired of clerks as to the whereabouts of a product known in advance to be on the fourth floor of the store. Predictably the clerks each responded to his query with *fourth floor*. Labov listened carefully for the pronunciation of the [r] in these words, and after each such brief interview he recorded the pronunication in phonetic notation.

The results of his survey of candid pronuncations of "fourth floor" in the three stores are listed below, with numbers indicating the percent of utterances with constricted [r] [for θ flor], versus unconstricted [r] [fo°θ flo°].

Percent of Constricted [r] in NYC

	FOURTH	FLOOR
SAKS	30	64
MACY'S	27	44
KLEINS	5	8

Geographical region and social class affiliation figure into the distribution of language systems. But even within regions and classes, the contexts of speaking elicit different language productions from the same individual.

Consider, for example, Labov's data on [r] production in casual, careful, reading, and "frozen" speech styles. These data show that [r] variation is continuous within individuals, and is correlated with the social context of their speaking. The more formal the social context of New Yorker's speech, the more frequent the production of constricted [r].

100

This context dependent variation, besides being systematically patterned, reveals speakers' attitudes towards their own speech. The speech of lower-middle class speakers (below) is especially revealing. As the context becomes more formal and affords lower middle class speakers more time to reflect on how they are talking, they manipulate their speech to produce far more than their predicted frequency of constricted [r]. This manipulation of speech, which Labov calls statistical hypercorrection, suggests a greater amount of linguistic insecurity in this group than in any other.

These findings show that intra-individual variation is both frequent and systematic. In the view of some linguists, these data suggest that speakers actually control multiple language systems, not just one. A description of the language of an English-speaking individual, for example, would require separate grammars for casual and formal styles. The separate grammars may overlap considerably, but still they must be independent language systems. As the situations of speech change from hour to hour or minute to minute, speakers must switch from one grammar to another so as to produce speech apt for the situation.

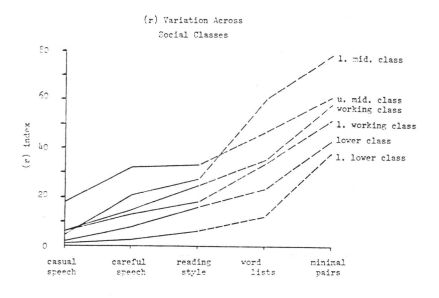

(r) Variation Across Social Classes

The notion of multiple independent coexisting codes or grammars saved--at least for the moment--the Saussurean doctrine of identical distribution of language systems from being completely swallowed up by the facts of geographical, social, and stylistic variation. Linguists were able to maintain the notion of individually possessed, identically shared language systems in the face of ubiquitous variation by postulating in speakers' heads as many different codes as were necessary to account for the variation in speech. But the costs of this theoretical move were tremendous. For one thing, given such multiple language codes, a description of any one language system could only be accomplished by analyzing the speech of a highly circumscribed group, if not of just one single individual. That is, a single grammar or a code must be a description of "the totality of possible utterances of one speaker at one time using a language to interact with one other speaker."

Bloch called this totality of possible utterances an "idiolect," and he argued that all grammatical description must ultimately be based on idiolects. A grammar of a language is really a grammar of one idiolect of a language. Since individuals control multiple idiolects, they must control multiple grammars.

This notion of grammar of an idiolect involves a curious paradox. A grammar is a social phenomenon, yet it is based on observations of purely individual behavior. Evidently we must accept this paradox if we are to preserve the Saussurean principle that a grammar is both social and mental.

Inherent Variability

William Labov was the first to break open this paradox and to propose a real alternative. He did so with the notion of inherent variability (1969). Twentieth century linguists, he argued, had been tying themselves in knots trying to preserve the Saussurean doctrine of mental language systems in the face of ubiquitous variation. The idiolect was their best solution to the problem, but even that solution leaked. Even idiolectal speech is variable. Single individuals, at one moment in time, produce varieties of phonological and syntactic tokens. Their grammars are evidently not systems of invariant rules. Narrowing of the focus of grammars even to single individuals can not accomplish the task of isolating invariant speech.

In the face of this fact, Labov proposed that sociolinguists should forsake the task of describing invariant rules of a language system and focus instead on processes of variation. Such processes of variation, Labov suggested, are always socially shared even if invariant rules are not.

Socially shared processes of variation can be illustrated by the case of the phonological deletion of the final consonants of English word-final consonant clusters. Within any idiolect, the final consonants of strings like [bold] and [mist], along with a host of other words that end in consonant clusters, are variably deleted.

At no time and under no conditions can the appearance of the consonant at the end of such words be predicted. But one can predict relative frequencies of occurrence for all speakers. For example, the deletion of the final consonant is always more frequent when the following word begins with a consonant than when not. Similarly, the deletion is always less frequent when a morpheme boundary exists within the final consonant cluster, as in words like "missed" and "bowled," than when not, as in words like "mist" and "bold."

The relative frequencies of consonant deletion in New Yorkers of different social classes, controlling for context of speech is as follows:

	no morpheme boundary		morpheme boundary	
	__C (mist dipped)	__V (mist over)	__C (missed Mary)	__V (missed a)
social class				
u.m.c	60%	28%	19%	04%
l.m.c	90	40	19	09
l.c.	89*	40	47*	32

This matrix presents the environments which constrain variation in final consonant deletion. "Environment" here means the linguistic condition for rule application (see chapters four and five). Some environments favor deletion, e.g. a following consonant and the absence of a morpheme boundary between the final consonant and the word root. Some environments inhibit deletion, e.g. a following vowel and the presence of a morpheme boundary. But in these data, the favoring or the inhibiting are not categorical. All environments are variably influential; their favoring and inhibiting effects are variable.

From within the displayed array of variable effects of these environments there emerges an interesting pattern. The environments to the right of the matrix generally inhibit deletion. And as you move leftward, the environments increasingly favor deletion. Moreover, while the absolute frequencies of deletion differ across social classes, this relationship between environments is maintained. In each social class, the environments to the left favor deletion more than environments to the right. Moreover, the pair of environments to the left (no morpheme boundary) as a whole favor deletion more frequently than the pair of environments to the right (morpheme boundary). From this pattern we can conclude: though any particular instance of final consonant deletion cannot be predicted, the average frequency of deletion in any linguistic environment for any speaker can be predicted

103

relative to average frequencies in other environments; and this pattern of relatively predictable frequencies of deletion is shared by all social classes. (Asterisks indicate deviant frequencies.)

Interestingly, this pattern of consonant deletion holds for all styles, all social codes, and all geographical dialects of English. Speakers of Black English, for example, typically apply deletion to a much higher frequency in all linguistic environments than speakers of even lower class non-Black English dialects in NYC. Many speakers of Black English even apply the deletion rule 100% in certain linguistic environments. But even so, the pattern of deletion frequencies displayed above still holds true. If a frequency of 100% were to appear in an environment to the right, you could be sure that all the environments to the left also favor deletion at a frequency of 100%.

From facts such as these Labov argued that language communities really share linguistic environments on processes such as consonant deletion. The linguistic environments with their relative powers to promote or inhibit a process span geographical, social, and stylistic speech varieties. And such constraints seem to be about the only phenomena that are realized homogeneously in a community.

Phonological units and syntactic structures are certainly not identically distributed. Contrary to the Saussurean doctrine, their realization is not even predictable in the speech of a single individual. Hence, language communities cannot be defined in terms of such units. However, environments in variation processes are identically shared. They, and not sounds and words, are the basis of the sociality of a language.

Labov's methods of statistical analysis are ingenious. And the thoroughness of his investigations of such variability (1972a; 1972b) are deserving of emulation. But his conclusions must be recognized as predictably structuralist. That is, Labov's variable rule describes superficial variability which hides underlying uniformity, and in this case, underlying sharedness.

Universal Constraints on Variation

Labov's account of the underlying sharedness of superficially variable aspects of languages has its drawbacks. The Saussurean theory according to which sharing consists of an identical distribution of systems of linguistic units had its wide and long-lived appeal largely because objects like phonemes and morphemes are phenomena which one can easily imagine are acquired in an identical fashion by individuals of a community. But when processes, not objects, are what is shared by speakers, one must struggle to imagine how those processes can be acquired so precisely by language learners.

Derek Bickerton (1971) pointed out the problem most clearly. To suppose that language learners acquire Labovian variation processes in the course of language acquisition is to suppose that each learner has both clairvoyance and superhuman analytic powers. Language learners must hold in their heads the relative statistical frequencies of the variation processes that Labov describes, and they must be able to know *in advance* frequencies of processes in a speaking event in order to "decide" whether to apply or not to apply the process at any point within the act of speaking. In short, to claim that language communities are defined by an identical distribution of processes of variation is to impute implausibly strong powers to the language learner.

Can This Language Be Acquired?

A gunsmith might shrug off criticisms of sloppy woodworking or erratic metal etching. But he has got to attend to someone who says that his rifles won't fire. Bickerton's criticism is of that trenchant sort. He takes his argument to the very heart of what any linguistic proposal is all about, namely, the universal language learning abilities of humans. Telling a linguist that the grammars that he or she describes is not acquirable is like telling a gunsmith that his weapons won't fire. Little wonder that the Labov-Bickerton debate quickly became a bitter one.

Bickerton's alternative is to maintain the Labovian view that processes, not objects, are identically distributed among speakers. But he deviates from Labov's proposal by hypothesizing that variation processes, and more specifically the linguistic environments which constrain inherent variability, are fixed and universal, i.e. part of the language faculty.

Speakers do not learn the processes or the relationships between linguistic environments. The relationships between environments for processes are fixed and provided to language learners in advance from the catalogue of universals of language to which everyone has access. Variation processes are identically distributed only because the constraints on the processes are universal and identically possessed even before language acquisition begins. They are pre-wired into the brains of language learners. Thus, for Bickerton, the acquisition of variation processes is not problematic because these processes are not so much acquired as inherited along with all other language universals.

Some of the evidence supporting Bickerton's claim is drawn from English Creole languages of the West Indies. Bickerton

105

found that speakers vary in their production of the complement-
izers *tu* (T) and *fu* or *fi* (F) sometimes even within the same
sentence: *jan riez di prais fi get di fish tu sen san andres*
(John raised the price to get the fish to send to San Andres).

Bickerton suggested that three universal environments constrain the replacement of F by T. The replacement occurs after
inceptive and modal verbs (I started to..., I have to...), after
verbs of desire (I want to...), and after verbs controlling
purpose clauses and others (I went in order to...). The abstract
model for the replacement of F by T shows that the replacement
occurs first and fastest after modal verbs (I), secondly after
verbs of desire (II), and finally after all other verbs (III).
This abstract model which predicts a specific pattern of F/T
variation is shown below.

Speakers	I	II	III
1	F	F	F
2	F/T	F	F
3	T	F	F
4	T	F/T	F
5	T	T	F
6	T	T	F/T
7	T	T	T

The empirical support for this analysis is weak (Washabaugh
1977). Bickerton fails to justify his claim that environments I,
II, and III are universal constraints. He fails to consider the
possibility that the shape of the complementizer as *tu* or *fu*
might be the result of associations between complementizer and
distinctively Creole or distinctively English verbs. For example, *fi* is always retained after the verb *fiil*, a type II verb,
even when it is replaced in environment III, e.g. *ah fiil fi go*
(I want to go). Here the retention is probably due to the fact
that *fiil* is a distinctively Creole expression which demands the
distinctively Creole *fi*. Finally, his model of variation fails
to apply to varietes of English Creole in which T or F are
frequently deleted, e.g. *Jameika en no pleis go* (Jamaica is no
place to go).

Empirical considerations aside, Bickerton's analysis has the
merit of accounting for inherent variation without imputing implausibly strong powers to language learners. Unlike Labov's
image of humans as statistic-generating machines, Bickerton's
picture of humans is one of speakers endowed with mental gyroscopes for steering their way through variation.

However, the cost of this plausible theory of language
learning is a controversial view of language communities. Bickerton's analysis implies that language communities do not exist.
They may seem to, but this appearance of different language

106

communities is just a mirage. Bickerton's structuralist analysis is the demystifying tool for banishing that mirage and for showing that deep down all language communities are one. If communities are defined by the identical distribution of variation processes, and if variation processes are controlled by an innate universal pre-wired language faculty, then it follows that the only real language community is the community of the whole human species. All speakers of all languages are part of one single language community. French, Hindi, and Tagalog speaking communities are merely untrustworthy appearances, tricks of time and space which lead us to think that human groups and languages are distinct from one another.

For Bickerton there are no distinct languages and no distinct language communities. There is only one language, the Human Language, aspects of which appear to one degree or another in geographically disparate populations. No language is qualitatively different from any other either by way of identically distributed objects or by way of identically distributed processes.

The Application of Sociolinguistic Knowledge

This chapter has focussed on theoretical sociolinguistics, spotlighting the problem of language variation. However sociolinguistics has a very practical side which needs to be appreciated.

Real Versus Ideal Linguists

In the abstract, structuralist linguists including sociolinguists are, as was stated in chapter one, philosophers. However, the real scholars who *do* sociolinguistics are complex people whose objectives are never simple and unitary. The very existence of practical and applied sociolinguistics research should be a reminder that the real world of real language studies is not divided neatly into philosophers and social reformers. There is a bit of philosopher and a bit of social reformer in every language scholar.

The theoretical discussion of language variation is carried on with data drawn from the lives of living people whose languages vary. And most of the time those living people are subject to highly charged forces that swirl about their own language varieties. Kids who speak the Creole languages of the West Indies feel a deep and wrenching shame when they open their mouths in school. Black speakers in the U.S. cling to their language variety as a symbol of their identity, but they also

107

regard it as an obstacle to getting ahead in the world.

Some sociolinguists are aware of the power of their research to both influence such feelings of speakers of stigmatized language varieties, and to shape social and political policies that have a bearing on those feelings. William Labov's variable rule, for example, was initially advanced with data drawn from Black English (1969). And, not to gainsay the theoretical significance of that proposal, Labov clearly recognized the practical social ramifications of his work. Black English abides by precisely the same rules as do all other varieties of Anglo-English, and therefore, Black English is a bona fide English, and not a degenerate language or a language apart. The speech of a member of the Black community is every bit as much English as the speech of an Edwin Newman or a William Safire.

Using this variable rule analysis for leverage, Labov made specific proposals toward revamping of educational programs that deal with speakers of Black English (1970). The objective of his proposals is to draw attention away from the so-called peculiarities of Black English and onto racial discrimination which he considers to be the real problem in American education.

Other sociolinguists, like J.L. Dillard (1972) and his colleagues at the Center for Applied Linguistics in Washington, D.C., pursued precisely the opposite line of argument. They tried to show that Black English is fundamentally distinct from English, being derived from a West Indian Creole. As such, Black English can and should serve as a flag around which the Black community can rally round and to which it can look with pride.

The literature (see, for example, Valentine (1972)) that discusses these different proposals on the status of Black English is both large and intensely argued. It is vast because Black English contains many nooks and crannies, of phonological and syntactic sorts, that can be explored from one point of view or another. It is complicated because the sociolinguistics explorers are operating, now as scientists with theoretical interests in the nature of grammatical rules and the problem of variation, and now as sympathetic advocates for the Black community.

Summary

Sociolinguists are ambivalent about the sharedness of languages. They shuffle between saying that communities are held together by a language shared in some manner by members and saying that local language communities are mirages which blind us to the existence of a larger community composed of all humans, specifically of humans made equal by their identical possession of a language faculty.

First among the high points in the history of these ambivalent sociolinguistic descriptions, is Saussure's proposal that a language is shared by way of an identical distribution of language states in the minds of members of a community. Secondly, sociolinguists demonstrated that no such identical distribution exists. Variability pervades language systems. Variability inheres in language systems so that, in the end, language systems cannot really be called states at all for they are never static. Thirdly, Labov reaffirmed the significance of local communities by arguing the linguistic environments of variable rules are shared by members of local language communities. Finally, Bickerton has undercut the significance of local communities by proposing that linguistic environments on variation are part of a universal language faculty.

Interestingly, the ambivalence in sociolinguistics matches perfectly the ambivalent political needs of the nation-state. On the one hand, the integrity of any nation-state needs to be bolstered by a stress on the sharing among its members of historical traditions and/or beliefs and values. But too much emphasis on such sharedness leads to a back-door support for potentially subversive activities of sub-communities within heterogeneous states. Stress on the importance of traditions and values licenses the IRA, the Basque separatists, the Quebecois, etc. in their struggles against Britain, Spain, and Canada. To counter such back-door support, the keepers of the state have had to carefully temper sociolinguistic stories of language sharedness which encourage patriotic commitment with emphasis on the universal language faculty.

Sociolinguists have not intentionally conspired to create myths and stories which serve the ambivalent needs of nation-states. Nevertheless, ambivalent sociolinguistic descriptions of language communities match those ambivalent needs nicely.

Chapter Eight

The Genesis of Language

The structuralist perspective on language is decidedly synchronic. Structuralists claim that you can know a language by understanding the systematic relations of its parts *at one moment of time.*

It might seem strange, therefore, that a chapter on language genesis, which implies a temporal or diachronic perspective, should be included here in the discussion of structuralist linguistics. The reasons for including this chapter are fourfold.

First, anthropologists have traditionally considered historical, developmental, evolutionary accounts to be significant. Disciplinary pillars like Evans-Pritchard considered anthropology to be a sub-discipline of history; and Boas said of anthropological studies of language, that they aim "to unravel the history of the growth of human language." However you reckon it, anthropologists favor diachronic accounts more than structuralist linguists do. Consequently, when anthropologists read about the works of structuralist linguists, they usually gulp whatever drops of history structuralists might offer. This chapter, in being devoted to language genesis, is intended to satisfy that anthropological thirst for historical studies.

Second, as Nisbet (1969) has argued, Western intellectuals have always held developmental explanations in high regard. You might question the knowledge of a botanist who describes the leaves, bark, and roots of an oak tree. But you are convinced when he or she describes the development of oak tress out of acorns. Genesis accounts have always had such power to convince. Partly in deference to this explanatory power of developmental descriptions, even structuralists, loath though they be to deal in such matters, describe language development.

Third, and besides the popularity of developmental accounts, an account of history and development is frequently as strong a justification for things-as-they-are as one can find. Whoever wishes to legitimate either a contemporary situation or a synchronic explanation can do no better than to describe the past in such a way that it seems to logically and inevitably lead up to that contemporary situation or the synchronic account. Ataturk, the shrewd ruler of early twentieth century Turkey, demonstrated the value of historical accounts as legitimators. He instituted language reforms that resulted in a massive infusion of European words into Turkish. However, he accompanied those changes with a revised language history that described European languages as originating in an early version of Turkish. His language reform, he argued, was taking back into Turkish what was borrowed out of Turkish centuries ago. The people of Turkey accepted Ataturk's

111

drastic language reforms partly because it was accompanied by a history that made sense to them.

Structuralists have no desire to legitimate language reforms. But they do have a very real desire to demonstrate the legitimacy of their principles. Specifically, they want to demonstrate the reality of *competence, universal language faculty, phoneme, deep structures,* etc.. When they present developmental accounts which describe how phenomena came, and continually come, into being, structuralists take giant steps towards making the structuralist linguistic perspective credible.

In a sense, the validity of a generative grammar is demonstrated by projecting that grammar with its assumptions about the language faculty onto a temporal developmental plane. Only when seen through time, can the full array of implications of the theory be appreciated. Lightfoot (1982: 142) says that "A principle of grammar is evaluated according to the extent to which the principle sheds light on the essential problem of language acquisition...One will prefer a theory illuminating the acquisition process."

Two quite different sorts of developmental accounts are possible. On the one hand, the description can focus on origins and evolution of the language capacity in the human species. This sort of description is called a *phylogenetic* description. On the other hand, the description can focus on the acquisition of language abilities by individuals, especially the acquisition of first languages by children. Such an account is called an *ontogenetic* account.

Structuralist linguists have relatively little to offer in the way of phylogenetic accounts of language genesis, but they have abundant descriptions to offer in the way of ontogenetic accounts of language acquisition. The present chapter will examine both.

Fourth, and perhaps most importantly, a diachronic account, especially a phylogenetic account, draws out fully and most clearly the big picture of the human condition which any explanation or theory implies. In phylogenetic accounts, all the assumptions and unspoken ramifications of a particular view of human nature are made apparent. For example, anthropological writings of all sorts have, since the beginning, been marked by a sexist emphasis on males and on male perspectives. Human origins accounts, like all other anthropological writings, have been marked, and marred, by such sexism. However, because the human origins accounts make assumptions clear, the sexist biases in these accounts have been identified early. Other kinds of anthropological writings are probably no less sexist than human origins accounts, but because origins accounts put on the table what other accounts keep under the table, human origins accounts

112

have been subject to early and severe criticism (Haraway 1986).

Language Phylogeny

Design Features   One way to approach language phylogeny is to use modern language competence as the basis for all comparisons and as the standard for all evaluations. Such an approach starts with an assessment of the "design features" of human languages and then proceeds to a comparison of human languages to other communication systems in terms of those design features (Hockett and Ascher 1964).

Among the prominent design features of human languages are arbitrariness/conventionality, discreteness, displacement, re-flexiveness, duality of patterning, and syntactical organization.

The arbitrariness and conventionality of language units make up one design feature. According to this feature, human languages, unlike all other communicative systems, are constituted of units which are not determined by communicative circumstances, but are arrived at by way of a tacit agreement among language users. "Dog" means a species of canine because a community of speakers have agreed on such a meaning. But a scream means pain because the scream is directly determined by the pain. The former expression is an arbitrary conventional epxression; the latter is not.

Discreteness refers to the fact that the units of human languages are types which are categorically opposed to other types. Displacement suggests that humans can communicate about a phenomenon in its absence. The feature of reflexiveness suggests that only humans can talk about talk. Only human languages include "metalanguages," and have expressions like "word," "meaning," and "name" which refer to expressions.

Duality of patterning refers to the fact that only human languages are constituted of a rather small number of phonemes which, when assembled in different orders and to different lengths, can produce an infinity of words.

Finally, syntactic organization refers to the fact that the relations between constituents of sentences regardless of word meanings can make a semantic difference in human languages.

Most speculation about primal human languages in terms of these design features concludes that primal languages are simplified and primitive. Naturally occurring non-human communication systems exhibit only rudimentary aspects of these design features. And, supposing that primal human languages arose out of non-human communication system, those primal languages themselves must have been rudimentary.

113

The Structure and Function of the Brain   Primal languages may have been simplified relative to modern languages, but it is more enlightening to consider the conditions in which those primal languages emerged and the processes that led to their formation.

The first observation to make regarding the earliest human languages is that whatever their form, they were acquired by speakers with brains that were just beginning to look like and operate like modern brains.

Language and the Brain

Since the nineteenth century, language study has been linked quite predictably to the study of brain structures and processes. Such a linkage is predictable because linguistics was born in response to philosophical concerns about mind and it matured in an era when empirical research was emphasized.   The brain is the measurable object which is most closely associated with mind and through which one might make sense of the mind without departing from the description of sensory phenomena.

Modern human brains differ from non-human brains in a number of respects.   First, human brains are proportionately larger than non-human brains, i.e. the ratio of brain weight to body weight is higher in humans than in any other creature, except perhaps the porpoise.   Secondly, human cerebral functions are uniquely interrelated, there being a multiplicity of connections between different cortical areas which enable information from various sense to be translated into a single cerebral code.   Finally, the human brain is asymmetrical in its functioning.   The left hemisphere performs analytic operations and the right hemisphere performs synthetic operations.

One way to appreciate the development of human language is to inquire into the evolution of the modern brain.   If a language is a kind of knowledge, and if the brain is the organ of knowledge, then we should be able to understand the evolution of language by understanding the evolution of the brain.   Accordingly, we will ask about the cerebral changes that had to occur in the primate order in order for humans to begin building and using languages constituted of arbitrary conventional discrete doubly structured expressions.

Lateralization of brain function is generally regarded as a stepping stone for cerebral specialization.   If the right hemisphere is set aside, so to speak, for synthetic functions, then special structures can develop there to enhance synthesis.   And if the left hemisphere is set aside for analytic functions, then

114

special structures can develop there for analysis.

The human capacity for language, being akin to the human computational capacity, is just the sort of cerebral specialization which one might expect to be facilitated by left hemisphere specializations for analytic operations.

How might analytic specializations like those associated with language have benefited evolving humans? What are the selective advantages of such specializations?

Some have argued that the advantage of specializations for analytic operations is increased facility and efficiency in information management and exchange. That is, left hemispheric cerebral specializations were selected for because they made economic and social life easier and more productive. A simple formula summarizes this argument: Analytic abilities make for clearer communicative expressions which facilitate understanding which increase cooperation which speeds social evolution.

Others contend that the adaptive advantages of specializations for analytic operations have nothing to do with communication, at least not at the outset. Ashley Montague (1976), for example, argues that analytic abilities facilitated activities like tool making rather than communicative efficiency. He has proposed that the making of stone tools requires an analytical neural capability quite like that required for language production. The fabrication of a stone blade involves numerous discrete steps which must be precisely ordered. Analytic functions of the left hemisphere were selected for because they enabled proto-human flint knappers to distinguish and order the steps of tool fabrication. The main advantage of left hemisphere specialization is that it facilitates stone tool production. Only later, and less significantly were the communicative advantages of enhanced analytic abilities realized in human evolution.

An even more radical view along the same line is that lateralization and the emergence of the language faculty had no adaptive advantages at all. The structures of the human brain were not directly selected for. Chomsky suggests, "There is no reason to demand, and little reason to suppose, that genetically-determined properties invariably result from specific selection" (1980b). The structures and functions of the human brain "might have arisen from the functioning of certain physical laws relating to neuronal packaging of regulatory mechanisms." Analytic and synthetic specializations may have conferred no specific selective advantages in and of themselves. Rather they may be merely entailments of other, now unknowable, developments which were selected for.

The emergence of left hemisphere specialization was crucial for the emergence of the human capacity for language. Specifically, left hemispheric specializations must have emerged during the course of human evolution--though with what selective advantage we cannot now say with certitude--to enable humans to manipulate discrete doubly structured expressions.

One way to identify the linguistic developments made possible by the lateralized brain is to compare the linguistic capacity of humans to the analogous capacities of non-humans. Peter Marler (1975), for example, has compared the acoustical productive and processing capabilities of contemporary species of primates and humans.

Within different primate species he has discerned two major types of call systems: the discrete type and the graded type. The discrete type of call system is characterized by different calls produced by completely distinct articulatory means, e.g., grunts, chirps, snorts, screams, roars, each different call bearing a distinct meaning. The graded type of call system consists of calls constructed from a handful of articulatory means, and the calls vary by degree of amplitude, frequency, etc..

Marler finds that the discrete call system is employed by highly territorial species for use in inter-troop communication, usually over long distances. But among other species, especially non-territorial species, for which most communication occurs within the troop and at close proximity, a graded system is more common. Notably, chimpanzees employ a graded call system.

Human speech, like chimpanzee calls, involves graded expressions. Spectrographic representations of speech show no chunked segments, no discrete units, but only flows of rising and falling frequencies of sound.

We can imagine that humans, initially at least, used systems of graded calls for communication in socio-ecological circumstances quite like that of contemporary chimpanzees, i.e., non-territorial and inclined to intra-group communication. But clearly something additional sets human communication apart from the graded call systems of other primates. Human speech, though acoustically graded, is processed into discrete units, that is, into sounds and words.

Some primates have discrete calls which are processed into discrete units. Others, like chimps, have graded calls which are processed, we suspect, into graded units. The meanings of the graded calls vary along continuous dimensions.

The human call system differs from both these. It is a system of graded calls analyzed into discrete units.

Marler argues that the distinctive character of human expressions is made possible by specific neural specializations for

116

discrete processing. Humans, early on, must have developed what he calls a "neural template" which enabled them to discern units within graded expressions. There must be some neural directive, he says, which enables human subjects to discern the difference between a [p] and a [b] regardless of experimental manipulations which reduce that contrast to its acoustic minimum. Moreover, such a neural directive must be innate rather than learned because, as Cutting and Eimas (1975) have shown, "segmental processing of speech sounds occurs in infants as young as four months or even one month, long before they have begun to speak or even babble."

In summary the evidence of the species-wide human characteristics of graded speech with discrete processing requires the postulation of a species-wide mechanism to facilitate that discrete processing. The postulation of an innate and universal neural mechanism, a neural template, in the left hemisphere of the brain seems to be the most plausible explanation. Notice that such an explanation allows for the obvious human capability to process sounds continuously as well as discretely. The right hemisphere can be supposed to discern the gradient value of non-linguistic expressions.

On another score, the postulation of an innate and universal neural template for categorical processing of sounds paves the way for the development of syntactic capabilities: "Once having accomplished the assemblage of discrete clusters of elements or words by recombinations of the same limited set of minimal sound segments, it is a natural step to recombine words in new ways, i.e. syntax. the two kinds of recombination may even employ similar kinds of physiological processes" (Marler 1975: 34).

Quite a different view of human cerebral evolution for language is offered by Derek Bickerton (1981). Bickerton contends, like Montague, that language emerged initially at least, as a system for conceptualization, not as a system for communication. "Language grew out of the cognitive system used for individual orientation, predication, etc. rather than out of prior communicative systems" (Ibid, p. 267). Specifically, analytic language emerged under the selective pressure for precision thinking. "Cognitive growth," he argues, "has always been the major thrust of evolution." Thinking-in-language gave humans an extraordinary advantage over other primates, especially when that thinking was hooked up to communicative expressions so that the advantages of precision thought could be shared.

The selective advantage of analytic language-thought is obvious, to Bickerton at least. And given this selective advantage, human brains were universally rewired for language. So began the evolution of the "linguistic bioprogram," the universal innate language faculty discussed in preceding chapters.

117

But the universal rewiring for analytic language-thought was not a sudden and abrupt development. Rather it emerged slowly with the accumulation of linguistic capabilities. Those capabilities were hardwired in the brain in an evolutionary sequence which can now be discerned in the order of the acquisition of linguistic structures by children. Using a modified version of the old principle that ontogeny recapitulates phylogeny, Bickerton argues that the first sorts of linguistic-conceptual structures which evolved in humans are the first to emerge in child language acquisition. Hence child language acquisition is a mirror in which to discern the progress of cerebral changes in human language acquisition.

The proposals of Marler and Bickerton are similar in that they postulate universal cerebral mechanisms to account for the emergence of distinctively human language capabilities. However, they differ in details. Marler is concerned to explain the human phonological capabilities, and he does so by postulating the rather abruptly evolved neural template. Bickerton is interested in explaining the human capability for precise conceptualization, and he does so by postulating a gradually evolved linguistic bioprogram.

The Human Pharynx   The brain and its evolution is the focal issue in structuralist discussion of the evolution of human languages. But extra-cranial developments also interest linguists, particularly those having to do with the human vocal tract. Among these discussions, none has been more provocative than the current debates about the evolution of the human pharynx.

The pharynx is the chamber which, in mammals, extends from the vocal cords to the back of the mouth. In humans that chamber is curved and elongated, whereas in non-human primates, it is rather short (see chapter 2). Perhaps bipedal locomotion and upright posture were factors which, more than others, conditioned the reshaping of the pharynx during human evolution. But, whatever the reasons, the reshaping seems to have had a significant impact on the evolution of language.

First of all, the reshaping of the pharynx during human evolution enabled humans to produce a distinctly human range of vocalic sounds. Most importantly, the pharynx enables humans to produce the sounds [i], [u], and [a]. These three sounds may be critical in human speech, for they function as demarcations of the human phonological field. Present in all languages, these sounds set the limits of phonological contrasts.

Philip Lieberman (1975; 1984) has argued that the development of the elongated human pharynx occurred rather late in the course of human evolution. His reconstructions of some Neanderthal crania show that the pharynxes of these specimens were not elongated and curved in the distinctly human manner. The conclu-

118

sion he draws is that Neanderthals did not have the ability to produce human speech sounds. Hence they did not command a oral human language like our own.

Neanderthals may not have spoken a language, but they may have signed a language. Gorden Hewes (1973) has gathered together evidence and even some centuries-old arguments to support the hypothesis that the first human language was a gestural language. Somewhere in the evolution of humans, perhaps around the era of the Neanderthals, the medium of language switched from gestures to sounds.

The work of both Marler and Lieberman suggests that the control of acoustic phenomena, i.e. the abililty to both produce speech sounds and process them, is intimately tied up with the fully evolved language faculty. They suggest that any account of the evolution of the language faculty which fails to note the intimate links between that language faculty and the control of speech sounds misses out on a fundamental aspect of that faculty.

On the other hand, Montague's and Bickerton's phylogeny both suggest that the language faculty evolved as a general cognitive faculty without specific ties to phonological capabilties.

There is dissension in the ranks, but that is to be expected for such a highly speculative issue as the evolution of the language faculty.

However, on one major point, all these scholars are in agreement. That is, the critical characteristic of the language faculty is, whatever its original evolutionary function, the ability to calculate, categorize, and produce/interpret tokens for types.

Scholars who pursue different objectives from structuralist linguists have different views on language evolution. I am thinking particularly of the Boasian ethnographers who struggle to understand language for what it can teach us about social life. In their view, a description of language evolution makes no sense if it does not explain how languages come to be used by communities of people. We will consider such an alternative phylogenetic account in chapter thirteen.

Language Ontogeny

Descriptions of child language acquisition play an extremely important role in Saussurean-Chomskyan linguistics. Generally, language acquisition is the bell-wether of grammatical theory. If a particular grammatical description with all its postulates accords with the behaviors of children in language acquisition, then that description is regarded as plausible. If a grammatical description fails to match that data, it is considered suspect.

119

Particular issues aside for the moment, the commonly shared view about language acquisition is that children are able to construct languages for themselves because they are guided by their innate language faculties. They unconsciously build grammars of rules in stages moving from phonologically and syntactically unmarked characteristics to increasingly more marked ones. And they do so systematically, guided by their cerebral gyroscopes. Most importantly, children perform the task of language construction for themselves.

Adults do not teach children a language. They certainly do not consciously instruct their children in speech as a school teacher might teach arithmetic. But neither do they teach language unconsciously, with covert instructions and subtle rewards.

Adults perform one task only with respect to language acquisition. They provide the raw material and the goal for children. They speak the utterances which children take to be examples and models of language. They present the children with illustrations of what they will eventually have to produce if they, the children, are ever to be considered authentic speakers of a language.

The task of becoming a speaker by building a language is something that each child undertakes alone. The babbling of infants is their way of experimenting with and acquiring an ability to produce speech sounds. Babbling of roughly the same sort is produced by children in all societies. When it comes to acquiring words and phrases, each child must summon his or her own sleuthing resources to discern, in the speech of surrounding adults, some orderliness and regularity. The child must work alone at the task of perceiving the tokens of speech, deciphering the types, and discerning the best ways--usually the simplest and most parsimonious ways--to represent those types in tokens of their own making.

The task of the child is similar in certain respects to the task of the linguists who set for themselves the task of describing the grammar of a language (see p. 45). The child, like the linguists, must decipher types in tokens and propose simple, but general, rules for the bewildering array of possible tokens from the paltry number of types available. The child and the linguist are doing the same work. And to underscore the similarity, linguists say that children, like linguists, produce grammars.

There are differences of course. The product of the child's efforts is an unwritten grammar, unconsciously arrived at and housed in the mind. The product of the linguists' efforts is a written grammar consciously labored over and housed between the covers of a book.

One other difference should be mentioned. The child labors at his/her task under the guidance of a universal language faculty, whereas the linguists, perhaps because their labors are so conscious, are not guided and assisted by that faculty.

This last difference may be exceedingly important. A child can produce a grammar with three or four years of apparently very casual labor, whereas linguists have been laboring together for years upon years to produce a written grammar of English, and they are still far from their goal.

These differences aside, the child and the linguists both produce grammars which accurately represent the organization of adult speech. Thus the term grammar is systematically ambiguous in the linguist's vocabulary. On the one hand, it represents the written product of linguists' efforts, and, on the other, the unwritten unconsciously constructed product of the child's efforts. But grammar, in either sense, is a product of, and a testament to, the linguistic sleuthing capabilities of individuals, whether children or linguists.

Under the guidance of the innate language faculty, the child proceeds in grammar construction by conjecture and refutation. The child guesses at grammatical representations and revises those guesses when they turn out to be faulty. This process is very much like that described for the "I'm going camping" game in chapter three. For example, children at the beginning of their efforts to acquire English, internalize irregular past tense forms as distinct lexicals items, e.g. *go* and *went*. But with more exposure to adult speech, children invariably conjecture that past tenses should be formed by adding *-ed* to the root of a verb. At that point they ignore the previously internalized expression *went* and form the past tense of *go* as *goed*. Further down the line, they revise this guess and reinstate irregular past tense forms like *went* as exceptions to the regular past tense formation rule.

Given this conjecture-refutation model of child language acquisition, the errors that children make in acquiring adult competence are necessary steps for learning. Each error, indicating an inadequate generalization--usually an overgeneralization--is a necessary prelude to formulating the more accurate generalization. Children overgeneralize and when they find that speech from adult models does not match their overgeneralized forms, they refine their grammars. Child language errors are not *faux pas* but symptoms of on-going grammar construction.

Why, one must ask, should children pursue so tenaciously the task of grammar construction? Why are children so unswervingly devoted to the project of revising their inadequate generalizations about their language?

121

One plausible, but ultimately unacceptable, answer is that persons around them pressure the children into disambiguating and clarifying their ambiguous and confused utterances. A two year old boy, for example, might produce an utterance *mommy socks*, and by that utterance he might mean a variety of different things. He might mean that the socks belong to mommy, or that mommy is washing the socks, or that mommy is holding the socks. In short, *mommy socks* is multiply ambiguous. Perhaps, the mother, on hearing such an utterance, requires of the two year old that he specify exactly what he means. Under such pressure the two year old struggles to disambiguate his utterances.

Such a hypothesis is plausible, but probably false. The people closest to a child, especially in the early years, rarely pressure the child to revise utterances. Mothers, "being in the same situation and familiar with the child's stock of knowledge, understand so far as one can tell, even the child's incomplete utterances" (Brown 1973: 410). In other words, caregivers usually accept the child's context sensitive utterances and interpret them properly, a process made possible by the fact that the caregivers are intimately aware of the context of the child's utterances. "We do not presently have evidence that there are selection pressures of any kind operating on children to impel them to bring their speech into line with adult models". (Ibid., p. 412).

If pressures to disambiguate expressions do not push a child to continually refine his or her generalizations toward an adult competence, what does? The answer--at least from those scholars who postulate a mental organ for language--is that children are driven by an internal juggernaut to develop an adult-like grammar. Most linguists discount the role of external and social circumstances in language acquisition, and appeal instead to internal and innate factors: "Children work out rules for speech they hear, passing from levels of lesser to greater complexity, simply because the human species is programmed at a certain period in its life to operate in this fashion on linguistic input" (Ibid., p. 412).

Innate programming may explain a child's relentless pursuit of language acquisition and may explain why so many different children learn so many different languages while following the same paths in language acquisition. However, these findings should not be interpreted to mean that social interaction plays no significant role in language acquisition. On the contrary "interactionists" argue that certain sorts of child-caregiver relationships and behaviors are necessary for language acquisition. For example, the simplified registers used by caregivers with children serves to highlight structures and focus the child's attention on regularities.

Some "interactionists" have argued that the processes of

acquisition is really supported in a substantial way by the actions of caregivers. When their children are infants, adults frequently take on the infant's role in interaction. They speak *to* infants, asking questions and making observation, and they then speak *for* the infants, responding to the questions or following up on the observations. All adults model speaking behavior in this way for their children. And the children use those models in their struggle to become competent speakers. Without such modeling, it is questionable whether a child would ever come to know what it means to engage in the social act of speaking.

Research among the deaf of Providence Island, Colombia corroborates such a view. The deaf there have not yet constructed a fully mature Sign language comparable to American Sign Language, and the reason seems to be that the deaf there have no models of mature signers to imitate. As a result their acquisition of a Sign language is stalled (Washabaugh 1986).

Genie (Curtiss 1977), a kind of modern "wild child," is another case of language acquisition stalled by inadequate social interaction. Genie is a child who was isolated from speech until she was a teenager. Only at that time did she begin her process of English language acquisition. She learned English word order rules fairly rapidly, but she continues to have difficulty with the placement of auxiliary verbs and negative particles in sentences. Such evidence suggests that certain directives of the language faculty operate regardless of social conditions. Other directives of the language faculty are less resilient and fail to operate under abnormal conditions.

Such cases as these suggest that a grammar may be a bundle of characteristics. Some of these characteristics are acquired under the rather direct guidance of the language faculty. Others require careful social guidance and support if they are to be acquired. Neither the language faculty in solipsistic acquisition nor social interaction without the guidance of the language faculty can successfully bring the language learner to a mature command of a language. Both directive forces seem to be necessary for normal acquisition.

Summary

Plenty of room for debate still exists on the issues of ontogeny and phylogeny. No one has the feeling that the work on these issues is anywhere near completion. Most scholars believe that research on both fronts is in its infancy.

While research may be just beginning, the assumptions behind the research are mature, widely shared and, within circles of generative linguists, seldom debated. Most structuralists consider language acquisition to be an accomplishment of individuals who are aided in the task by an innate language specific faculty.

That faculty may have appeared in the human species early or late. It may have been selected for because it facilitated communication or because it facilitated thought. It may be task-specific or a general faculty. It may be applicable to specific grammatical structures, or it may apply across the board to the acquisition of syntax. But whatever the answers to these questions, the language faculty is understood to have emerged as a distinctively human faculty which is now a component of human nature, a part of the bio-psychological legacy inherited by each and every human individual.

Critical Reflections on Structuralist Linguistics In these phylogenetic and ontogenetic accounts, we can discern two specific assumptions, both of which were apparent in the structuralist theory of grammar outlined in chapters three through five: the assumption of uniformity of languages and the assumption of individual competence.

First, structuralist accounts, especially the accounts of language phylogeny which focus on the emergence of universal language faculty, imply the uniformity of languages. Uniformly structured human brains evolve with uniform specializations for handling analytic processes. And all languages which are spun out of this uniform faculty are themselves uniform at an abstract level despite their superficial differences.

Second, structuralist accounts, especially accounts of onto-geny, imply the competence of individuals. Every normal individual has the tools for building a grammar, and every grammar which is built with those tools is of equal power and equal value. No grammar has any corner on logic, rigor, precision, abstractness, complexity, or sophistication. Every vernacular language is equipollent. Such an assumption of the equipollence of individual grammars flies in the face of the traditional grammarians assumption that vernacular grammars are, by definition, sub-standard, rude, and unsophisticated.

Being scientists who heel close to the standards of nineteenth century empiricism, structuralist linguists tend *not* to pursue the political implications of these assumptions of the uniformity of languages and the competence of individuals. They regard their discipline as "autonomous" (Newmeyer 1986), a discipline untainted by philosophy, politics, or art. They avoid all discourse that carries them beyond discussions of grammars, grammatical rules, and the language faculty.

However, claiming "autonomy" no more guarantees autonomy, than swearing an oath guarantees truthfulness. I have suggested that all of modern language study, including structuralist linguistics, is rooted in the political upheavals and reconstructions of the seventeenth and eighteenth centuries. Sprung from these political roots, modern linguistic theory carries a signficant political message. That message may be muted by claims of "autonomy," but it is not nullified. And that political message is evident in the assumptions of the uniformity of languages and the competence of individuals.

The political significance of the assumption of uniformity is complex. On the one hand, claims that language faculties are uniform, that languages despite diversity are uniform at an abstract level, and that grammars in a language community are uniformly shared imply the *equality* of all languages and of all speakers of all languages. Such linguistic equality promotes a political egalitarianism. And such egalitarianism contrasts with political positions which privilege one class of humans over another, e.g. racism, sexism, etc.. However on the other hand, claims that language faculties are uniform imply a condition of *expendability*. Every individual and every language, being uniform, is non-essential and replaceable. One can recognize this condition of expendability in Huxley's The Brave New World where individuals are cloned, and therefore replaceable, hence expendable.

Translated into political terms, the condition of expendability means that the loss of a speaker of a language is not a significant loss since all speakers possess uniform knowledges of their language. And the loss of a whole language community is not a significant loss for the human species since all languages are but variations on a single theme.

Depending on your political views, the political upshot of the structuralist linguistic assumption of uniformity has a bright side and a dark side. It promotes a progressive politics of individual and social equality. Such progressive politics can range from moderate, e.g. support for human rights policies, to extreme, e.g. anti-institutional anarchism. On the other hand, the assumption of linguistic uniformity can be used to justify the suppression of linguistic diversity that proceeds under the label of "modernization." The individual, collective, and linguistic losses that result from such suppression are tolerated because people and languages are expendable.

The structuralist assumption that individuals are competent has its own complex political ramifications. On the one hand, the stress on individal competence reinforces the politics of equality. However on the other hand, the stress on individual competence implies that the individual is the locus and domain of human nature, and therefore that human nature is not essentially social. Structuralists assume human nature can be described in terms of the qualities of the human individual and little remains to be said about human society.

The political ramifications of such a view are somewhat difficult for us to imagine. They are difficult to imagine

125

primarily because all modern political movements and positions operate as if human nature were an individual rather a social nature (Berger 1979). Hence, the structuralist assumption about individual competence reinforces this unchallenged aspect of modern politics.

We moderns, like the fish in the sea, live in an atmosphere that we are unaware of. Specifically, we live in an ideological atmosphere that vaunts the individual and discounts the social. And no significant political opposition to this individual-centeredness exists. Consequently, it is difficult to talk a human science or to do a human politics that emphasizes human sociality. But that difficulty does not at all diminish the importance of the tasks. Indeed, the very difficulty of imagining and talking about essentially social humans makes the enterprise all the more urgent.

The Boasian ethnographic linguists-ethnographers whom we are about to consider have faced, admittedly with mixed success, just this task of talking about the unimaginable and the unspeakable. They have attempted to describe cultures and languages in such a way as to assume that communities are the loci of human nature. It is in this respect more than any other that the work of Boasian linguists contrasts with the work of structuralist linguists.

PART II

BOASIAN ETHNOGRAPHY

Chapter Nine

Boasian Ethnography and the Study of Languages

Structuralist linguists are heirs to a rich tradition of philosophical thought and scientific practice. The philosophy centers on the issue of mind and has far reaching political implications. The science was shaped by the empiricists of the nineteenth century who made astounding progress in linguistic studies while boasting that their work was free from taint of philosophy and politics. The impact of this paradoxical legacy of philosophy and anti-philosophical empiricism is a structuralist linguistic discourse which is focussed on mind but which mutes the philosophical and political ramifications of that focus on mind.

The Boasian tradition of language study is an interesting contrast to the structuralist tradition. First, the writings of Boas and his followers generally ignore the central issues that dominate Western philosophical writings. Second, the Boasian tradition is rooted in that same anti-philosophical empiricism of the nineteenth century described above. But third, Boasian ethnographers have been anything but reluctant to voice criticism of modern social and political life. True, the contemporary continuers of the Boasian tradition study the same phenomena as structuralists, e.g. language differences, language variation, language acquisition. But the way they study and write is distinctively colored and flavored by the combination of their anti-philosophical empiricism and their ardent social critique.

Impatient Scientists

Franz Boas and his supporting colleagues, Edward Sapir, Ruth Benedict, Margaret Mead, Robert Lowie, etc., were scientific but impatient searchers for a nobler way of life. Anthropologists in the Boasian tradition are *scientific* searchers, and that means that they trust only what their senses tell them, all that they can perceive objectively, and nothing that they cannot perceive objectively.

But besides being scientific scholars, Boasians are *impatient* scholars. Specifically, they wait impatiently for their scholarly labors to bring about a moral transformation of modern society. Marcus and Fischer (1986: 129) tell us that "in the 1920s and 1930s, anthropology developed the ethnographic paradigm, which entailed a submerged, unrelenting critique of Western civilization as capitalism." Margaret Mead's work illustrates

127

this penchant for social criticism. Stephen Toulmin says that her "work was moral; her mission, to put her knowledge at the service of humankind. From the start she took pains to connect what she had seen abroad with what she found at home in America."

Two practical reasons account for this penchant for criticism. First, the group of anthropologists who followed Franz Boas into anthropology during the first third of the twentieth century included many immigrants and women. And these scholars found themselves at a disadvantage in traditional American scholarly circles. These early Boasians had a personal stake in seeking reform in their own society.

Second, the American Indian societies which Boasians described were societies in disarray and decline. That disarray was caused by the expansion of modern society which, like a juggernaut, crushed everything and everyone in its path. The disarray of Indian societies was a reminder that modern society was itself out of balance.

Considering America to be a culture out of balance, the Boasians never felt at home in or contented with America. Robert Lowie, for example, was an Austrian who emigrated to America at 10 years of age. But he never lost the feeling that Austria was his home. For him, "the United States was a foreign and shadowy land." And his work as an anthropologist was, in part at least, an effort at sorting through his own cultural allegiances. "In straightening out his own life and cultural position, he left cultural analysis of lasting value" (Bohannan and Glazer 1973: 58).

Here one can see that for Lowie, and for others, getting American culture back into balance began with his getting himself personally back into balance. Thus, the Boasians would agreed with Robert Pirsig's (1974: 267) argument that "The place to improve the world first is in one's own heart and head and hands, and then work outwards from there."

Boas's own experiences point up the sorts of oppositions which confronted reform-minded ethnographers. In 1919, Boas wrote a public denunciation of the use of anthropologists as spies in Central America. And for that he was censured and removed from his seat on the National Research Council by the "waspish" powers at Harvard and in Washington.

Political events like these, both in the small world of anthropological associations and in the larger world of international affairs, convinced the Boasians that life at home was in deep trouble.

What the Boasians found in the field only reinforced their discontent with modern American culture. The Indian cultures they studied were disintegrated. Everywhere ethnographers witnessed the aftermath of the oppressive imperialist behavior of their own society. Before the anthropologists had gotten to the American Indians, the land developers, the industrialists, and the politicians had already eaten them up. Very little American Indian culture remained to be described. The ethnographers responded by producing ethnographies which both eulogized the Indians and also presented their messages of social reform to the North American people.

In contrast to these American linguists-ethnographers, the British in Africa faced an altogether different situation and, consequently, produced quite a different kind of linguistic and ethnography writing (Henson 1974). Indigenous African societies were, by comparison to North American societies, much less severely crippled by culture contact. In consequence, British ethnographers developed different objectives for their work than the Americans. They described social behavior for the purpose of discerning the most efficient and humane ways of governing these subjects. American ethnographers, however, described American Indian life, at least partly, to illustrate the moral bankruptcy of modern North American society.

Critical of life at home, the Boasian ethnographers opened themselves to "the possibility of cultural worlds more harmoniously fulfilling the potentialities of the human spirit...Rejecting traditional 'American civilized morality', but still sustained by the earlier 'promise of American life', they struggled to find values upon which a genuine national culture could be found. In various ways, Boasian anthropology of the 1920's embedded in this intellectual context" (Stocking 1976: 31; 83).

Boasian ethnographers were reformers, but they were also hard-nosed scientists. These two features together account for the distinctive features of Boasian ethnography. Boasian ethnographers placed a greater emphasis on field experience than on deductive reasoning. They had neither the patience for deductive reason, nor faith in reason over the senses, nor an appreciation of the value of philosophy. Margaret Mead boasted that "there is no room in anthropology for philosophical concepts and deductive thinking...Papa Franz has always stood for empirical thinking." For these reasons the Boasians produced descriptions which were rigorously empirical but unsophisticated according to the standards of European scholarship.

In the area of language studies Boasian and Bloomfieldian linguists were much more concerned with getting reliable data on disappearing languages than in engaging rival scholars in debates over abstract issues. Their linguistic works are generally oriented towards data rather than towards theory.

The emphasis on field research affected not only what Boas-

129

ian linguists did, in their research, it deeply affected how they did it. Boasians were vulnerable to their research situation and were proud of that vulnerability. Their very objectives for research were often shifted in the field as ethnographers came upon new experiences. Contrast this Boasian attitude toward field research with that of the structuralist linguists who, with their deductive method, never lose control of what they are doing or of where they are going with their research.

Devotion to gathering data led Boasian ethnographers to throw themselves into their fieldwork with an enthusiasm that bordered on passion. But their Jeremiah-like criticisms of modern society and their impatience for change prompted them to mold the data which they gathered into nobler accounts than the data sometimes warranted. Their impatience for change led them to use their data of the rapidly disintegrating American Indian societies as the bases for constructing enhanced images of those societies as if they were undisturbed by contact with unbalanced modernity. Noble, balanced, and worthy of emulation, those were the ethnographic pictures which Boasian ethnographers composed. The noble Indian appears most clearly in Ruth Benedict's <u>Patterns of Culture</u> in the 30's, in Dorothy Lee's <u>Freedom and Culture</u> in the 50's, and in Gary Witherspoon's <u>Language and Art in the Navaho Universe</u> in the 70's.

Edward Sapir contributed more than anyone else to the creation of a distinct discipline of linguistic anthropology which exhibited all of these characteristics. He was passionately devoted to his linguistics to be sure. But, his linguistics was not the "autonomous" linguistics of his contemporary Leonard Bloomfield. Sapir's linguistics always described language in concert with the social life of the speakers--and for that reason Bloomfield labeled him "the medicine man."

Sapir was a reformer who, at one point, called American culture a "spurious culture...without harmony or depth of life." His early essays and his influential book <u>Language</u> (1921) are rigorous statements of a program for linguistic research. His "Time Perspective in Aboriginal American Culture" established clear criteria for the historical reconstruction of language groups, including guidelines for making use of data on frequencies of use and geographical distribution of linguistic phenomena. <u>Language</u> is widely regarded as the last word on a century-long debate over whether languages can be classified by gross syntactic characteristics (see pp. 77f) and then interpreted within an evolutionary framework. As to the matter of classification, Sapir pointed out the difficulty of the task by demonstrating the inability of existing classificatory schemes to handle the phenomena of American Indian languages. And on the matter of the evolutionary progression of languages from one type to another, he was decidedly negative.

Sapir's pursuit of psychology and personality theory helped to advance the Boasian goal of social reform. By describing primitive peoples in terms of personality theory, he was able to present aspects of primitive life in such a way that they could be emulated by modern peoples. Psychological descriptions of primitive peoples became lessons in living.

Benjamin Lee Whorf studied with Sapir and, more than anyone else, pursued Sapir's interest in "language as a symbolic guide to culture." And everywhere in Whorf's pursuit of this issue, the nobility of American Indian thought systems was played up. Whorf, for example, did not rest his case with pointing out that the Hopi verb system is tenseless and that the Hopi do not count abstract nouns. He moved straight away to contrast Hopi with English and to expound on our own preoccupation with temporal sequence and object definition and enumeration. The implicit message in this, and in the other analyses of Whorf, is that learning something about the noble logic of the primitive is morally edifying. "Through this sort of understanding of language," he claimed, "is achieved a great phase of human brotherhood."

The homily on brotherhood is usually implicit in Boasian linguistics, though it is unmistakable in the later writings of Sapir and in most of the work of Whorf. It is explicit also in the writings of Dorothy Lee. For example, her conclusions from a Whorfian analysis of the tenselessness of the Trobriand language leads her to conclude that we, unlike the Trobrianders, are always "looking forward to" something still in the future and hence in our culture we rarely appreciate the present for itself. The Trobrianders appreciate each situation and each event in and for itself. We, for example, labor at child birth with only one thing in mind, the arrival of the newborn. We pursue the erotic kiss with only one thing in mind, the sexual climax. And in all this we miss out on the sweetness of the present moment. The lesson here is to take time to smell the flowers, for then every experience overflows with its own joyfulness. "If it is not important to get to a particular point at a particular time, the insuperable puddle from the morning's shower is not frustrating; I throw stones into it and watch the ripples and then choose another path." The homiletic tone of Lee's account is unmistakable. A similar homiletic tone pervades most Boasian linguistics, though it hides between the lines.

Two Messages Towards Social Reform

Two major messages of social criticism dominate all this literature. The first of these messages consists of a celebration of the reality and significance of communities. The second concerns the autonomy and significance of individuals in communities.

131

The message celebrating community runs strong in the writings of Boasian ethnographers. It says, in effect, we in the West have lost what they--primitive people--still have. "They--primitive man (sic)--have sustained close, intimate, satisfying communal lives, and we have lost this way of life (the experience of community)" (Marcus and Fischer op. cit.). We have even lost the ability to recognize a distinctive community when we see it. We no longer know *that*--let alone *how*--communities can differ from one another.

On New Age Sociology

Popular sociology, especially "New Age" social criticism, walks its first mile with Sapir, Benedict, and other Boasian writers. Riesman (1949) was among the first writers of popular sociology to decry in Boasian terms the absence of community in the modern world. Since then, numerous writers have picked up the same theme, fingering the absence of community as the underlying cause of the ecological crisis (Capra 1983; Rifkin 1979; Roszak 1979), of nuclear madness (Peck 1987), of the uncontrolled growth of modern social institutions (Illich 1977; Lasch 1979), and of the modern sense of alienation and homelessness (Elgin 1981; Slater 1974; Thompson 1971). Unfortunately, much of this literature goes on to advance remedies which involve concepts of individual and community drawn from the same roots (p. 185) and flawed in the same way as the modern notions of individual and community which they set out to revise.

Though popular sociology has not successfully revised pivotal social concepts, it, like Boasian anthropology, has been successful at pointing out the emptiness and dangerousness of most political movements which aim at rekindling community in the modern world. Such movements often begin with the noblest of justifications, but they soon fall, like the life of Faust (Berman 1982), dreadfully out of balance (Tinder 1980). Or worse, they are transformed into the social monstrosities that have bedeviled the twentieth century (Bookchin 1982), social monstrosities which are especially terrifying because they are rationalized in the name of community.

The Boasians set for themselves the mission of rectifying this waywardness of us moderns. First, they constructed their descriptions so as to demonstrate the dramatic differences between cultural communities. Often they described the nature of those cultural differences in linguistic terms. Languages, they assumed, were both clearly variable and also central to cultural communities. Therefore descriptions of languages differences counted as demonstrations that cultural communities are fundamentally different from one another.

The vehicle of the descriptive grammar also allowed ethnographers to argue that the processes of culture change and differentiation are similar to processes of language change. To understand the flexibility and malleability of cultures, the Boasians argued, one must understand the variability of human languages.

The objective behind their language-centered cultural descriptions was clear. Their message was that we North Americans need not be the spurious non-communal people that we are. We can be taught to recognize both what community is and how it can be adapted to our own situation. A thousand alternative life ways are available for our edification. These alternatives are real life ways, not imaginary; and we ought not be put off by the fact that they are called primitive. In sum, the issue of cultural/communal distinctiveness provided Boasians with tremendous leverage for moral transformation.

The emphasis on cultural distinctiveness went hand in glove with the second major homiletic theme of Boasian ethnography and linguistics, namely, the autonomy and significance of the individual.

The standard view, made clearest in the work of Sapir and Linton for language and culture, was that a community is grounded in individuals. Each person in a culture possesses the culturally distinctive traits of his or her fellows. To each individual is distributed identical traits; the collectivity is distinctive because each individual is distinctive.

The most dramatic and convincing verification of this principle of identical distribution of traits across individuals of a community came with Sapir's demonstration of the psychological reality of phonemes. While working on the Southern Paiute language, Sapir took some time to teach his informant, Tony, to transcribe Paiute sounds with phonetic symbols. When presented with the task of transcribing [pa Ba], meaning "at the water", Tony "astonished" Sapir by recording the bilabial stop [p] and the bilabial fricative [B] with the single symbol "p." It seems that, though the phonetic difference between [p] and [B] is clear enough to us English speakers, the sounds are allophones in Paiute, and Tony was deaf to their difference. In the same way, English speakers would fail to note the differences in the "t" sounds in the words "tap," "try," and "writer." If called upon to transcribe such words, we would probably use "t" for each and never think to transcribe the first as an aspirated "t," the second as a retroflexed "t," and the third as a voiced flap.

133

Observing such phenomena, Sapir surmised that each individual possesses a mental system of phonemes that enables him or her to classify speech sounds systematically. These mental systems must be learned; they are not biologically determined because they differ from community to community. So, each individual in a community acquires the same phonemic system acquired by everyone else in that community. And in consequence, individuals, through their acquisition and possession of traits like phonemes, are responsible for the distinctiveness of their community.

The moral message of this emphasis on the individual is clear. Sapir makes that message explicit when he says: "A genuine culture refuses to consider the individual as a mere cog, an entity whose sole *raison d'etre* lies in his subservience to a collective purpose that he is not conscious of or that has only a remote relevancy to his interests and strivings." Varenne (1976: 237) restates this same message in abstract but succinct terms which, he argues, are generally embraced by Boasians if not by most American social thinkers of the twentieth century: "Subjects create communities through private personal movements."

The Role of the Individual

Boasian linguists and structuralist linguists may embrace distinct objectives for their scholarly research, but they all live in the same world. Specifically, the Boasians, for all their emphasis on communality, still live in a modern Western tradition that is shaped by a religious and philosophical history of devotion to the individual. That devotion was apparent in the psychological orientation of structuralist linguists. It is apparent too in the Boasian linguistic notion that the individual is the agent of social action.

The Boasian emphasis on community does not require a reduction of emphasis on the individual (Lee 1959), but it should require a redefinition of the notion of the individual. However, such a redefinition was not undertaken by the early Boasians partly because they wanted to appeal to the traditionally understood moral sensibilities of individuals in modern society in order to transmit their message. If any moral changes are to be wrought in a community, individuals, they felt, must bring them about. More pointedly, if the spurious American culture is to be transformed, only the individual, understood in the traditional sense, can transform it.

Boasian ethnography emphasizes both the community and the individual. But it should be admitted that the emphasis on com-

munity and cultural distinctiveness dominates. In Sapir's celebrated essay on the "Unconscious Patterning of Behavior in Society" (1949), for example, he admitted that individuals are often
unaware of psychologically real systems and, in that unconsciousness, subject to the external forces of history. In such a
case Sapir subordinates the doctrine of the priority of the
individual to the doctrine of the irreducibility of cultural
differences. Varenne (1984) finds the same tug of war in the
writings of Ruth Benedict.

Reformists are not always consistent. Even less often are
they complete in their efforts at reform. As Monday-morning
quarterbacks, we might be tempted to make use of current sociolinguistic findings (see chapter seven) and ask questions that
Boasian linguists never seemed to consider: whether the theory
of identical distribution of phonemic systems is born out by the
facts; whether so-called distinct cultural communities might not
blend into one another at the edges; whether the capabilities
that enable individuals to learn phonemic systems are not common
to all humans and are not grounds for emphasizing cultural and
psychological universals. All these questions are reasonable
questions. They are currently being asked and the answers are
having a profound effect on the shape of current linguistic
anthropological research in the Boasian tradition. But, if you
situate yourself in the inter-war period, and appreciate the
reformist motivation behind Boasian linguistic anthropology at
that time, you will understand that such questions deflect attention from the message that linguistic/cultural communities are
distinct in significant ways. And such questions detract from
the moral significance of the anthropologist's descriptions of
those distinct communities. The issues of cultural distinctiveness and individual autonomy provided Boasians with tremendous
leverage for moral transformation. The Boasians sidelined all
other issues that might weaken that leverage.

Summary with a Glance Forward and a Glance Backward

Boasian ethnographers-linguists were impatient scientists.
They were scientific Jeremiah's who criticized modern life on the
one hand, and who produced no-nonsense descriptions of primitive
life and languages on the other. They were linguists who, like
most in their era, stood in awe of the descriptive power of
linguistic methodology. But their descriptions leap beyond language to teach us all about worlds and lives which we desperately
need to know about if we are going to revise modern life.

The aspect of modern life that most frequently attracted
Boasian criticism was that same aspect identified by John Donne
in 1611. "T'is all in peeces; all cohaerence gone." Social ties
no longer bind. Social relations no longer command respect. In
short, modern life lacks community. The old God-centered foundations of community were eaten away during the long century be-

tween 1450 and 1600. And ever since then modern social life has suffered from fits of disintegration. In modern life, all relations are built on shifting sand; they are in danger of being broken apart by every next wave. No ground is solid. Anything you had thought was secure now melts into air.

The Boasians, then and now, don't deserve credit for recognizing this problem of ungrounded social ties. This problem had been recognized long before Boasians arrived on the scene. But they do merit applause for helping us to see the emptiness of most rationalizations of modern social life. The Boasians have seen through such efforts and recognized them to be little more than new ways of presenting the old foundations, ways of recovering community by falling back on the patriarchal and God-centered models of community of bygone eras.

The Boasian rejection of an "autonomous" linguistics might be interpreted as the rejection of an attempt to replace one divinity by another. The very quality of "autonomy" is one which is more plausibly attributed to divine affairs than to human. And, the structuralist pursuit of a unitary abstract principle, the language faculty, seems to resemble the theological pursuit of unitary spirit, God. Perhaps the Boasians reacted to both the emptiness of modern social life and of modern structuralist linguistics because they regarded them as, in Unamuno's words, (1921: 27) "social parasites." They draw their energy, their principles, and their high sounding philosophy from the very God which they deny.

When the Boasians in the early twentieth century launched their stinging attacks on nineteenth century evolutionism, they were doing much more than criticizing some esoteric writings of a clique of scholars. They were unmasking an aspect of the mythical foundation of modern society. They were exposing unilineal evolutionary thought for what it was, a justification for the subordination of the masses to a few powerful rulers, and a legitimation of efforts by those rulers to eradicate cultural diversity. Unilineal evolutionary thought was, in their view, an intellectualization which legitimated the same oppressive state of affairs which the name of God legitimated in the Middle Ages.

Now, more than fifty years later, modern bearers of the Boasian ethnographic legacy continue to unmask the intellectual forms of social parasitism. Their target is the structuralist perspective whose principles serve as a legitimation for modern social life. Specifically, the target is the structuralist principles which reinforce the modern location of human nature in the individual rather than in the community.

The *content* of modern Boasian thought is critical of the individual-centeredness of structuralist linguistics. For example, Dell Hymes, who as pioneered a modern version of Boasian ethnographic studies called "the ethnography of speaking" (chapter eleven) has been explicitly critical of the structuralist focus on "an abstract and isolated individual, not, except contingently, of a person in a social world" (Hymes 1971: 53).

But besides *content*, the *form* or style of Boasian research and writing has implied a criticism of the structuralist perspective. In structuralist science, as in most modern sciences, scholars cling to other scholars who share the same axioms. In this way uniform communities of scholars are formed all the members of which play off each other in elaborating the theory which they are developing. The shared theory and the uniform community of scholars who shared it can both be called a "scientific paradigm" (Kuhn 1962). In a scientific paradigm, the theory justifies research; no research is worth the effort unless it is devoted to elaborating the paradigm. One can interpret these conditions to mean that the social life of modern science parallels the social life of the modern world, with communities organized around uniformly shared ideas.

Boasian science has always worked differently. Specifically it has always been centered around the interdependence of scholars talking to one another rather than around the ideas which individuals might share. Boasian science has always been dialogical rather than individualistic and ideological.

The dialogical nature of Boasian science is apparent in the absence of theoretical principles shared by members of schools of ethnography. A dialogical style is apparent too in the absence of generally explanatory "totalizing" theories of human behavior. Finally, the dialogical nature of Boasian science is evident in the subordination of abstract theory development to fieldwork experiences in the shaping of ethnographic research. As Strathern (1987) points out, this dialogical style makes Boasian anthropology more like a feminist science and different from the ideological sciences which, like patriarchal religions of old, demand that members share beliefs. Hence the actions as well as the words, of Boasian ethnographers are opposed to the the style and conduct of structuralist linguistics.

Social criticism, as Jeremiah discovered, is an anguishing task. The critic is regularly filled with self-doubts and hesitations. And such is the story of Boasian ethnographic social criticism. Throughout this century, Boasian scholars have found themselves drawn by the siren call of the ideological scientific style. Regularly they have fallen back into the mainstream both in the style and the content of their work (Varenne 1984).

Maintaining an emphasis on the communal while simultaneously focussing research on language was, in the early twentieth century, like trying to walk a tightrope in a stiff crosswind. The assumptions that language abilities were housed in the individual continually tempted Boasians to emphasize the significance of the individual and the psychological over the social. Still anthropologists have not given up the struggle to maintain their balance as the following chapters on Boasian linguistic anthropology will show.

Chapter Ten

Meanings and Communities

For at least two hundred years, one aspect of language has served the purposes of scholars and politicians who have wanted to emphasize the social, the collective, and the communal nature of languages and speakers. That one aspect is meaning. Syntax and phonology together with semantics have served as vehicles for emphasizing universals and uniformity or for underscoring the individuality and creativity of language competence. But meaning and semantics has been the specially favored topic of scholars who want to emphasize the sociality of language.

Two hundred years ago Herder and Humboldt in Germany developed the thesis that the meanings of the German language formed the semantic capital of German culture (Schaff 1973) (see p. 257). Some German politicians, banking on that capital, argued that the German culture had a legitimate right to a unified German state because it had a language with a distinct set of meanings. In this way there was born the powerful hypothesis of *linguistic determinism* which locates language meanings at the core of a cultural community and consider those meanings to be the independent shapers of a culture.

This early version of linguistic determinism strongly influenced the Boasians who themselves were looking for ways to accord language a central place in culture while also preserving the sense that language differences are community-level differences.

Introduction and Background

Most great Western thinkers who have reserved a privileged place for language in their theories--and that means most of them--have had something to say about meaning. The Platonists had one theory of meaning. The Sophists had another. Aristotle's cognitive representational theory of meaning served the purposes of scholars and kings for centuries. But Augustine adjusted it to his own ends by giving God a role in the process of the interpretation of meaning. Medieval scholars pursued Augustine's theme, elaborating and embellishing it to glorious extremes as in the following analysis of the meaning of linear inscription:

> The Hebrews, the Canaans, the Samaritans, the Chaldeans, the Syrians, the Egyptians, the Carthaginians, the Phoenicians, the Arabs, the Aracens, the Turks, the Moors, the Persians, and the Tartars all write from right to left, following 'the course and daily movement of the first heaven, which is most perfect, according to the opinion of the great

Aristotle, tending towards unity'; the Greeks, the Georgians, the Maronites, the Serbians, the Jacobites, the Copts, the Poznians, and of course the Romans and all Europeans write from left to right, following 'the course and movement of the second heaven, home of the seven planets'; the Indians, Cathayans, Chinese, and Japanese write from top to bottom, in conformity with the 'order of nature, which has given men hands at the tops of their bodies and feet at the bottom'; 'in opposition to the aforementioned,' the Mexicans write either from bottom to top or else in 'spiral lines, such as those made by the sun in its annual journey through the Zodiac.' And thus' by these five diverse sorts of writing the secrets and mysteries of the world's frame and the form of the cross, the unity of the heaven's rotundity and that of the earth, are properly denoted and expressed" (M. Foucault 1970: 37).

Only analysts who let their minds be guided by divine light will uncover such deep-seated meanings in the signs that abound in language and in everyday life.

More recently Humean empiricists clashed with Cartesian idealists over meaning, a war which was delightfully satirized by Swift in Gulliver's Travels:

We went to the school of languages, where three professors sat in consultation upon improving that of their own country. The first project was to shorten discourse by cutting polysyllables into one, and leaving out verbs and participles, because in reality all things imaginable are but nouns. The other project was a scheme for entirely abolishing all words whatsoever; and this was urged as a great advantage in point of health as well as brevity. For it is plain that every word we speak is in some degree a diminution of our lungs by corrosion, and consequently contributes to the shortening of our lives. An expedient was therefore offered, that since words are only names for things, it would be more convenient for all men to carry about them such things as were necessary to express the particular business they are to discourse on. And this invention would certainly have taken place, to the great ease as well as health of the subject, if the women, in conjunction with the vulgar and illiterate, had not threatened to raise a rebellion, unless they might be allowed the liberty to speak with their tongues, after the manner of their ancestors; such constant irreconcilable

140

enemies to science are the common people. However, many of the most learned and wise adhere to the new scheme of expression themselves by things, which has only this inconvenience attending it, that if a man's business be very great, and of various kinds, he must be obliged in proportion to carry a great bundle of things upon his back, unless he can afford one or two strong servants to attend him. I have often beheld two of those sages almost sinking under the weight of their packs, like peddlars among us; who, when they met in the streets, would lay down their loads, open their sacks, and hold conversation for an hour together; then put up their implements, help each other to resume their burdens, and take their leave. But for short conversations a man may carry implements in his pockets and under his arm, enough to supply him, and in his house he cannot be at a loss. Therefore the room where company meet who practice this art, is full of all things ready at hand, requisite to furnish matter for this kind of artificial converse.

Twentieth century scholars of human behavior are no different. In this century which has carried on a love affair with language, scholars have devoted an extraordinary amount of attention to theories of meaning. Even Noam Chomsky, whose original intention was to produce a grammar of the forms of a language without getting into matters of meaning, found it necessary to advance a semantic theory in conjunction with his generative structuralist linguistics.

In the present chapter I will show that Boasian linguists, especially Sapir and Whorf found lexical and syntactic meaning to be especially congenial to their purposes of demonstrating the distinctiveness of cultural communities. Later efforts by scholars like Lounsbury and Goodenough showed that, what we shall call, taxonomic and componential analyses of meanings, served the same purposes; and, being produced by replicable scientific methods, these latter analyses promised even more reliable descriptions of the distinctive characteristics of cultural communities.

Chomskyans had an interest in meaning as well. But not a central interest, for, as we noted in chapter five, syntax is the kingpin of Chomsky's theory of language. However, in the early 1960's Chomsky was pressed to comment on grammar and meaning. And so, availing himself of the work of Katz and Postal (1964) he incorporated a theory of meaning into his so-called Standard Theory (Chomsky 1965).

The generative linguistic proposals on meaning were coincidentally quite similar to the proposals of Goodenough and Louns-

141

bury, but they were couched in a theory which emphasized the capabilities of individual minds rather than the distinctiveness of cultural communities. As a result, generative semantic analyses undermined the significance of ethnographic analyses of meaning.

The seventies witnessed a decline of interest in "ethnosemantics" and "ethnoscience," which are labels that were given to Boasian analyses of meanings. Scholars either devoted themselves to analyzing lexical material with an eye to supporting something like Chomksy's standard theory, or they ignored the subject of meaning altogether. If one were a cynic, one might interpret these developments to mean that the subject of meaning is one which is easily adapted to suit one's needs, but just as easily dumped when things go sour.

Whorfian Semantics

The bulk of Whorf's scholarly energy was devoted to documenting significant differences in form and meaning between languages. He assumed, as did the German romantics of the late eighteenth century, that such language differences were the root and source of the conceptual differences between speakers. The principle of *linguistic determinism* makes his proposal clear. Language structure, he contended, is identical to thought structure. People think the way they do because their language forms provide them with forms for thought.

The languages that he most often selected to exemplify the principle of linguistic determinism were American Indian languages. The diagrams on the next page (Whorf 1956: 235) illustrate Whorf's claim that two sentences which are semantically dissimilar in English (1, 2) are semantically quite similar in Shawnee. The second drawing illustrates his contention that "Nootka has no parts of speech; the simplest utterance is a sentence, treating some event or event complex. Long sentences are sentences of sentences, not just sentences of words." The obvious target for contrast to this Nootka sentence is English which expresses the illustration with subjects and predicates, i.e. He invites people to a feast.

(1) I push his head backward.
(2) I drop it in the water and it floats.

Whorf is contending here that Shawnee and Nootka grammars are distinct from English grammar, but also, and more importantly, that Shawnee and Nootka minds work differently from English minds. People think in their languages. When languages differ as dramatically as Shawnee and English, thinking differs in an equally dramatic fashion.

142

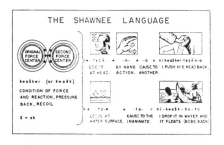

Such analyses as these accomplish the objective of documenting cultural differences. But, being fastidious scientists
in the tradition of Boas and Bloomfield, American linguistic
anthropologists needed verification of the results. So, in the
1950's numerous scientific tests of Whorfian hypotheses were
undertaken. Carroll and Casagrande (1958) for example administered the visual test (shown on the next page) to Hopi and
English speakers. The task for each subject was to match the
bottom picture in each of figures 2-4 with one or another of the
top pictures. Figure 1 is a test figure. The results of the
experiment showed remarkable differences between Hopi and English
associations, and the differences can be plausibly explained in
terms of language differences. Regarding Figure 2, the Hopi
subjects tended to associate pictures A and C, whereas English
speaking subjects associated pictures B and C. The explanation
for these differences is as follows:

> In Hopi there is a verb *'u'ta* which means 'to
> close an opening,' and this is the verb normally
> used for placing covers on open boxes, closing
> lids, closing holes in tubes or walls, etc, in
> contrast, placing a cover on something for protec-
> tion against dust or damage is represented by the
> verbs *na:kwapna* or *nonoma*. In English however we
> tend to use *cover* regardless of whether we are
> covering an opening or not, and we tend to reserve
> *close* for the situation where an opening can be
> more or less exactly fitted with a lid (Ibid., p.
> 495).

143

FIGURE 1

FIGURE 2

FIGURE 3

FIGURE 4

Regarding Figure 3, Hopis tend to pair A and C. English speakers paired B and C because they are both instances of painting. Hopi has a word for painting, but its use is restricted to cases where one paints a picture or a design rather than covering a surface with paint. Regarding Figure 4, the Hopis tended to pair A and C whereas English speakers tended to pair B and C. In the Hopi language accidental and intentional acts are not distinguished.

Ethnoscience

Some American linguistic anthropologists wanted their analyses to be, if nothing else, scientific. And, Whorf's semantic analyses, even when confirmed by experiments like the one above, seemed to be more artistic than scientific.

These scientists wanted more than verifications. In their view science is above all a method for true description. If an analysis is to be truly scientific it must be produced according to an explicit method and guided by an unambiguous set of procedures. Whorf used insight and intuition to discern language and culture differences, not explicit procedures. So even if his analyses be confirmed empirically, they still fall short of being

144

scientific. What the scientists wanted were clear procedures through which significant semantic differences might be discerned in the first place.

The requirements for a scientific analysis of significant semantic differences were as follows: a) First, any feature that renders a language/culture distinct must be located in the minds of individuals of that language/culture. This assumption is taken directly from Sapir's conclusion about the psychological reality of cultural phenomena. And it is an important assumption for it permits scientific analyses of cultural difference to be based on the investigation of individuals. b) Second, cultures--and therefore individuals--differ in how they organize experience. The Shawnee and the English do not see radically different worlds around them, rather they see roughly the same world but organize it in two quite different ways. This view that organization, rather than perception, accounts for cultural differences is akin to the Saussurean notion that systems differ in how their elements are related more than in what their elements are. A scientific analysis of cultural differences must explicate the distinctive organizations of linguistic/cultural systems. c) Thirdly, a people's experience is organized in the lexicon of their language. Specifically the relationships between words of a language bear witness to the cultural organization internalized by those who use those words. This final assumption is drawn directly from Sapir's view that language is "the symbolic guide to culture."

Those scientists who subscribed to these three assumptions are called ethnoscientists, or ethnosemanticists, or cognitive anthropologists, or the new ethnographers. The very proliferation of names is enough to demonstrate the prominence of this movement in the anthropology of the 1960's (Tyler 1969).

A closer look at ethnoscientific methods will show that those methods are consistent with the longstanding Boasian struggle to explicate cultural differences and with the equally longstanding emphasis on the role of the individual in maintaining a culture.

The first ethnoscientific method to be considered is componential analysis. One begins a componential analysis of the vocabulary, or more precisely of the lexicon, of any community by locating well-circumscribed sections of that lexicon and then subjecting those sections to a feature analysis.

Well-circumscribed sections of the lexicon are called "domains." A domain, in plain English, is a collection of words which elaborate a single concept or a single theme. In English, for example, the words *horse*, *dog*, *cat*, *cow*, etc. elaborate the domain of animals; and the words *tree*, *flower*, *bush*, etc. flesh out the domain of plants. Just such domains as these are sub-

145

jected to a feature analysis.

A semantic feature (componential) analysis is similar to, and borrowed from, phonological feature analysis---though American anthropologist are always happy to note that A.L. Kroeber precociously employed a kind of feature analysis in his 1909 analysis of kinship terminological systems. Recall from chapter four that, in phonological feature theory, phonemes are bundles of abstract elementary dichotomous features, e.g. English /t/ = [-voice, +dental, +obstruent].

Boasian Structuralist Linguistics

This text portrays Boasian ethnographic linguistics as if it were a program which is completely independent of structuralist linguistics. Such a portrayal is motivated by my desire to clarify what are complex realities in the development of modern research on languages and communication. However, the fact is that American anthropologists were deeply involved with structuralist linguistic methods if not with structuralist objectives. The use of phonological theory as the model for ethnosemantic analyses is one illustration of that involvement.

Componential analysts took over this phonological notion and applied it to the lexicon. In the lexical application, features are understood to be abstract components of meaning, conceptual atoms that combine to constitute molecules of word meaning. In a componential analysis, a set of features is devised to account for all the meanings of words in a domain. For example, in (A), the features [adult] [male] and [bovine] resolve the meanings of the very small domain of cow words. The statements in brackets [ ] represent the meanings of the words to their left as abstract semantic features. Or, in the jargon of linguistics, one can say that the words to the left are "lexicalizations" of the semantic components in brackets.

> (A) cow [+adult, -male, +bovine]
> bull [+adult, +male, +bovine]
> calf [-adult, +male, +bovine]

This semantic analysis of English cow words shows that specific semantics features, e.g. [adult] and [male] and [bovine], combine together to constitute the English words for cow. The beauty of this sort of analysis is that it allows one to compare and contrast domains and even languages in terms of features. (B) for example presents a feature analysis of horse words. And you can see from this analysis that it takes advantage of two of the same features used in (A). Analyses of pig

146

words, sheep words, etc. take advantage of these same features. These abstract meaning features are extremely productive; they enter into the constitution of many different words and recombine with many different features.

(B) mare   [+adult, -male, +equine]
      stallion   [+adult, +male, +equine]
      foal   [-adult, ±male, +equine]

Animal terms are used here to illustrate the analytic power of this method. But the domain of kinship terms has been worked over more thoroughly than any other. One reason for this is that kinship relations are generally considered to be close to the core of every community's social life. It follows that analyses of the meanings of kinships terms are doubly revealing, revealing of core meanings and of core aspects of a community's social life.

In analyzing kinship terminological systems, ethnoscientists assume that kinship terms in different cultures are constituted of components in different combinations, and are therefore indicative of different cultural organizations. And with componential analysis, such differences in organization can be pinpointed precisely. For example, English kin terms employ a feature for sex and generational difference only for those relatives who are "near kinsmen" to the speaker. By near kinsmen I mean those persons who are not far removed from the speaker in descent, in generation, or in collaterality. So we distinguish our female parents from our female children as *mothers* and *daughters* and our female parents from our male parents as *mothers* and *fathers*. But our *cousins* may be of any sex or generation. Contrast this situation with the Njamal of Australia or with the Burmese for whom generational and sexual distinctions are made for every kinsmen named. The lexical differences in these three cases make clear the cultural difference between the English and the Njamal and Burmese systems.

Critics of componential analysis point out three difficulties with this method. First, componential analysis still leaves room, as Whorfian analysis did, for the analyst's insight in discerning features. Second, componential analysis enables one to make cross cultural comparisons only if semantic features are shared across cultures. And to say that features are shared seems to run counter to the very objective of ethnoscience which is to document cultural distinctiveness. Finally, componential analysis implies static unchanging unevolving meanings. But the notion of unevolving meanings is counter-intuitive. Let me discuss each of these criticisms in their turn.

First, componential analysis leaves room for the analyst's insight in the selection of features for the analysis. Granted the features, whatever they are, must be plausible atoms of

147

meaning for the words being analyzed. But still, the analyst can exercise a good deal of latitude in selecting the number and quality of features. In other words, the method for selecting features is not explicit. And when procedures in an analysis are not explicit, bias and error can enter.

The Mind in the Machine

The empiricist sees science to be a machine invested with rationality. It is no longer humans who think. It is the scientific method that thinks for humans. Hence it is desirable to build a maximum amount of rigorous thinking into the scientific method and leave a minimum amount of creative thinking to fallible humans.

Such a view of science as machine is implied by seventeenth century images of humans as thinking machines. During the succeeding two hundred years such images have become a reality in the form of empirical scientific methods.

Second, componential analysis facilitates cross cultural comparisons and contrasts only on the condition that features be shared. The contrast between the English and the Burmese/Njamal system of kinship terms illustrates my point. Because all three systems employ features for sexual and generational differences, they can be compared. Because they employ those features differently, we can pinpoint their differences. But if these different languages had employed totally unrelated features, then no conclusions could be drawn about their distinctiveness. The cross cultural sharing of features seems to be a prerequisite for getting the most out of componential analyses. However, the very assumption of cross cultural sharing of features runs against the grain of the Boasian assumption that language communities are distinctive.

Finally, critics point out that componential analysis implies the fixity and static character of meanings. Features, being dichotomous, are either present or absent. And if present, features can be assumed to be available for constituting messages anywhere in the lexicon. If asked how features originated, ethnoscientists would have to say that, being dichotomous, they must have popped fully formed into speakers' heads and been immediately available for constituting meaning. However, critics with an evolutionary bent say it is more likely that features come into being gradually and spread slowly from some domains of the lexicon to others. And if this evolutionary account were to be accepted, then the dichotomous features, the major building blocks of componential analysis, would have to be scrapped.

An alternative ethnoscientific approach to semantic analysis avoids these three problems. This alternative is called taxonomic analysis. Taxonomic analysts subscribe to the same three ethnoscientific assumptions described above. But they avoid postulating abstract semantic components in their analyses of meanings. Instead they build analyses out of existing lexical relations of inclusion and contrast. Like the componential analyst, taxonomic analysts begin with a speaker's lexical domain. After having identified that domain, they plot the relationships of items in that domain by asking speakers "What kind of a _____ is a _____?" and "Is a _____ different from a _____?".

If such questions are addressed to urban dwelling North Americans regarding the domain of fruit, the responses will probably lead to an analytic diagram like the one on the next page. Each unit in this diagram is, in common parlance, a word, but in strict terms, a taxon. As a taxon, a unit occupies a slot in a system which relates both horizontally and vertically to other taxa in the system. Horizontal relationships are relationships of contrast, e.g. a melon is different from a berry. Vertical relationships are relationships of inclusion, e.g. a cantaloupe is a kind of melon and a melon is a kind of fruit. The totality of relationships among taxa in the domain of fruit present, in visual form, a representation of the culturally distinctive structure of the experience of fruit for North Americans.

Taxonomic analysts assume that lexical organizations are always changing and shifting in response to environmental pressures. They assume for example that highly elaborated aspects of a domain are correlated with culturally focal experiences. The most often cited illustration of this phenomenon is the frequency of Eskimo terms for snow. Snow, a focal experience among Eskimoes, is a candidate for a larger and more diversified ensemble of taxa in Eskimo. In communities where snow is not central to daily life experience, it is represented with a small and less diversified ensemble of taxa. (This example of terms for snow amongst the Eskimo is a plausible and easily understood example, but unfortunately, it has been employed carelessly in anthropological writings. The empirical foundation for many of the claims about Eskimo words for snow are hazy, if not non-existent.)

The example of Eskimo words for snow aside, the reasoning behind the example is credible. That is, when communities have ample terms for their experiences, they can manage those experiences more handily. Brown and Lenneberg (1954) demonstrated the plausibility of this assumption by showing that speakers who have lexical labels for colors are better able to recall those colors than speakers who do not. In summary, a distinctively sculptured lexicon is the evolutionary product of the struggles of a people to survive in an environment.

149

A Taxonomy of Fruit

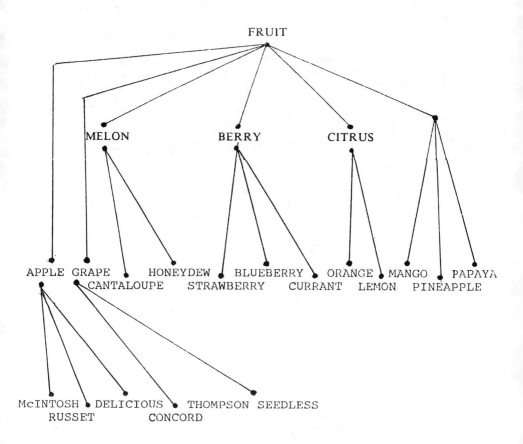

Semantic evolution proceeds by the multiplication of contrasts within a lexical domain. A complex domain, such as my domain of fruit words, can be expected to develop multiple levels of inclusion, and within each level, multiple relationships of contrast. For example, a Russet is a kind of apple which is a kind of fruit. And a Russet is different from a Macintosh which is different from a Delicious.

The objective and perceptible characteristics of a particular edible do not determine its position in the diagram. If it did, the word *berry* in the lexicon of North Americans would dominate or include the terms *grape* and *tomato*. In botanical terms, grapes and tomatoes are both kinds of berries.

The relationships which are described by a taxonomic analysis represent cultural, not objective, connections. For most North Americans, grapes are in a class apart from strawberries and blueberries; and tomatoes are vegetables, not fruits.

Cultural usage has everything to do with the organization of lexical domains. In the Anglo-Saxon tradition, for example, the grape was, at one time, the prototypical berry. But as grapes became specialized for wines, their place within the domain of fruit shifted until grapes and berries are now quite distinct.

Other words have an insecure place in the taxonomy because they are infrequently used. Tomatoes have been used as food only recently in our history, and some still disagree as to whether they are fruits or vegetables. Avocado is, for most of us, an exotic food, and again we find disagreement over whether it is a fruit or a vegetable. No such disagreements arise over potatoes as vegetables, oaks as trees or apples as fruit. Potatoes, oaks, and apples are too solidly entrenched in our everyday activities not to be agreed on. They are our prototypes of vegetables, trees, and fruits.

Prototypes

The literature on prototype analysis has grown rapidly in recent years. Tyler (1978: 76) discussed prototype analysis as an alternative to componential or taxonomic analysis. Lakoff (1987: 58ff) has suggested that prototype analysis together with fuzzy set theory makes for a powerful alternative to prior forms of semantic analysis.

Taxonomic analyses avoid the criticisms leveled at componential analysis. They do not arise out of an analyst's intuitions. They imply no cross-cultural sharing. And they imply

151

dynamic rather than static meanings. But they have drawbacks of their own. Unlike componential analyses, they lack anything like clear and explicit semantic features which facilitate cross cultural contrasts. Hence they do not serve so well the Boasian purpose of demonstrating the distinctiveness of languages/cultures.

Standard Theory Semantics

On Theories of Meaning

These generative linguistic proposals on semantics are presented in this chapter in Part II which is devoted to Boasian ethnography because they have shown themselves to be generally more powerful and more consistent examples of the very research tactics which anthropologists had been laboring at independently. As a result, semantic analyses, though somewhat peripheral in the structuralist program, have exercised a powerful influence over the directions taken by ethnographic semantics (see Keesing 1972).

The method of componential semantic analysis was independently developed by Boasian linguistic anthropologists and by generative linguists. In the hands of the former it was a tool for describing cultural differences. In the hands of the latter it is a tool for both explicating a speaker's competence and for suggesting the innate endowments through which that competence is made possible. In other words, one and the same method of semantic analysis serves two quite different goals in these two quite different approaches to language study.

In the generative linguistic perspective, a componential semantic analysis is conducted in much the same fashion as in the Boasian linguistic tradition. And it produces the same sorts of results, i.e. explications of word meanings in terms of dichotomous distinctive features. The important thing to note, however, is that the three characteristics which were noted as weaknesses of componential analysis in linguistic anthropology are advantageous characteristics which boost the worth of the method for generative linguists.

First, and regarding the matter of the analyst's insight in selecting features, generative linguists argue that insight is as good a source for scientific hypotheses as any. Embracing the method of deduction rather than induction (see p. 144), they argue that the source of a hypothesis is unimportant. All that matters is the testing to which a hypothesis is put after it is formulated. The testing, not the hypothesis formation, qualifies an analysis as scientific.

Second, and regarding the question of the cross cultural sharedness of features, generative linguists are happy to affirm that cross cultural sharedness. For such a notion of sharedness accords perfectly with the generative principle of innateness. All speakers of all languages are endowed from birth with exactly the same set of semantic features. Features, they say, must be shared by all humans; they are universals, part of the biologically inherited endowment of speakers which enables them to acquire meanings in the first place.

Fixed universal features do not preclude cultural differences in meaning. Generative linguists argue that those cultural differences are matters of feature combination. To appreciate how feature combination can produce dramatic semantic differences, consider the expressions for *kill* in English and Cupeno, a Uto-Aztecan language of the American southwest (Jane Hill, personal communication):

English	Cupeno
They died.	*nekuung chixe-pe* My husband die he
He killed them.	*mi chixe-ine ga-le-pe* them die cause he
He murdered them.	*ʔetaxmi mi-chix-ni-ne-t* *ʔelelʔish* people them die cause volition bad

The English sentences make use of different verbs to indicate die, "kill" and "murder," but Cupeno employs a single verb *chix* which means die. In Cupeno, the meaning of the word "kill" is formed by the addition of a causative particle *-ine* to the verb *chix*. And the sense of murder is conveyed by adding both a causative particle and a volitional particle to the verb for die. In short, the Cupeno do not say "kill", but they say its semantic equivalent "cause to die." The English "kill" and the Cupeno "cause to die", like the English "murder" and the Cupeno "intentionally cause to die" are constituted of identical features. The English word <u>assassinate</u> would probably be expressed in a similar fashion, that is, with the Cupeno root *chix* and separate particles for realizing the five meaning features of *assassinate*, [+political figure, +volition, +cause, +become, -alive].

The third and final problem incurred by componential analyses, the implication of static unchanging meaning, presents no difficulty for generative semanticists. In their view, universals can be dynamic and responsive to experience as well as static. Just because a characteristic is universal does not mean that it is independent of experience. Children, after all, are born with the universal language acquisition device but they must take advantage of social experiences if that acquisition device is to become active. Similarly, different peoples can be said to have the capability of using the features of the fixed universal semantic feature system, but they activate that capability only in real situations and in response to concrete experiences.

Berlin and Kay (1969), for example, demonstrated that the lexical domain of color is one for which a universal feature system must be postulated, but different languages make use of different numbers of those features. The claim for universality of the feature system is based on the universal path of the development of color terms in languages. All languages, they found, contain color terms for white and black. But if a language contains three terms, the third term is invariably red. And if a language contains four terms, the fourth is either green or yellow. If a language contains five terms, then the fifth is yellow or green. And if a language contains six color terms, the sixth is blue. The consistency of this path of development suggests a universal mental gyroscope in the minds speakers which guides the evolution of color terms.

Cecil Brown (1984) has found similar universal paths of development in other lexical domains. For example, in the domain of plants, if a language has only one term for botanical life forms, that term means tree. If a language contains two terms, the second term means grass. If a language contains three terms for botanical life forms, the third term means bush or vine, and so on.

Language Use and Whorf Revisited

The excitement that greeted the unveiling of ethnoscience as the new ethnography was quashed when standard theory semantics, with its rigor and elegance, demonstrated itself to be both powerful and consistent. The response of the majority of American anthropologists was to cut their losses and to look for less problematic ways of carrying on the Boasian project of cultural criticism and reform.

Most found the "ethnography of communication" to be a suitable vehicle for continuing the Boasian project, and consequently this latter discipline burgeoned in the 70's. The ethnography of communication is a discipline aimed at producing cross cultural descriptions of the users and uses of language, as the next chapter will explain.

However, the growth of the ethnography of communication among American anthropologists seems, on the surface, to be a strange turn. True, twentieth century European scholars had longstanding interests in matters of language use as part of their overall program of language planning and political modernization. And British anthropologists had been interested in language use since the time of Malinowski (Henson 1974). But American anthropologists had scarcely addressed the issue of language use before Gumperz and Hymes proposed it as a field of study in the 60's. Hymes himself admits that the stimulus to explore language use came from a lecture by the Prague school linguist Roman Jakobson (1960). In short, the discipline of the ethnography of communication seems a strange choice for the task of continuing the Boasian project.

More recently, however, scholars like Silverstein (1979) and Friedrich (1979; 1987) have shown that the explicit objectives of the ethnography of communication are not just consistent with, but are the truest renderings of, the spirit of Whorf's semantic theory and therefore of Boasian linguistic anthropology. In other words, the ethnography of communication is an altogether appropriate standard bearer for the Boasian project and not at all some bandwagon that attracted scholars in search of a program.

Silverstein contends that Whorf's discussions of meaning really aimed to uncover the mind-bending effect of language at a deeper level than word and phrase meaning. It is not word meanings and the thoughts conjured up in speakers that Whorf was after. Rather he was interested in the presuppositions about reality that grammatical categories led competent speakers to make. When speakers of English say *three large scoops of sugar*, their language presupposes for them that *sugar* is a formless substance which requires some externally imposed form (scoops) if it is to be numbered and sized. However, *tree* in *three large trees* has both a substance and a form which enables it to be numbered and sized. Cultural presuppositions about the form or substance of realities, like *tree* or *sugar*, are the sort of presuppositions Whorf was interested in. Silverstein points out that such presuppositions become apparent only when speakers use language in the world.

The prevailing Western use of language to represent the world predisposes Westerners to certain presuppositions about the world. But cross culturally, language uses are not at all restricted to representation. Language uses vary, and so too cultural presuppositions vary. Therefore only a study of language use will reveal the presuppositions about the world which follow from those distinctive uses of language.

Friedrich argues a similar line when he says that it is not language structure but "poetic processes of language that massively model, constrain, trigger and otherwise affect the individual imagination" (1979: 473). By "poetic processes" Friedrich means the non-literal, non-representational uses of language

155

which, he contends, provide the food which imagination consumes, the potential which imagination realizes.

The proposals by Silverstein and Friedrich demonstrate that Boasian anthropology has a buoyant, resilient spirit which persists through the waxing and waning of specific research programs. Boas, Sapir, and Whorf established goals for American anthropology which endure even when their own research methods and procedures are discarded.

Conclusions

Post-war Boasian linguists set out to make Whorfian descriptions of languages/cultures more scientific. As scientific reformers, they aimed to dramatize the distinctiveness of cultural communities, but they wanted to do so in the most rigorously scientific manner possible. As a result they developed componential and taxonomic analyses of lexical systems.

Both these analytic techniques could be counted as advances over the more impressionistic Whorfian techniques of analysis, but both had their drawbacks. Componential analysis, for its part, left room for the analyst's insight in selecting features; it implied a cross cultural sharing of features; and it implied static systems of meaning. The method of taxonomic analysis avoided these difficulties, but it could not easily be used to demonstrate cultural contrasts.

Generative linguists, for their own reasons, were searching for methods of semantic description in the 1960's. And they latched on to some of the same techniques used by ethnoscientists. But what ethnoscientists found to be difficulties and drawbacks of semantic analyses, were benefits to the structuralists. Being deductive scientists, they valued the role of insight in hypothesis formation. They gladly accepted the implication that semantic features were universally shared. And they found ways to talk about meaning in dynamic and evolving systems. And in so doing, they turned semantic analyses into powerful support for their theoretical activity.

The theoretical goals of structuralist generative linguistics are different from those of Boasian linguistics. And so too are the emphases of these two traditions. The former, being philosopher linguists, emphasized individual innate endowments supporting linguistic competence which, it is said, are crucial components of a human nature. The latter, being reformist scientists, aim to emphasize cultural distinctiveness for the moral transformation of modern societies which it promises. In other words, the structuralist's emphasis on the individual contrasts with the ethnographer's emphasis on the community.

Semantic analyses, we have seen, turned a profit for the

156

interests and emphases of the structuralists, and therefore detracted from the Boasian linguistic program. Little wonder, then, that the anthropological interest in ethnoscience waned in the late 1960's. Though the anthropologists had developed ethnoscience to serve their purposes as reformer scientists, it got away from them. In the hands of structuralist linguists, it was turned against the Boasian objectives.

Chapter Eleven

Ethnography of Communication as Cultural Critique

When language is king, a predictable assemblage of lords holds sway in the kingdom. It is no accident that, in the realm of American anthropology, the concepts of individual, mind, cognition, and sharedness have been the theoretical lords.

Anthropologists, by and large, have modeled their culture theory on the language theory of structuralist linguists, and this modeling of culture on language accounts for the psychological and cognitive leanings of American anthropology. When anthropologists assume that language is king, they find themselves bowing in the same direction and to the same lords as structuralists. And like them, the anthropologists end up describing the mind and its processes.

But at the same time that anthropologists have hailed language as king, they have struggled against the implications of its reign. Something in the soul of American anthropology objects to the focus on the mind. The reformist in the anthropologist suspects that too much has been made of the individual's mind and that not enough has been said about human communities, about their operation and their significance.

As far as the critics among the anthropologists are concerned, anthropological linguists have, in the past, made too much of the individual and not enough of the community. And, in so doing, anthropological linguists have supported, rather than criticized, the roots of alienation in modern culture. Far from mounting an effective reform, anthropological linguists have actually aggravated the problems of modern life.

In the 1960's, Dell Hymes and John Gumperz fingered the concept of language, till then undisputed king of the realm, as the villain. The problem with language and language theory, they argued, is not so much what it *says* about humans as what it *fails to say*. What language theory *says* about humans is that each speaker possess a systematic, though unconscious, knowledge of forms--and from chapters four and five we know that such a knowledge of forms means, in phonology, the ability of individuals to produce and interpret phonetic tokens for phonemic types, and in syntax, the ability to produce and interpret transformational variants of deep structures. What language theory *fails to say* is that speakers also know what is appropriate to say, when, how, and to whom. Hymes, Gumperz, and the "ethnographers of speaking" who followed their program set themselves to describing just such know-how among speakers. They described rules of language use to be added to rules of language form so as to make up a complete grammar of a language. With such an addition of rules for lan-

159

guage use, they reasoned that a grammar would present the social face of language as well as the individual face. Grammars, so augmented, would reflect the analytic quasi-computational form-knowledge of the lone speaker, but also the sensitive and mutually accomodating use-knowledge of speakers in a community.

The purpose of this chapter is to explore the descriptions of ethnographers of speaking. The first section will show that ethnographers of speaking have tried to maintain the structuralist's form of grammatical descriptions while altering the content. They continue to describe speaking behavior in terms of rules of grammar, only their rules are rules of knowing how to speak appropriately (use-rules) rather than rules of knowing what tokens can instantiate what types (form-rules). The second section will show that their descriptions are mirrors in which ethnographers can see and appreciate themselves and their practices.

Describing the Rules of Communicative Competence

Still under the sway of king language, early ethnographers of speaking reasoned that producing appropriate communication was a matter of knowing situations and of knowing what kinds of speech match those situations. Both sorts of knowledges, knowledges of situations and knowledges of behaviors, were assumed to be *categorical* knowledges. That is, categories of situation and speech knowledge, like categories of phonological knowledge, were assumed to contrast sharply with one another. Moreover, like phonological knowledge, situation and speech knowledge was assumed to be shared, that is, identically distributed, in a speech community. In these respects use-knowledge was supposed to be similar to grammatical form-knowledge. To make that similarity clear, ethnographers of speaking coined the label *communicative competence* for the use-knowledge which complements form-knowledge which is called grammatical competence.

An illustration of such categorical descriptions of communicative competence will be helpful. Frake's (1964) study of Subanun drinking talk embodies the assumptions of categoriality and sharedness described above. The Subanun of the Philippines are *cognizant* --cognizant here means more than just aware; cognizant suggests a well-defined conceptual knowledge--of the differences between festive gatherings and informal gatherings. Only the festive gatherings provide occasions for the drinking of beer.

Subanun beer, unlike American beer, is sipped through a straw inserted into a Chinese jar of fermented mash. The jar is passed from person to person. Jar passing and beer drinking on festive occasions proceed in three major substages of which the Subanun are cognizant: tasting, competitive drinking, and game drinking. Tasting involves brief moments for sipping beer; competitive drinking involves careful measurement of amounts of beer consumed; and game drinking is accompanied by drinking games with their own special rules.

Alongside this knowledge of beer drinking events, the Subanun are cognizant of different kinds of speaking which are appropriate for the different substages of beer drinking. All of these kinds of speaking are performed by drinkers for the purpose of monopolizing both drink and talk and thereby establishing a position of esteem and power amongst their peers. The strategies for talk vary with the different substages of drinking. Invitational speech is appropriate for the tasting stage of beer drinking. Here hosts invite drinkers to partake, and drinkers request permissions of other drinkers to join in. "Jar talk," which focuses on the quality of the beer and the performance of the drinkers, is appropriate for the stage of competitive drinking. Game drinking is accompanied by songs and verses that display poetic ability.

Communicative Competence & the Individual

This description of Subanun beer drinking and of the talk appropriate for that beer drinking illustrates the best of the early work in the ethnography of communication.

You should note from this description that Subanun *social* life is being described, but in terms of the communicative competence of *individuals*. This tension between the individual and the social is not unique in the ethnography of communication; it runs throughout Boasian ethnography.

All the members of the Subanun speech community are assumed to possess a cognizance of both the beer drinking substages and of the forms of speech that are appropriate for each stage. The appropriate forms of speaking convey the intentions that a speaker has in mind as he plays his part in the beer drinking. Such appropriate speakings can also be called *speech acts*.

The study of speech acts has a long history outside of anthropology (Searle 1969; Levinson 1983); the point of such a study is to make clear just how humans convey their intentions with a wide variety of expressions. In our own practices of beer drinking one can get a beer by saying, "Please pass me a beer," which expresses a requesting intention quite clearly. But one could also say, "How's the beer today?," or "Boy, am I thirsty!," or even "Sure is a hot day!," each of which can operate in a systematic way to convey the same intention of requesting a beer.

161

Thus, speech event descriptions reveal the conventional social circumstances in which speech acts are used. Speech act analysis reveals the conventional means for conveying intentions in those speech events. Here ethnographic description goes hand in hand with speech act theory. Together they create a package of descriptive methods that enable us to comprehend the communicative practices that are shared by the members of a community.

Just as a knowledge of speech events and of speech acts is assumed to be shared by members of a community, so too the knowledge of all other aspects of language use are assumed to be shared. Let us first examine the variety of aspects of communicative know-how, and then sample the descriptions of some of those aspects.

Hymes makes it easy to remember the variety of aspects of communicative competence by offering the mnemonic SPEAKING, each letter of which indicates a distinct aspect:

S	setting or scene of communication
P	participants in communication
E	ends or purposes
A	act sequence; the ordering of events
K	key or manner, e.g. ironic, serious...
I	instrumentalities; grammars
N	norms for appropriate expression
G	genres, e.g. greeting, praying, story telling ...

These different aspects of communicative competence will be discussed and exemplified below. The discussions are intended to show how the different aspects of communicative practice, varying as they do from community to community, can be described with language-like rules (see Farb 1974; Saville-Troike 1982).

Setting Knowledges of settings are basic aspects of communicative competence. *Settings* are the social locations in which speech occurs, e.g. a church, a ball park, a school.

In any *setting*, a communicative *situation* can occur, e.g. a church service, a baseball game, a class in school, a festive gathering, etc.. A communicative <u>event</u> is a spate of talk all components of which involve roughly the same participants, the same function, and the same key. ("Talk," "speak," "speaking," "speech," etc. will often be used in place of "communication" in view of the fact that humans typically communicate by talking. Such terms ought not be taken to mean that humans must speak in order to communicate. Often enough people communicate by gesturing, signing, etc., rather than by talking.). For example, the purchase of a newspaper from a vendor is an event; and the Subanun beer tasting substage of beer drinking is an event. A com-

162

municative *act* is a communication that results from a single intention of a single participant in an event, e.g. a request, a description, a compliment.

A baseball game will help distinguish *situations* from *events* and *acts*. Within the *situation* of a ballgame, a number of *events* of communication usually occur, e.g. fans purchase snacks, umpires call plays, catchers direct players, and fielders encourage each other by their chatter. The speech acts in each of these *events* are distinctive.

Similarly, the *situation* of a classroom in a school involves many different *events* of speaking, e.g. teaching, praying, playing, pledging allegiance to the flag. And again, each involves distinctive speech, though to a child the speech differences between *events* of pledging allegiance to the flag and praying may seem minimal. The recitations of any one person or group during these events are <u>acts,</u> analyses of which can reveal the nature of that speaker's intention.

Situation, event, and act analyses can reveal deep-seated characteristics of the social life of a people. Consider, for example, the study by Abrahams and Bauman (1971) of the situation of the West Indian tea meeting. In St. Vincent, the tea meeting is a public display which involves performers and audience. Usually the tea meeting becomes a contest-like performance marked by verbal jousting between officially designated orators and boisterous "rude boys" in the rear sections of the audience. On the whole, the tea meeting performance is a display of individual verbal virtuosity within the context of a social whole. Abrahams interprets this effect broadly, arguing that it reveals the essence of the Black aesthetic: "Each individual gets to do his own thing, yet, in vying with others, each affirms the social whole" (1976: 83).

Norm Situations, events, and acts provide one perspective on the communicative practices of a community. The norms for speech provide another. Norms refer to sanctioned ways of speaking in any situation. Speakers may be conscious of such norms; that happens most often where the norms are encapsulated in spoken rules, e.g. "Don't talk with food in your mouth!," or "Don't interrupt while another person is speaking!." But sometimes, norms are non-conscious and cannot be discovered by just asking. For such non-conscious norms, the ethnographer must observe and record regularities of behavior. For example, Zimmerman and West (1975) tell us that North American males interrupt in male-female conversations more frequently than females. This difference suggests a difference in norms for interrupting.

When ethnographers describe *norms* for speakings, they are describing individually felt obligations for social behavior. Deborah Tannen's discussion (1984) of conversational styles helps

163

us to appreciate both the individual feelings involved as well as the sharedness of those feelings among members of a community. By careful observation, Tannen unearthed an interesting normative difference in the speech of east coast and west coast communities. Her own New York way of speaking is, she says, a "machine gun" style in which she demonstrates interest in a person by asking a flurry of questions, one after another, and allowing little or no time for responses between. Californians, she says, find that style abrasive and controlling, preferring instead a longer duration between turns at talk. The difference between the two coasts is a matter of different norms for speaking.

As with distinctive events of speaking, distinctive norms for speaking can sometimes reveal the nature of a community. Bauman's (1983) description of British Quakers of the seventeenth century shows that distinctive norms for speech lie at the heart of the culture of this community. The Quakers believed that all speech should reveal the Inner Light which is God speaking through them. However, God's voice is easily hidden by the noise of everyday talk. Therefore, the Quakers counseled "plain speech" and frowned on laughter and idle jesting. They eschewed speech that bore the trappings of social, as opposed to Godly, distinctions, and so they avoided the pronouns that implied social respectability. (Prior to this era, English maintained two sets of second person personal pronouns, just like those found in Spanish, French, German, Italian, Russian, etc.. First, there were pronouns used among intimates, e.g. *thee/thou*; second, there were pronouns used in formal and polite relationships, e.g. *ye/you*. The distinction between the intimate pronouns and the formal pronouns which implied respect may well have disappeared from English in the seventeenth century as a result of the pressure brought to bear on the language by groups like the Quakers.) Quaker plain speech was to be sober truth-telling and was to be produced with a serious demeanor befitting truth: "Our words were few and savoury...our countenances grave and deportment weighty" (Ibid., p. 23).

The Quaker norms for speaking are similar to the norms of two other communities, gnostics of the second century and fundamentalists of the twentieth century. By describing the norms for speech in these two other communities, we will arrive at a deeper appreciation of our own cultural tradition.

First, the gnostics, heretics of the second century, believed that the spirit is good, but the world is evil. They were convinced that that all goodness emanated from a spark of God's "light" which resides in the soul of each human. They prescribed cultivated, serious speech so as to nourish that spark into an illuminating flame.

Second, fundamentalists, or conservative evangelical Christians of the twentieth century, are convinced that careful and serious talk, on the one hand, and a speaking-in-tongues, on the other, is a significant component of a personal relationship with the Lord within. Jerry Falwell and Jimmy Lee Swaggert tell us to avoid the frivolous chatter of the world and embrace the talk of the Spirit.

The relationship of Quaker, gnostic, and fundamentalist norms for talk to our own can be made clear by considering a fourth community which, like these three, prescribes serious truth-telling at the same time that it shuns worldly chatter. That fourth community is the scientific community amongst whom all talk is to be pure and untainted--Did not Bacon in his <u>Novum Organum</u> of 1620 advise scientists to avoid idolatrous talk? It is no accident that the norm for "plain speech" amongst scientists arose in the seventeenth century, at the same time as it arose amongst puritanical religious peoples like the Quakers. Both the Quaker community and the scientific community, prescribed non-worldly and therefore illuminating talk. Basically neo-gnostic in embracing this norm of illuminating talk, both Quakers and scientists celebrate words that are "few and savoury" (Berman 1981: 105).

Such a description of norms invites us to reflect on our own scientific communicative practices. And towards the end of this chapter we will take up such reflections. In the meantime, however, we will continue to explore the ethnographic descriptions of aspects of language use.

Act Sequence Speakers in a community are assumed to share a knowledge of events and a knowledge of norms for communicative conduct during those events. Speakers are also presumed to share a knowledge of the ordering or *sequencing* of talk. The clearest illustration of rule-governed sequences of talk are to be found in ritual events as opposed to informal interaction. In ritual events like the Subanun ritual drinking, speakers often have names for specific speech events and are quite conscious of the order in which those events are to proceed. In the same way, we are aware that in a championship professional football game, the players are introduced to the crowd; the introductions are followed by a coin toss which involves a few players and the referees; both the crowd and the players listen to the national anthem; then the crowd attends to the game as it progresses. Each of these rigidly sequenced events focuses on certain speech events, i.e. introductions, anthem singing, play by play talk. Other talk is permitted during most events, i.e. members of the crowd can order beer during the introductions, coin toss, and play-by-play, but not during the singing of the national anthem. For situations that are as ritualized as these, it seems plausible to believe that all participants share explicit rules that prescribe the sequences of events and talk.

In other less formal circumstances, the sequencing of talk

is far subtler, though no less regular. Explicating rules of these subtler cases begins to become problematic. If a person passes a stranger walking in the opposite direction on the sidewalk, and if, in approaching each other, the two persons establish eye contact, it is appropriate for them to voice a minimal greeting, "Hi!." The greater the duration of the eye contact the stronger is the prescription to proceed to a voiced greeting. If the passers-by are acquaintances, eye contact is prescribed as is a voiced greeting. Presumably speakers share a knowledge of these different conditions as well as a knowledge of the different strengths with which these conditions favor a greeting. The relative duration of eye contact and the relative familiarity of the individuals must both figure into any rules which account for such greeting behavior.

The Unconscious

Subtle regularities like these are aspects of an unconscious communicative competence and are analogous to aspects of the unconscious grammatical competence imputed to speakers by generative structuralist linguists.

Subtler yet is the rule for the production and sequencing of back-channel utterances. Back-channel utterances are a loosely defined set of words and sounds, like Uh-huh, mmm, okay, yea, etc. which listeners produce to show a speaking partner that the listener knows that a spate of talk is underway and that it is not yet complete (Schegloff 1982: 81). Competent listeners produce back-channel utterances only up to the point where the speaker completes an extended utterance.

How it happens that listeners recognize that an extended utterance coming to a close is hard to say, and harder still to represent in a rule. Whatever rule one might imagine, A, in the tion below, fails to follow it. A is an announcer/host for a radio talk show. His failure to follow a conversational rule causes the confusion in the last of the caller's utterances. The existence of such confusion is a sign that something is amiss in this conversation.

B: This is in reference to a call, that was made about a month ago.
A: Yessir?
B: A woman called, uh sayin she uh signed a contract for huh son who is--who was a minuh.
A: Mm hm,
B: And she claims inna contract, there were things given and then taken away, in small writing.

A: Mm hm
B: Uh, now meanwhile, about a month eh no about two weeks
     before she made the call I read in, I read or either
     heard-uh I either read or hoid onna television, where
     the judge, hadda case like this.
A: Mhhm,
B: And he got disgusted an' he says 'I'--he sick of these
     cases where they give things in big writing, an' take
     'em, and 'take 'em away in small writing.
A: Mhhm,
B: Uh what I mean is it c'd help this woman that called.
     You know uh, that's the reason I called (Ibid.).

The last pair of utterances in this conversation is the site
of a miscue.   B has been holding the floor for some while, and A
has been acknowledging B's extended conversation with *uh huh*.
But, for whatever reasons, A also produces a *Mhhm* after B has
completed his/her topic and come to the point that s/he had to
make about the judge's decision.   A's last *Mhhm* throws B off
balance.   This last *Mhhm* says, "I'm listening," but B has nothing
more to say.   So B finds it necessary to state his/her intentions
explicitly and somewhat awkwardly.

Schegloff and his colleagues have suggested some ways of
accounting for sequencing regularities, particularly the sequencing of turns at talk in conversations.   These scholars are
called *ethnomethodologists* because they assume that speakers
organize talk in and through the talking and with common sense
methods rather than with the rational methods of a scientist.
They point out that in most conversations turns at talk are
highly regulated.   Less than 5% of conversational talk involves
overlaps of speakers.   The rarity of overlaps suggests that
speakers usually succeed in allocating turns at talk in a regular
fashion.   The task of the ethnographer is to describe the know-
how behind such success.

Ethnomethodology

Ethnomethodological research may not itself be anthropology,
but ethnographers of speaking have certainly benefitted from
ethnomethodology in their search to understand communicative
competence.

A first observation is that some regularities of turn-taking
in conversation are established by the existence of adjacency
pairs.   Adjacency pairs consist of utterances the first unit of
which requires a responding second unit.   If Joe calls to Mary,
Joe and Mary will both expect that Mary will take a turn at talk

to acknowledge Joe's summons. If Joe asks Mary a question, Mary will take a turn of talk to respond. If Joe says "hello" or "goodbye" to Mary, Mary will take a turn of talk to match Joe's. To review the behaviors involved in an adjacency pair, when Joe has completed his summons, question, greeting, or farewell, he will leave the floor open for Mary to talk. And upon hearing the first utterance in such an adjacency pair, Mary prepares herself to take the floor with a turn at talk.

The smooth transition from Joe's talk to Mary's talk is not simply a matter of a lead utterance mechanically commanding a second. A variety of intonations and movements accompany the transition. Gaze is a particularly significant dimension of such transitions. Though a speaker's gaze may wander during a turn at talk, his/her eyes recontact the listener's when a potential transition point is reached in the conversation. Bodily orientation also plays a significant role in the sequencing of turns at talk. The speaker's orientation helps to nominate the next speaker who will assume the floor when the speaker's turn is complete.

Even with the assistance of gaze contact and bodily orientation, transitions from lead utterances to seconds in adjacency pairs are not uniformly smooth. In general, a second utterance that is known by both parties to be a preferred response is produced more quickly and smoothly than are dis-preferred seconds, which are usually marked by delays, hesitations, apologies, and/or explanations:

A: Uh, if you'd care to come and visit a little while this morning, I'll give you a cup of coffee.

B: Hehh, Well that's awfully sweet of you. I don't think I can make it this morning. hh, uhm, I'm running an add in the paper and-and, uh, I have to stay near the phone (Levinson 1983: 333).

To this point, the regularities regarding sequencing in adjacency pairs seems to be straightforward enough. It is not hard to imagine that such regularities result from shared rules for the sequencing of turns at talk. However the principle of *conditional relevance* adds a piquant spice of complexity to these regularities, making possible an almost unlimited number of ways of shaping seconds in adjacency pairs.

The principle of conditional relevance states that the second utterance in a pair must be relevant to the first and lead utterance in a pair. Interestingly, what counts as relevant is not always clear and obvious. Relevance is entirely in the hands of communicators, and the task of drawing up boundaries of relevance often defies scientific rule-making.

168

Some illustrations are in order. Levinson (1983) points out that questions can be happily followed by partial answers, rejections of the presuppositions of the questions, statements of ignorance, denials of the relevance of the question, and so on.

A: What does John do for a living?
B: a.   Oh, this and that.
     b.   I've no idea.
     c.   What's that got to do with it (Ibid.).

One need not search high and low to find examples of how generous speakers can be in deciding if a second is relevant. The actually occurring conversations that each of us enter into daily will tell the tale. Consider this brief conversation between Bill, a university professor, and Tony, a campus policeman.

Tony: Hi
Bill: Hi
Tony: Did you move?
Bill: I was just taking my child to a day care center over on Hampshire.

Two questions about relevance arise here. First, in what respect is Tony's lead question appropriate and relevant in a fleeting exchange of greetings? Second, in what respects is Bill's response to Tony relevant to his question.

In order to answer these questions you will need to know a bit more about both Tony and Bill. First, Bill had not seen Tony walking his beat for a couple of months. Typically, whenever they do see each other, they exchange a greeting. It has been that way for about ten years, ever since Tony rented Bill's home while he and his family were out of the country. The house is one block away from Bill's office on campus. On this day when Bill was riding his bike on campus toward his office, he saw Tony and said, "Hi." Tony, with his gaze fixed on the bicycle rather than on Bill, asked, "Did you move?." Bill found relevance in his question by putting it together with his gaze. The question about moving was actually germane to a more direct, but unasked question, about why Bill was riding his bike, seeing as he had but one block to walk. Bill responded to that unasked question. That is, Bill explained that he was riding because he had been delivering his child to a day care center. All of this happened in the time that it took Bill to glide past Tony.

The lesson in this anecdote is that speakers tend to be maximally generous in determining the contextual relevance of the utterances of partners in conversation. Speakers look far and deep to find relevance in what often seems to be pure nonsense. They may go so far as to see sense where there is, in fact, only nonsense (Garfinkel 1967).

169

The upshot of this principle of conditional relevance is that actually occurring adjacency pairs may not themselves display objective regularities of sequencing. The logic of the sequencing is not to be found in the utterances. Rather the speakers impose the logic as they allow or disallow utterances to pass as relevant.

At this point I suggest that we begin wondering how such mental processes might ever come to be shared among a community of speakers. It is easy enough to imagine that a word can be shared; even a meaning. But how does a child go about acquiring a mental process that imposes a logic on utterances?

On Sharedness

Raising questions about sharedness is tantamount to raising questions about the language-model on which descriptions of communicative competence are based. Here again we see that ethnographic descriptions are leading us Western scientists to critical reflections on our own assumptions and practices.

Also problematic in the realm of sequencing regularities, are the issues of topic coherence in conversations. The general rule for appropriate sequencing in conversation is that anyone who adds to any conversation is under some obligation to make their addition relevant to what has already transpired in the conversation. In other words, the principle of conditional relevance applies to the matter of the continuation of conversations.

But, even as the sequence patterns for conversations vary across cultures, so too the calculation of conditional relevance varies from community to community. That variability is correlated with other differences like those which exist between oral and literate communities.

Literate communities value a turn at talk if it is a logical conclusion to what precedes, or if it is an additional premise that leads to a logical conclusion. In such communities, talkers find themselves compelled to construct their talk so that it leads to a point, a conclusion, a logical finale. Fred Erickson (1984) has demonstrated that at least some members of the Afro-American speech community see the task of developing a topic to be one of blending details into an emotionally powerful rhapsody, rather than one of premise-to-conclusion logic. The rhapsody need not have a general moral, or a lesson or a point, nor do the details of the rhapsody need to be justified by their relationship to any propositional conclusion:

Leader:	What do you mean by a slum.
Jim:	Well, when we first got here there was a lot of ...you know there was a lot of white over here.
Ed:	Yeah.
Jim:	They started moving out.
Al:	Ah'm hip.
Jim:	'N then, 'n then everybody started coming in...
Ed:	'N they just, 'n they just...'n everybody jes' fall down.
Denise:	That's right.
Ed:	Used to...They used to come by...and they used to sweep the streets all the time...
Jim:	Now they won't even do that...won't even come in keep the garbage cans (Erickson 1984: 105f).

In this excerpt from a conversation of some members of an Afro-American speech community, the leader's question is phrased in a literate fashion with the expectation of a definitional response. But instead of responding with a definition, Jim and the others weave a rhapsody of emotionally powerful details that are echoed back and forth between them. Such rhapsodic sequencing runs by rules that differ from those that apply in a predominantly literate speech community.

Once again I suggest that you try to imagine the form which a rule for rhapsodic sequencing might take. And as you struggle to imagine that form you should remember that the form of a rule should be clear and simple enough so that the rule can be naturally acquired.

Key Besides describing the sequencing know-how of speakers, the rule-like descriptions of communicative competence are also intended to be plausible presentations of *keys* that speakers use and of the cues which mark those keys.

A key is a tone, or manner, or spirit in which an utterance is produced. A literal key of speaking differs from a joking, ironic key. A clear illustration of keys and of key switching is provided by Keith Basso (1979) in his description of Apache jokes about white folks. On one occasion involving J and L, both of whom are Apache men, J enters L's house and says: "Hello my friend. How are you doing? How are you feeling, L? You feeling good?" L responds to this utterance with laughter.

Basso helps us understand L's laughter by pointing out a cue which establishes the key for J's utterance as a joke. J uses the phrase "my friend" which "Apaches think Anglo-Americans bandy about in a thoroughly irresponsible way." The use of this phrase between these two Apaches marks the utterance as a playful and mocking imitation of Anglo behavior.

171

J continues his utterance with unsolicited queries about L's health and emotional state. L responds, once again with laughter. Basso explains that "if an Apache wishes to discuss such matters, he or she will do so. If not, they are simply nobody's business. But Anglo-Americans make them their business." Again, J lets L know that he is not serious but only pursuing a mocking joke. The use of these irksome but distinctively Anglo phrases between two Apaches is a cue to the mocking key that is being set up. Such a key-establishing signal can also be called a *contextualization cue.*

Contextualization cues can be extremely subtle; they are probably not at all the categorical, all-or-nothing signals that conform to the language-rule format. John Gumperz (1982) has been working for a number of years trying to describe the subtle powers of contextualization cues. He notes that they often consist of little more than rising or lowering intonations, or of strategically placed pauses or stresses. But such subtle cues regularly perform the powerful labor of distinguishing polite requests from brazen demands, etc..

Though subtle, contextualization cues are significant. Conversations, especially those across boundaries of speech communities, often break down because of a failure of one party to appreciate such a cue (see Gumperz's video documentary Cross-talk). Indeed, Gumperz searches out such breakdowns as indicators of the operation of a cue. Where talk breaks down, there, as often as not, is a contextualization cue operating which one party has misconstrued.

Descriptions of Communicative Practice

The ethnographic description of communicative keys offers an opportunity for self-reflection. A comparison of the keys of speaking in the traditions of peoples who are, on the one hand, similar to us, and on the other, different, leads to a deeper appreciation of our own communicative keys.

First, we should be prepared to recognize that the ethnographic practice of describing the communicative behavior of humans creates a curious conundrum. As in the situation depicted in Escher's Drawing Hands on the next page, ethnographic description is included in the very objects which it describes. Ethnographic practice is at once description and object of that selfsame description. This situation sets up the conditions that lead ethnographers to use their descriptions to arrive at a deeper and clearer appreciation of themselves describing. Such self-reflective and self-critical activities have always been integral aspects of the Boasian project of ethnography.

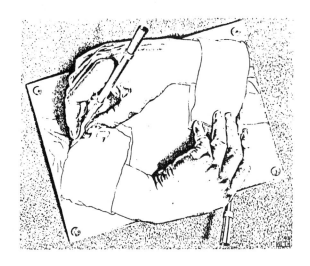

On the whole, and controlling for situations and events, all modern American speech communities, as well as second century gnostic communities and seventeenth century Quakers, attribute the highest significance to the serious, literal, truth-telling key and to the informative functions of talk. Talk, in these traditions, is for exchanging thoughts.

Predictably, these traditions rank talk that provides maximally clear and accurate expressions of thought above all other differently keyed talk. Predictably too, they regard mind, the fountain of thought, as the essence of humanity. Humorous speech, or phatic speech, which, like a "Hi, how are you," just makes contact with others, or speech which, like psychobabble, celebrates a social identity, ranks lower and is sometimes disdained. The abbott in Umberto Eco's The Name of the Rose demonstrates characteristic Western disdain for less-than-truth-telling talk when he hides the sole copy of Aristotle's treatise on humor in the labyrinthine library of his monastery.

Living, as we do, in a tradition that values truth-telling, we have a hard time believing that anyone anywhere could really value any key other than the literal truth-telling key. It is hard for us to believe that the Malagasy are really suspicious of informative speech because it draws attention to the speaker and causes him/her to stand out from the rest. Even the poignant example on the next page is not powerful enough to thoroughly disabuse us of the belief that secretly the Malagasy don't regard truth-telling as the epitome of speaking.

173

On returning to your village late on night, one of
the peoples appear at your door. (It is most
unusual to visit after dark, so you know something
is up.) And you ask him, "What's new?" to which
he responds, "Nothing." Then after some inconsequential discussion, it emerges that your neighbor
who was expecting has had an unsuccessful labor,
the child died and the woman is in the town
hospital (Keenan (1979: 151).

As this example suggests, the Malagasy are comfortable only when
they can relate to one another without having to inform or give
news. In this scene, the details about the unsuccessful labor
came out only because Keenan, with his Western penchant for
information, pressed his visitor for news. On their own, however, the Malagasy prefer the bland anonymity of ritualistic
communication. Just as the Balinese run in shame from the prospect of revealing their inner feelings (Geertz 1973), so too the
Malagasy run from situations where they must speak informatively.

A Reflection on Incredulity

The fact that a behavior is "hard for us to believe" is an
indication of the presence of an ethnocentric bias, here specifically, a bias about the possible keys and functions of speaking.
Such a bias, when unearthed, is food for critical self-reflection.

When we come across a people like the Malagasy, or the
Maninka (Bird and Shopen 1979) of West Africa, who speak in
proverbs that circle around a concept but never hit it on the
head, or like the Burundi (Albert 1972), whose legal debates are
decided more on the elegance of arguments than on their truth, or
like the Minang (Errington 1984) of Sumatra, whose speech is a
bundle of ritualized but uncriticized explanations of happenings,
we become impatient. We suspect that the proverbs, the legal
arguments, and the uncritical explanations are just cultural
clothing for the real meanings and concepts that lie underneath.
If pressured, the Malagasy, Maninka, the Burundi, and the Minang,
would, we suppose, dispense with that clothing and would present
the naked and literal idea behind their talk.

However, an alternative state of affairs is also possible.
That alternative is that literal, representational, informative
speech--simply, truth-telling--is not a high ranking key in some
non-modern communities like the Maninka, the Burundi, and the
Minang. The possibility is that in such communities non-literal
keys and non-informative functions are more highly valued. The

174

possibility is that truth-telling is not a universally valued kind of speaking.

These non-Western peoples may produce literal speech that resembles our literal speech. They may even do so frequently. But still their perceptions of what they are doing may be quite different from our self-perceptions.

Valuing Communicative Keys

Cross-cultural descriptions of keys lead to the conclusion that, while all communities make use of literal, humorous, ironic, formulaic, etc. keys, different communities might value those keys differently. Such differential valuations make for dramatic differences in communicative practices as a whole. And they provide ethnographers with abundant food for self-critical reflection on their own keys of speech and its value.

We modern Westerners value truth-telling over formulaic speech, humorous speech, and instrumental speech, i.e. speech which gets things done. That is not to say that in our daily lives we do not make abundant use of formulaic, humorous, and instrumental speech. We do. Indeed, some studies of Western language use show that the young children among use make far more frequent use of instrumental speech than of truth telling (Halliday 1973).

However, when--and this happens often in formal circumstances--we take the time to reflect on how we ought to speak, we then employ the characteristics of truth-telling as the model for our behavior. And we select our words--often self-consciously--mindful that our words will be judged according to their value as tellers of truth.

The Malagasy, the Maninka, the Burundi, and the Minang may speak a truth-telling speech as often as they speak in a formulaic key. But when put on guard in a formal setting, they look to formulaic speech as the model for their behavior. They select words--again self-consciously--mindful that those words will be judged by others according to a formulaic standard.

Truth-telling is our key of keys, the most highly valued of our keys for speaking. Ironic and humorous speech, for us, are understood in terms of truth-telling. They are intentional departures from truth-telling. The elementary principles of all modern theories of human action rest on the centrality of the truth-telling key (Grice 1968). Indeed, the whole of modern philosophy (Rorty 1979) rests on this key. Were this our key of keys to change, the number and depth of the ramifications of such a change would be staggering.

In other cultural communities, the highly valued keys of keys is often a key other than the literal key with its representational function. In such a case, humor, irony, etc. is understood differently from our humor and our irony, even if they be accomplished in the same way. The perception of speech is shaped by the values attributed to speech.

What might be such an alternative key of keys? The possibility is that the *cosmogonic* key might be such an alternative, for this key is far from being uncommon cross culturally. Cosmogonic speech is world-creating speech, speech that recreates and reshapes the cosmos. The Navaho (Witherspoon 1977), the Dogon (Calame-Griaule 1985), and the ancient Hebrews (Ong 1967), all consider language to be a device for such cosmogonic speaking. The Navaho contend that "by speaking properly and appropriately, one can control and compel the behavior and the power of the gods" (Witherspoon 1977: 60). All less significant keys in a such a community revolve around this central key, and are significant only insofar as they realize this world-creating power of speech in diminished degrees.

If, as Witherspoon suggests, the cosmogonic, world-creating key is the most highly valued key in Navaho communicative practice, then the possibility exists that other Navaho keys of speaking, including the literal and ironic keys, are understood to be departures from that world-creating key. To a naive Anglo, a Navaho who is speaking in the literal key might seem to be speaking naturally, using speech for its God-given purposes. But to the Navaho, such speech might seem to be inane disturbing chatter. And to a naive Anglo, a Navaho speaking in the cosmogonic key might seem to be mumbling mumbo jumbo. But to the Navaho, such speech is the most serious and significant of all speakings.

Instrumentalities A description of the instrumentalities of communication, and especially of that most celebrated instrumentality, writing, will cap off this survey of the ethnography of communication and provide us with yet another occasion for self-reflection. In this final section, we will, by a careful study of the impact of writing on the Western world, come to a deeper appreciation of how our truth-telling speech came to be so highly valued and of why this literal key came to be nominated as our key of keys.

The instrumentalities of communication are the channels and media through which people communicate. They are the expression-making and expression-carrying devices used by speakers and the sensory receptors used by listeners. Face-to-face speaking involves multiple channels which interact in complex and system-

176

atic ways for the success of the speaking. When those channels are extended or deleted, the events of speaking are dramatically changed. Changed too are the relationships of the persons communicating, if not the very fabric of their social life.

Expressions are produced and received through productive and sensory channels. Consider, for example, the channels employed in face-to-face communication, the voice and the ears, the bodily, manual, and facial movements and the eyes, even smell and touch. In face-to-face communication, the contribution of the various channels is relatively fixed. No single channel ever carries the communication beyond the range of others. The visual channel is not drowned out by the audial, and the tactile cannot cover over the olfactory. Listeners not only hear the voice, they see the movement, smell the excitement, and feel the vibrations. Hence face-to-face speaking is an act of the whole body and certainly not just the mouth. In face-to-face communication, all of the five senses are called into play.

These channels can be modified to a degree. Humans can hide their eyes when talking and wear perfume or cologne to mask their scent. They can cover their faces as do women in the Islamic tradition.

These popular sorts of modifications are superficial and temporary. Other adjustment are permanent or more dramatic in the way that they alter channels. People can permanently alter their visage with scars or tattoos. Egyptian beggars mutilated their bodies to enhance the force of their begging and medieval women ingested pupil-dilating nightshade to alter the impact of their eyes. But the range of such adjustments, even the permanent ones, is severely limited.

Face-to-face communication, even with its channel adjustments, answers many, but not all human expressive needs. Sometimes a greater spatial range is needed. A voice can carry, say, a hundred yards to reach the ears of those close by. But suppose the crowd stretches out for two hundred. A megaphone may be the answer, for it extends the voice beyond its natural range. Or perhaps semaphore flags are appropriate, for they can be seen from all directions whereas a megaphone restricts the voice to just one. Or perhaps the choice may fall on drums or whistles which can extend communication across expanses where vision is obstructed. (The Lokele of Africa and the Mazatecans of Mexico use these two devices. Pitch in the drumming and whistling represents lexical tones. And when repeated in formulaic and easily recognized phrases, those tones indicate words. See chapter four for more on tone languages.) More recently, radio and television extend communication across unlimited distances.

In the same way communicators may need to extend the temporal range of utterances. In this case, graphics, painting, and

177

sculpture can be used to preserve static visual images in time. Writing, print, audio, and video recordings are modern methods for extending both static and kinetic visual images. They too are media extensions.

It should be evident from this short catalogue of media extensions that a great variety of extensions are available, that almost all humans make use of some such extensions, and that there is a great deal of intercultural diversity in the use of such extensions.

But besides all these observations, one other is of crucial importance: every time a communicative channel is extended, the contribution of all channels to the process of communicating is altered. The various channels in face-to-face communication form a system of channels such that an extension of any one channel requires accomodating changes in other channels. Generally the more one channel becomes extended, the less do other channels participate in the communication.

Communications which involve a dramatically extended channel operate differently from those that do not. The most frequently cited illustration of this condition is written communication.

Writing is a distinctive form of communicative activity, one which extends static visual images in time and space. As an extended medium of communication, its most remarkable characteristic is its single channeledness. Face-to-face communications involve multiple channels orchestrated into an ensemble by context-cueing actions. But written utterances, being single channeled, are simpler in certain respects. No orchestration of channels is necessary. Moreover, no pointings and other references to the circumstances of communication are possible since the written words come to the reader with an already manufactured context: the covers of a book remind us of the book seller-publisher-author establishment which serves as the context for a writer's communication with a reader. In these ways single channeled writing is simpler than face-to-face communication.

But the simplicity of the written word is purchased at a price. Specifically, all that lies in a context, everything in the circumstances of the communicative event to which attention is steered must, in writing, be packed into a single channel. Wherever speakers might use a reference to context, writers must pack that reference to context into their context independent words.

The task is managed, of course, and managed well according to traditional historians of writing. Huey (1916:19) calls alphabetic writing "one of the greatest and momentous triumphs of the human mind." Writers accomplish the task by employing a distinctive packaging system for their messages.

The key to the distinctive packaging of messages in writing is analysis and synthesis. The writer, using his single channeled medium, breaks face-to-face expressions down into discrete semantic units--analysis--and then strings those units together on a line--synthesis.

Written language is language broken down into discrete parts. Indeed, the only reason we can think of a language as a system of words (and phonemes and morphemes) is because it has first been written. Jacques Derrida, the French philosopher, has argued that linguistics would never have gotten off the ground if it had had to describe languages without the aid of writing. Writing is a basically analytical activity, a distinctively computational, left-hemispheric behavior. [Not to gainsay the significance of Derrida's argument, it should be mentioned that Panini's grammar of Sanskrit was an oral grammar of the fourth century B.C. which was only later recorded in writing. That grammar was an aspect of Hindu worship, undertaken specifically in order to facilitate the precise articulation of Vedic hymns and mantras.]

No hearers are present to participate in this analytic process. Audiences are absent. Writing is not a participatory activity. Listeners cannot cooperate in the production of writing as they do in face-to-face communication. Writing is a solipsistic endeavor. The writer must march to self-generated rhythms. Honore de Balzac certainly appreciated the need for drumming up his own rhythms: he dressed for each writing occasion. Always he wrote in the dead of the night robed in a Carmelite monk's habit, all so as to establish for himself just the right ambience for writing.

The analysis/synthesis and the solipsism of writing were, initially at least, just part of the mechanics of writing. But when writing became popular in Hellenic Greece, and more importantly, when it became the prototype of communication in the modern world, then analysis/synthesis and solipsism became valuable in themselves. When written philosophical debate and composed drama replaced improvizational and memorized performances, the way was cleared for the installation of analytic/synthetic solipsistic writing as more than just one technique among many. Writing became *the* model for all other communicative acts, and *the* measure by which other communicative acts were assayed.

Writing about Writing

This description of the instrumentality of writing is driving us to look at our own communicative practices in a new light. It tempts us to set aside our common sense perspective which takes

179

our writing practices to be *natural*, and it suggests to us that our practices are unusual by reason of our cultural norms modeled on writing, our *writerly* norms.

At this point, our cultural style as communicators has become more than just a writing style. It has become a *writerly* style. That is, because writing has been a valued mode of communcation for such a long time, the analysis/synthesis and self-conscious solipsism, which are aspects of the writing process, have became valued in themselves and have been applied well beyond the specific situations that involve pen and paper.

In a writerly community, all aspects of communicative practice are reshaped into writerly practice. The very meaning of talk is redefined. Specifically, when analysis/synthesis become valued in themselves, the process of composing talk becomes a solo process and is moved to center stage. Composition proceeds with analytic precision, detached and removed from listener participation. Only in the presentation of talk does the listener enter into the communicative act. Goffman (1981a) tells us that all good public speakers exhibit in a dramatic way this writerly commitment to the detachment of composition. They compose in advance and usually on paper and they talk with a feigned candor and freshness. They only pretend to speak straight from the heart (see p. 234).

With writerly detachment, members of modern literate communities employ an inner light (see p. 164) rather than audience participation to guide their composition. Following the inner light of logic, writerly speakers cannot help but move step by step from premises to conclusion, and from situation to climax.

Speakers in other kinds of communities might weave "rhapsodies" of discourses out of the interplay of participants in a conversation. A storyteller in eastern Europe plays off the responses of listeners: "Often the smallest motion among his listeners influences the narrator and influences the shape of his narration" (Degh 1969: 113). And a Flamenco performer in Andalucia would be incapacitated if his or her audience didn't shout out their participation in the Flamenco event. However, writerly speakers tune out listeners, and construct their discourses with detached logic. Such a logic may be interpretable by anyone anywhere, but it is available only to those who first detach themselves from their listeners.

Writerly detachment allows speakers to heed an inner light and to commune with the introspected world of their consciousness. They must enter into such introspection if they are to see clearly the inner light of logic. Truly writerly talk requires speakers to be in touch with themselves, to cultivate their

180

inner life, their self-consciousness. Critical self-reflection is a writerly mandate because self-reflection is the sole guide to analysis/synthesis during writerly detachment. And just as analysis/synthesis become valued in themselves, so too self-consciousness becomes a highly valued and cultivated aspect of writerly discourse.

In every community, the notion of person is defined according to valued skills and competences, especially communicative competence. In a writerly community, the notion of person is defined in the terms of the valued analytic/synthetic skills and self-reflecting practices of lone individuals. For us, a competent person is the loner in whom units of meaning are housed and who exercises, by him/herself alone, the power to organize semantic units into sentences. The writerly person emerges as an "independent, autonomous and thus essentially non-social moral being" (Dumont 1965: 15).

Such a notion of writerly person is disturbingly consistent with the notion of a language competence, both form-competence and use-competence, possessed by essentially independent speakers. Language competence is yet another inner light which is available to essentially detached individuals as they construct talk in isolation from others. What is disturbing is the notion of an individually acquired language competence which is systematically consistent with a writerly perspective on communication. The disturbing possibility is that contemporary theories of language and communication are the children of our peculiar writerly style of communicating.

The disturbing possibility is that the writerly communicative style of the elites at the formative stages of modern culture established a way of talking which in turn established a specific content of talk about human nature. Alternative, differently styled discourses (Ginzburg 1980; Strathern 1987) have competed, and still do compete, with this vaunted writerly style. But writerly discourse together with its favored topic of language seem to have gotten a lock hold on the attentions of the elites in the modern world.

Summary and Prospect

At the beginning of this chapter we noted that ethnographers of speaking set out to counterbalance the individual-centeredness of structural linguistics. Their hope was to describe, not the context-independent language-forms that speakers know, but the context-sensitive, socially shared regularities of language-use which speakers know in concert with others in their communities.

Accordingly ethnographers of speaking describe speakers' knowledges of communicative events, speakers' knowledges of the norms for speaking, and of the appropriate sequences for speaking, including knowledges of turn-taking rules. They describe the context-sensitive knowledges which enable speakers to use and switch keys, and which constitute their common sense appreciations of language functions. And throughout such descriptions, ethnographers of speaking struggle to represent such knowledge in competence rules which individuals might be supposed to acquire.

However, these descriptions also prompt us to think further about our own speaking--even as the Boasian objectives for anthropology suggest that they should. Cross cultural descriptions of keys and norms and instrumentalities of speech make us wonder about our own traditions of speaking, about how they came to be, and about how they shape our relationships to each other.

These self-reflections tell us that the very ethnographic project which has generated our reflections falls short of its goal of describing cross cultural communicative practices unless it criticizes its own writerly perspective. At the very least linguistic anthropology must criticize and revise the central notion of a "rule of communicative competence" because that notion is so deeply implicated with a writerly concept of person.

Ethnographers of speaking set out to emphasize knowledges which hold people close to one another in a community, but their use of the structuralist notion of rule to formalize such knowledges, works against their goal. Instead of counteracting the structuralist emphasis on the detached, autonomous individual, rule-centered descriptions have only contributed to that emphasis. By adopting the format of a rule of competence, ethnographers of speaking confirm the writerly concept of the speaking subject.

PART III

TRANSLINGUISTICS

Chapter Twelve

An Introduction to Translinguistics

Mihail Bakhtin was shaping translinguistics at the same time that Franz Boas was shaping American anthropology. And the forces that drove these two pioneers were similar. Both scholars were acutely aware of the oppression and suffering that had been wrought in the name of modern progress in science and technology. They recognized that modern progress means plush living for some, but to everyone modernity brings a sense of homelessness, of groundlessness, and, specifically, a sense of the loss of community. Bakhtin and Boas both shared the view of John Donne who in 1611 wrote:

> T'is all in peeces, all cohaerance gone;
> All just supply, and all Relation:
> Prince, Subject, Father, Sonne, are things forgot,
> For every man alone thinkes he hath got
> To be a Phoenix, and that then can bee
> None of that kinde, of which he is, but hee.

Gone, Donne says, are the ties that bind people together. In modern times each person stands alone, self-generated and self-grounded, significant by reason of what is *within* rather than by what is *between.*

Driven by a thirst to reconstitute the lost coherence of social life, both Bakhtin and Boas developed utopian disciplines. Boas, anthropology; Bakhtin, translinguistics (literally, beyond linguistics). Both their disciplines aimed to portray the nature of human community and to move modern humans a step in the direction of recovering a sense of being at home in the world, and of knowing, as Chief Dan George says in the film <u>Little</u> <u>Big</u> <u>Man,</u> "where the center of the earth is."

Boas's program was, we have seen (chapter nine), an ingenious blend of scientific method, of a Romanticism that celebrates the nobility of primitive peoples, and of language-centeredness. Being language-centered, Boasian anthropologists assumed that a common language was the foundation for shared values, thoughts, and feelings. And, in his view, shared values, thoughts, and feelings are the core of human communities.

Bakhtin's program differed from Boas's on all three fronts.

183

Whereas Boas confronted the problem of modern social life as a scientist, Bakhtin did so as a theologian/philosopher/literary critic. Whereas Boas's program is shot through with backward-looking Romanticism, Bakhtin's program is forward-looking in the sense that it finds communal potential in the bustling jostling noise of modern life. And finally whereas Boas's program is language-centered, Bakhtin's is communication-centered.

Bakhtin's Theology

Bakhtin's translinguistics arises out of a tradition of Russian Orthodox theology (Clark and Holquist 1984). And, as we are about to see, this specific tradition of Russian Orthodox theology is diametrically opposed to the theological tradition that undergirds the practice of modern science. If we are to understand Bakhtin's aversion to a **science** of language and society, we must explore the contrasting theological foundations of translinguistics and of science. As these foundations contrast so too do translinguistics and the scientific language study contrast.

We have seen, in chapter eleven, that the practice of science in the seventeenth century had a great deal in common with the religious practices of the Quakers in that same century. Moreover, both the scientism and the Quakerism of that era had a great deal in common with gnosticisms that preceded and fundamentalisms that followed--the root of the word "gnosticism" is the Greek word *gnosis*, meaning knowledge. All these "isms" share a common feature: they all assume a dualist world in which God, mind, and knowledge are essentially good while world, body, and society are essentially evil.

Along with this dualism, these "isms" all assume that Christ bridged the division between God and world through his resurrection. The resurrection is nothing less than a divine intervention into the world, specifically for the purpose of elevating humanity above the level of the world and the body and above the mortality that is characteristic of the world and the body. In this view, Christ's resurrection is the central mystery of Christianity; the resurrection is God's gift to humans, a divine liberation from the threat of death.

The gnostics had a very clear sense of how this divine gift of the resurrection fitted into the scheme of human life (Pagels 1979). First, they reckoned that every human being is born with a spark of divine Light, a share in God's life which was primordially lured down into the world by the forces of evil in a time before time. The resurrection is, in effect, God's promise that if each individual cultivates that spark, then God's Light will spring into a bonfire whose power is so great as to virtually raise the individual beyond the worldly level of human mortality.

The gnostic prescription for proper cultivation of divine Light is this: first, one must flee the world, the flesh, and all that is associated therewith; and second, one must cultivate the mind through prayer, meditation, and study. Hermitages, monasteries, convents, and later, of course, universities, arose as institutions through which to pursue a gnostic salvation through the cultivation of mind, consciousness, and knowledge.

In the Renaissance we can see a resurgence of gnostic thought and practice. The counsel of the fifteenth century spiritual guide, Thomas à Kempis, summarizes the antagonistic stance of resurrectional Christianity towards worldly human relationships: "Everytime I go out into the world, I come back less a man." The great Thomas More's life is, in a sense, a study in gnosticism for he inveighed against the sham and pretense of courtly life on the one hand while he searched for a more substantial inner reality on the other. He was thus "poised between engagement and detachment," tortured by "perpetual self-estrangement" and "forever aware of (his life's) own unreality" (Greenblatt 1980: 31). Such is the gnostic way.

The Quakerism of the seventeenth century is founded on a similar resurrectional Christian principle of salvation through the cultivation of divine Light within. However, the Quakers did not flee the world by erecting artificial communities for meditation. Instead they confronted the world head on by speaking God's truth in the face of worldly, societal iniquity. Their calling was to witness to the Light within. No human relationship was to stand in the way of such witnessing. For example, since, in God's Light, all humans are equal, Quakers refused to employ conventions of politeness which implied social distinctions. They would not doff their hats to others, because such behavior failed to witness to the message of the Inner Light, a message of human equality.

Scientists, too, like Quakers, aimed to speak the truth...no matter what. From the mid-seventeenth century to the present, scientific practice has implied a flight from human relationships because human relationships are sources of bias which cloud one's clear vision of the truth. For Quakers and scientists alike, human relationships are worldly distractions from life's central task of nourishing the growth of God's Light in the mind.

The current practice of science has dispensed with the talk of God's truth and of Inner Light, though, as Carl Becker (1932) demonstrates, such talk was not far from the lips of scientists through the eighteenth century. However, the view that human relationships are distractions from proper conduct of science remains as sturdy a pillar of science today as it was in the seventeenth century. Modern science, like the theological foundation on which it rests, is thoroughly anti-social at least in its approach to data-gathering.

185

Bakhtin's kenotic Russian Orthodox Christianity starts from a Christian mystery different from all the "isms" described above. And it leads to a different understanding of the human condition and to a different perspective on human knowledge. In the simplest terms, Bakhtin's kenotic Christianity celebrates, rather than obviates, human relationships.

The central event in kenotic Christianity is not the resurrection but the incarnation, the event in which God becomes human. Kenotic, incarnational theology focuses on this event of God becoming human--the root of the word "kenotic" is the Greek word *kenosis* which means an emptying, as in Christ's emptying himself of all divinity. Kenoticism finds in that event a distinct promise of salvation: because of the incarnation, the world is sacralized; the world is transformed into a world-full-of-God. Just because of the incarnation, there is no longer a dualism of God above and world below, but only a monism of divinized materiality. In the kenotic world view, the humblest aspects of life become holy; the blackened pot becomes a sacred vessel.

The human challenge, seen from the perspective of kenotic Christianity, is not to flee the world, but to embrace it and celebrate it. The human challenge is not to avoid human relationships or to convert them, but rather to give oneself over wholly to human relationships even as God gave himself over wholly to the human.

The kenoticist's commitment to the world, however, must be a searching commitment, not by any means carefree or hedonistic. An unsearching embrace of the world may be a misplaced embrace: the Romans, according to Augustine, certainly embraced their city and all that it stood for; but, failing to search for the "city of God" within their "city of man," their celebration of the city and its tradition was inappropriate. It is for that reason, he argued, that Rome fell. In summary, the kenoticist must live in the world while searching for the divinity within it.

Kenotic, incarnational Christianity has had its moments in the limelight, but, in Europe at least, it has been overshadowed, in the course of the past 2000 years, by resurrectional Christianity. Many of the earliest Christian communities on record were decidedly kenotic in their operation, but Paul's resurrectional theology gradually came to dominate the early Christian scene. One example of that domination: early on, the Eucharistic celebration involved a communal feast, but Paul's reprimand (See 1Cor. 11: 20ff) separated out the worldly feasting from the sacred celebration.

Augustine, as suggested above, championed a subtle and carefully thought-out kenotic sociology/theology in his City of God

186

(P. Brown 1967). However, he is most often remembered either for his early Manichean, dualist views, or for his role in laying the groundwork for the consensus in Christian theology that persisted in Europe for a thousand years and which became increasingly dualistic and resurrectional as it ran its course.

Recently, Teilhard de Chardin (1959) worked out an extraordinary kenotic theory which portrayed the divine as evolving through biological and social evolutionary processes. For that theory, he was sanctioned by the Church. Today, Teilhard is most often thought of as a utopian dreamer and a gullible dupe in the Piltdown hoax.

Again, and even more recently, kenoticism has emerged in what have been called "Death of God" theologies. Harvey Cox (1965), for example, described modernization, with its homelessness, anonymity, and its commitment to science and technology, as part of the working out of the divine plan, a plan which was set into motion with the mystery of the incarnation. The jury is still out on such proposals, but if press and publicity are any indication of trends, then "Death of God" theologies are dead, and fundamentalisms of all sorts are thriving.

Russian Orthodoxy, in contrast to European Christianities, has long been kenotic and incarnational in its perspective. And, not accidentally, Bakhtin turned to that kenotic Christianity for the principles of his translinguistics. Between 1918 and 1929, during which time the bulk of Bakhtin's ideas were drafted, he was searching for the utopia which the Revolution was supposed to introduce to the world. He did not look in the direction of a resurrectional Christianity which discouraged human relationships. Instead he turned to his own Russian Orthodox kenotic tradition which celebrated human relationships and human community. Like the Rabelais he wrote about, Bakhtin reached out and wrapped his arms around the world with all its carnivalesque noise and laughter and struggle. Bakhtin's program for living is summarized in his counsel: strong drink, tireless sex, and conversations long into the night. With this counsel, Bakhtin was not advising loose living. Rather he was advancing a kenotic celebration of human relationships and all that goes with them.

The Style of Theological Discourse

The styles or interactional manners of kenotics and gnostics influenced succeeding generations far more than the contents of their theologies. The *immersion* of the kenotic sage in relationships and the *detachment* of the gnostic seer established models of behavior, prototypes of social life which were performed, invested with value, and perpetuated in the social lives of the generations of people who lived under the sway of these Christ-

187

ianities. In concrete terms, it is not so much what Augustine wrote that was significant. It was how he wrote, always collaboratively while immersed in long conversations with his friends. Similarly, it was not what Thomas à Kempis said. It was his ascetic and detached demeanor that helped to encourage the rebirth of gnostic detachment in the modern world.

Unity and Diversity

The utopian community that Bakhtin envisioned and towards which his translinguistics is directed is a world of diversity rather than a world of unity. In this regard, Bakhtin's kenotic utopia differs from the gnostic utopias that have dominated Western literature.

Since Thomas More's Utopia in 1516, Western utopian writers have sought to outline the perfect community. And always their outlines have circled around the issue of unity. One reason for this fixation on the unity of the ideal community is that religious thinking strongly influenced those utopian writers (Manuel and Manuel 1979), and, in religion, communites have almost always been reckoned in terms of shared beliefs (Bellah 1958). Hence, guided by their religious assumptions, utopian writers generally assumed that the sharing of beliefs is the first step toward the perfect community.

The problem with this view is that no real human communities anywhere show signs of consistent sharing toward perfect unity. As Haraway (1986: 82) has observed: "The tragedy of the West is rooted in number: one is too few and two are too many. To be one should mean to be unified, whole; that should be enough, yet it is lonely. But all human community involves difference. Difference is a challenge to autonomy, to wholeness. Memory, always about the origin, is about a lost oneness imagined as sameness. The telos or goal is about perfect union. The origin and the purpose, then both are about the desire to be One."

Like the early utopian writers, Boasian linguists-anthropologists have usually dreamt of harmonious communities whose members were all of one mind. However, their descriptions of social life continually turned up diversity, rather than uniformity; and as a result, Romantic utopians have always been on the defensive, trying to justify their assumption of unity in the face of their findings of diversity. Sometimes the justifications simply did not work, e.g. the field of culture and personality studies in American anthropology, a field which was closely linked to linguistic studies (Aberle 1968), foundered on the problem of diversity (A.F.C. Wallace 1961). Sometimes the justifications involved the principle, usually associated with structuralisms, that abstract unities lie beneath the surface of concrete realities, e.g. the history of sociolinguistics (chapter seven) is a history of explaining away diversity as a superficial and accidental condition which hides the sharedness and uniformity which are central to a human community.

But by far the commonest strategy used by anthropologists, has been to portray diversity and conflict as inventions of modern life. In contrast to modern communities, primitive communities were unified and coherent. To the anthropologist, the clearest form of a unified utopian community is to be found by looking backward in time. The primitive community of the past, uniform and stable, has been the flag around which utopian American anthropology has rallied.

Bakhtin was vehemently opposed to this "orientation toward unity," whether in the form of backward gazing anthropology or inward gazing structuralism. Regarding programs of language study which emphasize unity, he said that they are "in service to the great centralizing tendencies of European verbal-ideological life" (1981: 274). And he reckoned that if there were ever to have been such a unanimity it would have led nowhere but to "an endless silence of homogenizing harmony" (Ibid., p. 136). In this regard, the utopian translinguistics developed by Bakhtin differs from most Western utopian programs: translinguistics celebrates diversity rather than unity.

Bakhtin's translinguistics expects to find diversity in social life. Translinguists expect the interactions of people to be filled with struggle, conflict, and interruption (Silverman and Torode 1980). Translinguists expect that individuals will continually vy with one another for control of the interactions in which they come together. And translinguists expect all this because they consider individuals themselves to be a jumble of conflicting voices, each in competition with others for the floor within a single skin. In short, the struggle of diverse voices characterizes life within the community even as it characterizes life within the individual.

Bakhtin points to Dostoevsky for an example of the struggle of diversity within the community and within the individual. First, Dostoevsky's novels are showcases of utopian diversity where community life is a carnival of zanies bouncing off one another as if they had eluded the power of the author to hold them to the orderly behavior required for his story. Second, Dostoevsky's very method of writing attests to the diversity of voices within Dostoevsky himself. That is, Dostoevsky wrote his novels by dictating while lying on a couch as if spinning out the conflicts of his own personality to a psychotherapist. The effect of this writing is a radical shift away from an "authoritarian" voice to dispersed voices.

Just as Dostoevsky's novels suggest that individuals, like

communities, are diverse and fragmented, so Bakhtin's translinguistics implies a blessed diversity and holy fragmentation of the individual. Boldly waving aside what some scholars have considered to be the "intuitively unvanquishable" principle that persons are unities, Bakhtin sees person to be a convergence of heterogeneous communicative experiences. For Bakhtin, person is no metaphysical unity, but a memory-stored sedimentation of the diverse communicative experiences. A person is unified in the same way that a piece of slate is unified; a person is a compressed result of events that have occurred through time.

On the Unity of Person

Many of the New Age writers who took up the Boasian banner of social criticism (see p. 132) are themselves deeply invested in the gnostic view of the unity of person (Lasch 1987). The meditative, self-sounding, unity-discovering, self-actualizing practices which are so much a part of that New Age literature, spring ultimately from the gnostic principle that God is within and God is one. On the other hand, Bellah et al. (1985) offer us some popular sociology which implies a heterogeneity of the individual (see p. 204).

Communication

For Bakhtin, communication, not abstract language, is the foundation of social life. With such a focus on communication, Bakhtin's translinguistics is a logical brother to the discipline of the ethnography speaking.

According to Bakhtin, the life of a community pivots on behavior rather than on knowledge. It is the behavior of persons interacting that gives life to a group. Saussurean linguists, by abstracting linguistic knowledge from communicative behavior, and by adducing rules of grammar rather than describing the give-and-take of interaction, have given away the opportunity of tracking the most important component of community life, the impact of persons on each other through communicative behavior. Translinguists aim to correct that fault by an intense focus on behavior in interaction.

The model for Bakhtin's description of communicative behavior is the discipline of rhetoric. Rhetoric, in Roman antiquity, was a culturally pivotal discipline because through it individuals (the raw material) learned to become Roman persons (the cultural product). That is, by slavishly imitating the communicative behaviors of cultural exemplars like Cicero, the Roman individual, "not only draws encouragement and validation from the

190

moral exemplars of the past, but is actually able to make himself transparent to the values summed up in these exemplars: this is a 'person made into a classic' with a vengeance!...a system of discipline working relentlessly from the outside in" (Brown 1983: 4). Like Roman rhetoricians, translinguists expect persons to be formed from "the outside in" by way of communicative behavior.

While Bakhtin takes one chapter on social formation from the classical rhetoricians, he rejects their companion chapter on prescription. That is, the rhetoricians of antiquity sought to impose one set of rhetorical forms on a group so as to shape the group into a unity. But Bakhtin's translinguistics, far from imposing, or even expecting to find, a single set of communicative practices in a group, celebrates the diversity of behavior in interaction. For Bakhtin, the natural course of social life leads individuals to be formed "from the outside in" by the cacophanous welter of their communicative experiences. Any stifling of the noise and diversity of their communicative experience, bespeaks a dominating, stultifying political force imposing unity from above and operating against the natural life of a community.

Conclusion

Translinguistics is an alternative to structuralist linguistics and to Boasian linguistic anthropology. As a program for language research it is attractive to American anthropologists because it pursues objectives akin to the objectives of the Boasians and because it focuses on communicative practices like the ethnography of speaking, rather than on grammatical competence.

Translinguistics is founded on a kenotic Christian theology which celebrates human relationships. In this respect it contrasts with both structuralisms and Boasian linguistic anthropology which, in their adulation of scientific procedures, show themselves to be consistent with resurrectional Christian theology.

Translinguistics contrasts with Romanticism of modern language theory in its expectation that diversity rather than unity lies at the heart of all human communities. Whereas structuralists assume that grammars are shared, that is, identically distributed, translinguists assume no such sharedness. And whereas anthropological linguists cast a wistful glance backwards to the harmonious communities of noble primitives, translinguists suppose that the only unified and harmonious communities to be found amongst humans are the social monstrosities like Nazi Germany which have intentionally taken leave of the noise and disharmony that are natural to human groups.

Finally, translinguists focus on behavior rather than on knowledge or competence. In contrast to Chomsky (1977: 75), who blithely suggests that human nature is a matter of private individual mental faculties and is independent of social and historical experience, translinguists suppose that human nature arises in and through the behavior of persons in interaction.

Distinct in these three ways, the program of translinguistics is converging with currents of kindred thinking to form a truly alternative language theory. The two aims of the following chapter will be to describe translinguistic principles and methods, and to point out the convergence of translinguistics and other self-critical social theories.

Chapter Thirteen

Aspects of Translinguistics

In Bakhtin's view, the ground floor of every human community is a crawling knot of unique individuals. Not a neat knot, but a tangled web of diversity, heterogeneity, and individual differences. The knot is held together by noisy talk that spins out cultural projects. Individuals move against, and respond to each other. By repeated struggles with the assertions of others, interlocutors construct projects which hold self and community together.

Towards a more precise description of the cultural projects that emerge from the noisy talk of social life, we can say that humans both "experience" and "bespeak" projects in what they do and they frame those projects in what they say.

I will try to phrase this. "perceiving" and "bespeaking" of projects carefully so as to leave open the possibility that our experience may find projects whereas, in reality, there are none. And I will try to allow that the phrases and stories that we speak are somewhat independent of both the reality of our lives and of our experience or perception of that reality (Bruner 1986: 6).

Self and *community* are held together by cultural projects which almost always teeter between the confusions and disarray of noise and the oppression of unity. Social life is a hyperextended struggle of countervailing forces which simultaneously create and disband the experiences of self and community. The task of a translinguistic anthropology is to understand this dramatic teetering interaction of reality, experience, and expression.

This task of a translinguistic anthropology is complicated by the fact that two of its three objects of study are invisible. Expression can be heard and seen, measured, and calculated. Its uniformity and heterogeneity within a community of speakers is a matter for empirical consideration. However, (a) reality can only be approached through experience: there is no objective standpoint outside of experience from which to view reality. There is no knowledge of anyone's actual living except by way of a perception of that living. And (b) experience can only be revealed through a telling. Perceptions are, after all, invisible mental processes which are revealed only through speech. Hence the task of exploring the interaction between reality, experience, and speaking runs into the problem of the inaccessibility of both reality and experience.

Translinguists work around this problem of the inaccessibility of reality and experience by making two assumptions. First, regarding reality, they assume that it is variable and heterogeneous. And second, regarding experience, they assume

193

that it is torn by countervailing tendencies to see unity, on the one hand, and heterogeneity on the other.

Now let us turn to the relationship between inaccessible reality and experience and accessible speaking. What, we want to ask, is the relationship between speaking and reality together with our perceptions or experiences of reality? In the following section, I have tried to answer this question by contrasting the common sensical model of communication and the translinguistic model of communication.

Two Models of Communication

For most of us, the common sensical model of communication involves a sender and a receiver mediated by a message (see the model below). The *message* in this model is a linguistically structured message. That is, the message is encoded according to the grammatical competence shared by the sender and the receiver. Moreover, the content of the message is recoverable by a syntactic/semantic analysis of elements of the message. In this process, the receiver breaks the message into parts, analyzes the parts for meanings, and reassembles the parts to arrive at the meaning of the whole.

The objective of communication, according to this common sense model, is conceptual unanimity. Communicators start, supposedly, from the condition of sharing just a language code. They use their shared language code to build bridges to one another. They find common ground. They come to acquire the feelings, values, and concepts of the others with whom they talk. In the ideal end, all who engage in communication come to possess those feelings, values, and concepts identically, each in the same way as the other so that all share a uniform experience.

THE COMMON SENSE MODEL
OF COMMUNICATION

| sender dominant agent | ---> | messages | ---> | receiver subordinate patient |

194

In this model, senders convey messages so as to enlighten receivers with the information and conceptualizations that they, the senders, already have. The hope is that when the communication is completed, both senders and receivers will share the same enlightenment.

As they set out to achieve this utopian goal of unanimity, communicators find that, before they can share their enlightenment with others, they must first identify it for themselves. Hence they enter into the give-and-take of talk in order to clarify for themselves what it is that they know. This clarification process takes up the lion's share of communicators' time and energy in everyday life. But ideally, these self-clarifications are only appetizers compared to the real meat of communication which is the process of enlightening others toward unanimity.

The goal of conceptual unanimity is clearly evident in our religious and political oratory as well as in the mass-communicated advertisements of our hawkers of merchandise. Our most serious communications aim towards the creation of unanimity between sender and receiver. Certainly the discourse which you, the reader, are presently participating in is oriented toward this goal of unanimity.

Confession

Though I have tried to write this book in a style other than that modeled above, no one can speak or write in a manner too very far removed from that dictated by past experiences sedimented in memory. My efforts here are subject to the condition so clearly described by Augustine fifteen hundred years ago, that individuals are constituted "by the sum total of unique past experiences" (Brown 1967: 170).

With unanimity as a goal, receivers struggle to reconstitute in their minds the minds of the senders, and they do so by analyzing communicated messages. When the process of communication is completed and interpretation ceases, the minds of the receivers are supposed to replicate the minds of the senders. And then there is silence.

Bakhtin would have wanted us to recognize the resurrectional-gnostic-scientific spirit of this model of communication. As a model, it is mind-centered and hell-bent on unification. Its goal of unanimity is a flight away from the messiness of worldly heterogeneity and into the purity of mental consensus. According to this common sense model, discord is the "before" in a "before-

and-after" picture of social life. Disagreement is a social illness to be remedied. In such a view, the communications of all persons follow the ideal communication of the monastery, the convent, the university, and of all the other similarly oriented utopian communities which have aimed at achieving a blissful silence through communication toward like-mindedness. Such is the communication of Woody Allen's Leonard Zelig who found sweet security in identifying completely with whomever he was talking.

Bakhtin's translinguistics suggests quite a different model of communication (below). Notice that this model involves multiple senders and receivers rather than one of each. In Bakhtin's view no word belongs to one person only, but rather every word arises from amidst the experiences of multiple individuals: "Language lies in the borderline between oneself and the others. The word in language is half someone else's. Language is not a neutral medium that passes freely and easily into the private property of the speaker's intentions. It is populated--overpopulated--with the intentions of others" (Bakhtin 1981: 294).

THE TRANSLINGUISTIC MODEL
OF COMMUNICATION

senders   <-->   messages   <-->   receivers

Bakhtin's thought here about words always being "half someone else's" is shared by peoples like the Kaluli and the Samoans, for whom ideal communication always involves multiple participants. For them, as for Bakhtin, the situation of a single speaker and a single listener is an aberration, a parasite situation that relies on the more nearly ideal situation of multiple speakers and listeners (Ochs and Schieffelin 1984).

The *message*, according to the model above, is a symbolic action that senders perpetrate on receivers. Being actions, messages operate as wholes. Their value cannot be appreciated when they are broken into parts by an analyst and later reassembled.

196

Messages even though they be multi-voiced and heteroglot, are whole actions that are to be perceived and responded to as wholes. They are like the jabs of a boxer, constituted, it might seem, of parts, e.g. an eye flinch, a leg movement, an arm extension, and a wrist snap. But they operate as wholes, which is apparent when they land on their targets. The boxer responds with ducks and feints to whole actions rather than to parts; and if he does not, he is stung. Similarly, words advance on receivers and, as whole actions, invite responses from them.

Finally, the goal of communication is not unanimity but the conjoint labor of action-response. And each such action-response aims to promote further actions-responses in the future. Actions-responses are good in themselves. Interaction is "the trial of itself and needs no other touch" (from Ben Jonson with apologies). Any expression which threatens to put an end to the chain of acting-responding is inappropriate. Any action or response which promises to maintain or intensify the conjoint action of communication is appropriate and desirable.

The value of communication for itself, talk for talk's sake, suggests that conflict is more than just a tolerable aspect of communicative life. Conflict here is exceedingly valuable. Conflict stimulates communication whereas agreement quells it. Struggling talk breeds more talk whereas harmony breeds silence and sleep. In Bakhtin's view, good conversation is, and should be, a struggle: "The importance of struggling with another's discourse, its influence in the history of an individual's coming to ideological consciousness, is enormous" (Bakhtin 1981: 348).

The struggle of words is especially important because that struggle gives birth to experiences, i.e. the perceptions of self and community:

> The word "is not so much interpreted by us as it is further, that is, freely, developed, applied to new material, new conditions; it enters into inter-animating relationships with new contexts. More than that, it enters into an intense interaction, a struggle with other *internally* persuasive discourse. *Our ideological development is just such an intense struggle within us for hegemony among various available verbal and ideological points of view, approaches, directions and values*" (Ibid., p. 346, emphases added).

For Bakhtin, noisy struggle, not harmonious silence, is both a factual and an ideal condition of speaking. The translinguist's task is to appreciate how that noisy struggle is managed, on the one hand, and how it contributes to cultural projects on the other. A first step towards that appreciation is to consider the social nature of all instances of speaking and expression. That social nature of speaking will become apparent in the following descriptions of the (i) collaborative, (ii) context-sensitive, and (iii) bivalent nature of speaking.

(i) **Collaborative Speaking** Communicative action is always collaborative, negotiated action (Pearce and Cronen 1980). Speakers may think they are acting as independent agents, but not so. The ubiquitous synchronization of the movements of inter-actants is evidence that they are all involved in a conjointly orchestrated action. The facial expressions, body positions, gestures, and rhythms of talk of persons in conversation move together as if those persons were Astaire and Rogers on the ballroom floor. X shifts position at the same time that Y begins a gesture. X raises his eyebrows at the same time that Y turns his head. Sarles (1978) argues that this synchronization of communicative action is so regular and so powerful that if peo-ple, e.g. husbands and wives, spend enough time talking to each other, their synchronized movements will realign their facial musculature, and they will begin to look like each other!

Conversationalists are hardly ever aware of the coordination of their behaviors. And being unaware, they enter into their synchronized "dance" with a grace and ease that belie the com-plexity of what they are doing. Such grace is made possible, in part, by unconscious acts of metacommunication. Astaire and Rogers dance as if they were one body, but they can do so only because their eyes, hands, and body postures are cueing each next step. No one can dance a step without knowing a "lead," and similarly no one can converse without using metacommunicative cues.

A metacommunicative cue might be a type of smile. Kendon (1981), for example, found that a "closed lip smile" was a criti-cal cue for the couple whom he filmed as they sat kissing on a park bench. The young man advanced, retreated, and advanced again, but he only kissed the woman when she met his advance with that particular smile.

A metacommunicative cue might, strange though it seems, be silence. Rosenburg (1981) observed that, during the recorded conversation between a husband and a wife (on the next page), a series of head nods (at twenty-six seconds into the bout) and a silence of twenty seconds--all of which follow an interchange in which the husband made a pun and the wife ignored it--, cue the talk that follows. With his silence, the husband is, in effect, saying, "We are not communicating." The wife, trapped by this tacit meta-communicative cue, goes through a variety of non-talking maneuvers to elicit some sign from her husband that talking can be resumed. Reading the newspaper, she slaps her head; she laughs aloud; she exclaims, "God!;" and finally, she reads aloud, though not to her husband. A full ten seconds after these maneuvers, the husband responds with a barely audible grunt which indicates that talk can be resumed, which it does.

W: I got a hot apple turnover today and it was ghastly. I mean it was hot, but that's all you could say for it--just awful.
H: Did it turn over? (pause) I mean did it turn over in your stomach afterwards?
W: No, it wasn't that bad. It was just mushy.
H: (mumbles)
W: They have this microwave oven. It's really great. They make hot sandwiches and they stick, I mean they make the sandwich and stick it in for about two seconds and it goes bing and it's done and the cheese is melted and it's hot and it's good.
H: Mm hm.
W: But it sure didn't do anything for the turnovers. I guess you have to have something to start with. (twenty seconds of silence)
W: (laugh) God! (laugh)
H: Mm.
W: "What would happen if there were no rules? Please be specific." (laugh) Oh well.
H: Mm.
W: (whistle) Oh.
H: Mm.
W: Dick, what is it? What kind of metal?

The husband, in this conversation, like Astaire on the dance floor, leads. He calls the shots. However, in most conversations, "calling the shots" is a reciprocal activity. "One party takes action in account of what another party has just done, and then in the next moment, another party takes action in account of what was done the moment before" (Erickson and Shulz 1982: 71f). Thus conversational partners are usually *interdependent*. Moreover, the "leading" and cueing that they do, is not usually a matter of turns at the helm but rather a "mutual entrainment of all conversational partners within an overall pattern of rhythm" (Ibid.). It is as if partners were laboring together at establishing a synchronous rhythm that neither controls completely. That synchronous rhythm does not arise from what any one partner plans or intends or indicates. Rather it is usually "an emergent phenomenon, explicitly specifiable only in retrospect" (Dore and McDermott 1982: 374).

Talkers might think of themselves as independent agents in cooperation with other independent agents, but the reality is that they are interdependent. The only truly independent talkers are schizophrenic persons whose completely independent and ultimately private behavior is recognizable as "crazy talk" (Rochester and Martin 1979).

199

If persons in conversation are typically engaged in a conjoint action, then it stands to reason that actors, on their own, do not really know what a conversational action is accomplishing as it proceeds. Conversations are emergent phenomena; they are actions that are beyond the knowledge or control of solo actors. Talkers do not know what has really happened in a spate of talk, until it is completed. As Goffman (1974: 2) says, they "must wait until things are almost over before discovering what has been occurring."

Until they make that post-hoc discovery of "what has been occurring," talkers must operate from moment to moment with trust in the capabilities of a partner to co-accomplish the act of talking. Such trust is apparent in the willingness of talkers to find contextual relevance in even the most nonsensical utterances by a partner (Garfinkel 1967).

The collaboration described above is natural to humans. It is a central aspect of interaction. People fall into dialogue-like collaboration effortlessly and from the first moments of life. Newborns move in collaborative synchrony with adult speakers as if their movements were muscular reflexes. And in the seemingly simple act of breastfeeding, sophisticated collaborative negotiations take place between mother and infant (Kaye 1982). The infant pauses in its sucking; the mother tries to jiggle it back into feeding. But it takes a jiggle of a certain duration, neither too lengthy, nor too brief, to accomplish this effect. So the infant teaches the mother the appropriate duration for her jiggling and, at the same time, the mother teaches the infant to empty her breast. Thus breastfeeding is a sophisticated give-and-take activity which infants enter into collaboration as naturally as ducks take to water.

In such collaborations, caregivers coach children into interaction just as master swimmers coach their young apprentices. The swimming masters put their hands on their apprentices, simultaneously protecting them and molding their behaviors while they flop around in the water. The apprentices play off of the protective arms of the masters and, in time, form routines of action that lead, first to floating, and then to swimming. They cling to the masters when necessary, but, in time, they let the masters know that they can back off a bit. So it happens that the skills of apprentice swimmers are forged in and through interactions with their masters.

In just the same way, the habituated skill of interacting and speaking takes place during collaborative interactions between caregivers and children. We North Americans introduce our children to collaborative interaction by talking for them (see chapter eight). In conversations, caregivers play both their own roles and those of the infants, speaking words that are appropriate for infants, and often in the tones of infants.

200

The Kaluli of Highland New Guinea make use of a similar tactic for introducing their children to conversation (Ochs and Schieffelin 1984). Kaluli caregivers, like American parents, start out by speaking for their children in interaction. Most often a mother will hold the infant facing another infant, rather than facing herself. And the two infants will be spoken for and moved about like dummies by ventriloquists. In this way, Kaluli mothers speak for their infants while infants are interacting with other infants.

Once a Kaluli child acquires some facility with speaking, the parents begin shaping the child's speech towards adult models. As the Kaluli see it, the child must gain command of proper forms of speech; it is less important that a child understand the meaning of those forms. The mother inculcates proper speech forms by commanding the child to speak words that the mother provides. When the mother speaks and adds to her words the phrase *elema*, which commands a repetition of what has been spoken, the child reproduces, the mother's words exactly. In this way, Kaluli children learn routines for interaction by doing interaction under the guidance of their caregivers. Such a learning exhibits the collaborative nature of the acquisition and use of communicative expressions in a way that our own meaning-centered learning does not.

(ii) **Context-Sensitive Speaking** Communicative collaborations are habitual, but they are not blind habits. They are sensitive to surroundings and intimately connected to experience. Pointed fingers and demonstrative pronouns are obvious indications of such context-sensitivity, but they barely begin to reveal the intricate ties of talk to context.

Writerly peoples tend to overlook the indexicality and contextuality of talk. One reason for this oversight--an interesting but not necessarily a complete reason--is that their attentions are focussed so intensely on their partners in communication rather than on the situation surrounding the communication. Writerly communication is carried off as if speakers, listeners and their messages were the sole significant aspects of the act. When accomplished orally, rather than in script, writerly communication is carried off in a face to face fashion as if two souls were locked together for an exchange. The communicators labor to maintain this facade of direct exchange by attending only to each other, locking into an eyeball-to-eyeball orientation. This orientation leads them to expect that all that is communicatively significant passes back and forth between speakers and listeners as if traveling on a conduit that transmits messages from mind to mind (Reddy 1979). Such an eyeball-to-eyeball orientation inclines writerly peoples to ignore the communicative importance of the situation and the circumstances of their speaking.

Non-writerly peoples are often more keenly aware of the communicative importance of the situation and circumstances of speaking. Perhaps their oblique bodily orientations facilitate such an awareness. Oblique bodily orientations include an L-shaped orientation in which straight ahead gaze scans the surroundings while peripheral gaze maintains contact between communicators. Even more radical is the oblique orientation said to have been preferred by the Bororo (Argyle and Cook 1976) in which participants are shoulder to shoulder gazing outward. Such oblique orientations incline communicators to connect their speakings with their situations, and to recognize links between what is happening in their worlds and what is being said in their words.

All talk is sensitive to context. Writerly peoples simply downplay that sensitivity. And what this means is that all our talk is related to our experiences of reality. As Goffman (1981b) shows, a finger pointed at a parked car is really indicating an experience of the car, not the car itself. The finger may point to the car *as* left on the street for a long time, in which case the pointed finger might well be combined with the utterance, "Well, they didn't steal it." Or, the pointer may indicate the absent owner of the car in which case it may be combined with, "He'll get a ticketed." Or the finger may point to the car *as* an example of a new model, in which case it could be paired with, "That's the new one." The lesson in this example is that all talk is relevant to a constructed, experienced context rather than to a simple physical context.

(iii) **Bivalent Speaking** Objectively seen, human social and expressive realities form a heterogeneous, fractious, crawling knot. Any coherence and coordination in human social life must be collaboratively constructed in subjects' experiences of those realities. The objective everpresent fractiousness of social life is a continual threat to the experience of coherence.

Communicative life is a face-off of forces of diversification, **centrifugal forces**, and forces of unification, **centripetal forces**. Centripetal forces tend to create coherence by transforming the heterogeneous realities, perceptions, expressions of social life into unities. Centrifugal "keep things various, separate, apart, different from each other" (Clark and Holquist 1984: 7). No interaction is ever free of the clash of the centrifugal and the centripetal. Every interaction is shot through with a struggle for unity against diversity.

Bakhtin exemplified the operation of centripetal forces with the history of attempts at classifying literary works into genres. The Greeks, for example, tried to contain literature with the genre labels like lyric, tragedy, and epic. Each genre was supposed to include its own canons of style. But, according

202

to Bakhtin, literature spilled over these categories with a welter of voices that washed away the clarity of the genre distinctions.

The rise of the novel testifies to the great centrifugal force of multiple and noisy voices. The novel was an anti-genre, so to speak. It defied all the canons of the classical literary genres. The continually shifting forms and styles of the novel made it impossible to cling any longer to the fiction of fixed literary genres. With no fixed rules of form, the novel is, in effect, a subversion of the canons of literature.

Not that different eras have not tried to impose canons of form on the novel. They have, and the history of the novel is a history of just such attempts. But each attempt at codification is met with a yet more subversive version of the rule-rocking novel, Dostoevsky's novel being the paragon of such subversiveness.

All of Bakhtin's work implies this struggle of the centripetal and the centrifugal. But his work on the history of the novel, and particularly on Dostoevsky, reveals as eloquently as any the value he placed on the centrifugal with all its noise and conflict.

Dostoevsky's characters are drawn with individuating characteristics and with unique styles of speaking. Those individuating and distinctive speech styles seem to hide the fact that one individual, Dostoevsky himself, created all the characters and all their discourses. It is these unique speech styles of characters that led Bakhtin to label Dostoevsky's novel "polyphonic" and to argue that, with this "polyphony" Dostoevsky's novels constitute a major advance of centrifugal forces over centripetal forces in literature. In art as in life, "cacophanous difference is what he (Bakhtin) valued most" (Clark and Holquist 1984: 136).

For Bakhtin, both forces, the centrifugal and the centripetal, are natural and inevitable and their clash is inescapable. But, given the dangers of oppression which are inherent in stressing the centripetal, Bakhtin embraced and celebrated the centrifugal.

Storytelling

Storytelling is the name used here to label the operation of the three aspects of speaking, i.e. collaboration, context-sensitivity, and bivalence, in the creation of cultural projects. As a label, storytelling has the advantage of bringing to mind familiar narrative practices. However, storytelling, as used here, is not restricted to narrative discourse. In the course of the following discussion, storytelling will be used to label the conferral and use of names, the use of pronouns, the use of politeness behaviors, the collaborative action of ritual dialogue, language borrowings, the use of verbal abuse and finally the use of various strategies of resistance through words.

Obviously, storytelling is not a single kind or type of speech act. Rather it is an aspect of speaking that operates in and through all speech acts to create projects that enable people to hold themselves together.

To say that speakings involve cultural projects is only to say that speakers are headed somewhere with their talk, that they are about something, that they are acting with a purpose and are pursuing an adventure of some sort. A most basic aspect of social life, says Hauerwas (1977: 13), is "a sense of participation in an adventure." Individuals need not be conscious of their purposes or of their adventures. Indeed, most often they cannot be. Cultural projects are usually unconscious (Giddens 1984: 117).

Besides being unconscious, cultural projects are rooted in the past. And they are rooted in the past despite their orientation toward the future. Wollheim (1984: 131) says that "we live under the influence of the past...the past influences our lives through obtruding itself into the present." And according to Bellah and his colleagues (1985: 153), "In order not to forget the past, a community is involved in retelling its story, its constitutive narrative, and in so doing, it offers examples of the men and women who have embodied and exemplified the meaning (or project) of the community. These stories of collective history and exemplary individuals are an important part of the tradition that is so central to a community of memory." In other words, the memory of the past sneaks into present stories, and once there, that memory give coherence to the lives that stretch forward into the future.

Storytelling in Social Theory

The label storytelling has the advantage of linking the hypothesis that discourses create unified experiences among speakers with the already abundant literature on the social function of narrative discourse. Claims that the world is "story-shaped" and "story-formed" have been advanced by students of myth (Campbell 1959: 467), of folktakes (Bettelheim 1975: 5), religion (Hauerwas 1977), of literature (Wicker 1975), of psychology (Gergen and Gergen 1983), and of history (White 1980).

Storytelling is a human universal, a necessary component of human communicative behavior. A clear and helpful illustration of the essential role played by storytelling is to be found in the novel <u>Watership Down</u> by Richard Adams (1972).

<u>Watership Down</u> suggests that humans, like the rabbits of Watership Down, maintain continuity through time together with a responsiveness to change by continually telling stories that tie the present to the past. More than just enjoying stories, the rabbits of Watership Down itch for stories that reframe for them their experiences (Ibid, p. 99). Such stories renew their courage, and enable them to interpret their misfortunes and to celebrate their successes. Stories that are up-to-date and relevant to current experiences prevent them from lapsing into the dangerous stupor of the rabbits of Cowslip's warren (Ibid., chp. 16), who, though well-adjusted in appearance, are, because of their inadequate stories, dangerously out of touch with one another.

From the rabbits of Watership Down we learn that storytelling is collaborative action through which persons construct for each other the world in which they live. In short, storytelling is their central cultural action; it is their process of building reality.

Storytelling performs this integrating task in real life just as it does in <u>Watership Down</u>. Witness, for example, the storytelling of the nineteenth century Bedouins of North Arabia (Meeker 1979) who, with very little social structure, hold themselves together by their tales of raiding and camel stealing. And in the same vein, the potentially divisive behaviors of Cretan sheep thieves (Herzfeld 1985) are woven into social bonds by their storytelling. Evenings find Bedouin camel thieves and Cretan sheep thieves gathering together to exchange tales of derring-do. Such storytelling has the affect of reaffirming for each the importance of their "life together."

Storytelling gives shape to the routines of life. It also establishes the reality of persons and communities. As Drummond tells us in his study of Arawak myth (1981), the action of celebrating the myth of Arawak origins actually creates the distinction between the Arawak and the Carib. It renders the Arawak people real.

Storytelling, it must be emphasized, is itself a collaborative action. Stories are negotiated in the telling. To understand this negotiated character of storytelling, one might examine the description by Ochs (1973) of the negotiations of ritual speechmaking among the Malagasy speakers of Madagascar. Malagasy speeches are negotiated in the telling. They are not shared in advance and just retold on ritual occasion. People debate and argue over what, when, where, and how to perform their

205

ritual speakings. In the end, speeches proceed only because participants in ritual events allow them to.

Storytelling, in general is a negotiated activity. That fact is important, but it is potentially confusing. The confusion is encountered in reflecting on the fact that stories, though negotiated, are the primary means of integrating negotiated routines. Stories give form and coherence to negotiated activity. But if the stories themselves are negotiated, what gives form and coherence to the enforming stories? The answer is stories, which invite more stories, which invite more stories. And it is stories all the way down. Cultural life is a profusion of stories on stories. And while the stories do form a system, it is a system that has no apparent beginning or first cause. Cultural life is a system of mutually constructive stories.

A Communicative Theory of Culture

The consistent emphasis on communication as collaborative practice--rather than as "language" use--leads to a definite and distinctive theory of culture. That theory of culture is being outlined in this present discussion of the formation of community through storytelling.

No storytelling in any cultural system escapes the condition of being negotiated. There is no detached autonomous position from which to tell an unnegotiated story. True, a people might argue for such a position. For example, in a Christian era, believers regard the Bible as the supreme story. Scientists too struggle to make their descriptions into ultimate truth-tellings. But all claims for a coign of vantage for storytelling are themselves negotiated claims. There is no story about which a story cannot be told.

Having described the coherence-creating function of stories, we are now in a position to explore the diversity of stories and their operations. Cultural stories come in a variety of shapes and sizes. They do not all conform to a "Once upon a time...happily ever after" format. Some stories are narratives that describe a situation from crisis to resolution. Other stories have a non-narrative form, e.g. a name is a story of sorts. All stories, however, can be put to the service of creating experiences of coherence.

Reservations about "Storytelling"

"Storytelling" is perhaps an unfortunate term because it conjures up images of the telling of fictional narratives However, it is a helpful term insofar as it implies a display of some sort.   All storytellings are collaborative, emotionally enthralling, cognitively satisfying displays.

The untidy house of cultural storytelling can be provisionally ordered by distinguishing the storytelling that pertains to the creation of experiences of coherent persons from that which pertains to the creation of experiences of coherent groups.

Storytelling and Person Formation   A preliminary assumption in this theory of storytelling is that folks do not just walk into experiences of themselves as coherent persons.   They have to work at creating those experiences.   And they work at creating such experiences by storytelling.

Without storytelling, an individual is a bundle of actions, awareness, and remembered events.   As such, individuals are capable of behaving and of being conscious of their behaving.   But, they are not able to experience themselves as coherent persons participating in a cultural project that extends over a period of time.   Storytelling, however, creates extended historical projects and inserts individuals into them and in that way creates experiences of temporally continuous persons.

Names are stories which create persons by conferring a trans-temporal continuity on actions and a coherence to self-awareness.   Names do this by giving an individual a linguistic dimension of existence so that when the name is uttered in the context of a story, the individual himself or herself become part of the project implied in the story. Wilshire says that "A name is in some way an equivalent of the person: it carries his presence far and wide through the world of persons...The name is not merely a sign related contingently to the person--so that we can easily imagine it to be changed and the person to remain the same--but rather is integral to that presence of the person to the world and to himself which is integral to who he is.   He *becomes* the named being" (1982:62).

Names create experiences of personal coherence in two ways. First, names are "rigid designators" of essences (Kripke 1972); the conferral of a name is an historical act which *fixes* the essence of a person (Bean 1980).   That is, a name declares and authenticates the *being* of the person independently of the superficial characteristics of the person.   In short, a personal name

207

establishes the inner self of a person. Secondly, names serve the function of associating the named individual with things, events, or other people in the world. Names thereby install named persons in history, and give them a place in the scheme of things.

In some societies people play. up the essence-fixing function of names; and in other societies they play up the associative function of names. Thus experiences of personal unity are created in different ways in different societies.

The Balinese are a people who mute the essence-fixing function of names while playing up the associative function. Balinese personal names are little known and seldom used, a sign, says Geertz (1973: 369), that "the more idiosyncratic merely biographical and consequently transient aspects of (an individual's) existence" are muted and downplayed. More frequently used are the birth order names, the kinship terms, and the technonyms which give individuals roles to play in the staging of the theatre-like life of the Balinese.

Similarly, the New Caledonians (Canaques) described by Leenhardt (1979: 155), the Tanimbarese described by Howes (1980: 26), and the Dobu described by Fortune (1932) are peoples whose naming practices mute the essence-fixing function while playing up the associative function of names. For all these people, names serve to relate people to others. When their relationships, or the circumstances surrounding their relationships, change, their names are also changed. For the Tanimbarese, "A youth will call upon his namesake to sit upon the tips of his arrows to ensure a good hunt. If the namesake is unhelpful in this respect, then another is found. This involves yet another change in name. The importance of this slippage from one name to another is that each denotes a different orientation in relation to the universe. From the condition of illness one passes to health. Each name signifies a different appearance" (Howes op.cit.).

Modern Americans play up the essence-fixing function, but mute the associative function of personal names. In America, a unique name authenticates a person's uniquely real status as a person. In earlier eras, a name had to be associated with an ancestor or a saint, but in modern times, even these associations have gone by the boards. A unique name is *de rigeur*; hence Rip Torn, Coke Izit, Mr. T, all are names which go to great lengths to tell the story of unique persons. "Every man alone thinkes he hath got to be a Phoenix."

Most societies fall somewhere between the extremes of the Balinese and modern Americans. For example, Bororo names both create persons and associate them with others (Crocker 1985). The Bororo child is not considered real until it is named in a ceremony some eight months after it is born. Until that time, no one speaks publicly of the infant; the birth is ignored by most village members. But with the naming, the Bororo family celebrates openly: their name giving has brought about the indwelling of a soul (*aroe*) in the Bororo child, and, as a result, they have, for the first time, a new person in their midst. However, unlike American names, Bororo names define a individual partly by establishing associations with others. Membership in a kinship group, for the Bororo, is not a matter of blood ties, but of name ties. "Name-giving defines all collective and individual identities."

Besides names, metaphorical talk also serves to create experiences of personal coherence (Lakoff and Johnson 1980). Specifically, the metaphorical talk, which is used in any society to discuss abstract realities like language, knowledge, and power--quintessential aspects of personhood--, creates experiences of the coherence of persons in that society. We modern Americans talk about language as if it were a message-transmitting conduit (Reddy 1979) and we talk about knowledge as if it were a landscape which knowers oversee (Salmond 1982). And both of these metaphors reinforce our culturally distinct sense of persons as unique and independent beings. In other societies, different metaphors are used in talk about language, knowledge, and power (Strathern 1985) with and different impact on the persons who do the talking.

Naming and metaphorical talk are short stories that people tell themselves with the effect of constituting themselves as coherent persons. Pronouns are even shorter stories that operate in a similar fashion.

Pronouns may seem to be simple indices. Operating like pointed fingers, they direct the listener's attention to the world in which discourse occurs. But, far from being simple in their operation, pronouns presuppose the existence of significant realities in that world. In the case of personal pronouns, the significant realities that are presupposed are persons.

Pronouns accomplish this complex presupposition dialogically. "The speaker's *I* becomes the listener's *you*," says Crapanzano (1979), "and the dialogue of *I* and *you* thus presupposes at once the consciousness of the *I* and the objectivity of the *you*. Thus, persons, as presupposed by pronouns, are compounds of interiority and exteriority, of consciousness and action.

Pronouns do not create personal coherence once for all, but rather they enter into a process of negotiating persons, a process which re-occurs in every interaction. Consider the following bit of talk as a re-negotiation of the persons of the teacher-speaker and of the students-listeners: "I know you've just had swimming, and it's not very nice to come back to the classroom, but the sooner you get used to it the better" (Silverman and Torode 1980: 29). In this utterance, the *I*, the subject of the independent clause, syntactically dominates both the *you* of the students and the *it* of their desires. "In this case...the grammatical structure of the sentence, i.e. its breakdown into specific kinds of clauses linked by specific linguistic relations, achieves its ideological effects" of subordinating one person to another" (Ibid.).

A pronoun-as-story creates, by way of its links to other pronouns, a world of pronominal relations. When that world of pronominal relations is uttered, it creates a well-defined experience of personal coherence for the pronominal referents. Thus, a pronoun is a person-creating story.

Storytelling and Group Formation   Cultures include in their work self-presentations to their members. On certain collective occasions, cultures offer interpretations. They tell stories, comment, portray, and mirror...Since these constructions are intentionally designed, they are not only reflections of "what is"; they are also opportunities to write history as it should be or should have been, demonstrating a culture's notion of propriety and sense...The central challenge to such performances is that of conviction. They must play well and persuade players and audiences that what is seen is what is...When such performances are successful, we receive experience rather than belief...The performed order is explicit, realized, and we are *within* it" (Myerhoff 1982: 103-105).

Myerhoff's theses statements present the case clearly and economically: stories create experiences of coherent groups. Goffman's investigations of impression management (1957) and face work (1967) shed some light on some features of this coherence-creating process.

Individuals, according to Goffman, are players in the game of social life. They are charged with the double responsibility of playing like winners, but also of playing in such a way as not to jeopardize the images of others as winners. This is a tricky task because selves-players are liable to a double jeopardy. One the one hand, they may destroy the images of themselves or others as competent players in the game of life. On the other hand, they may fail to move themselves forward in the practical business of living. A play that is too timid, too careful, and too reflective may move a player nowhere. But a play that is too brash and unreflective may damage the face of oneself or another.

One plays at social life by manipulating the images (Goffman calls them "faces") of oneself and of others. Storytelling enters into this picture in the form of gambits which players perpetrate

210

on others in order to manipulate faces. Players produce gambits in order to respond to threats to face. These gambits serve, in effect, as needle and thread to repair the rends in the fabric of their experience.

Threats to face may arise from the physical context of living, from the social context of interacting, or from within expressions used in interaction.

The physical and biological conditions of living often present us with face-threatening anomalies. Frequently, such threats are handled with brief face-managing stories called "response cries." When someone misses an easy shot on the tennis court or trips over a small crack in the sidewalk, he or she usually utters an expletive of some sort. The effect of such a brief "response cry" is to proclaim that his or her *real* self, and not the flawed self of a moment ago knows better than to miss such a shot or to trip while walking. Response cries verbally reassure others that the speaker is a competent person who deserves the trust that is necessary for social life.

Besides the threats that arise from the physical context of living, face-threatening anomalies can arise in the social context of interaction, as for example, when a request is made by one individual to another of different social standing. In such a case, the requestor must deal with the social difference between self and other as he or she requests some potentially burdensome favor. Politeness expressions are maneuvers or gambits which soften threats to face in such cases.

A request can threaten a person's desire to have his or her actions be unimpeded by others, "negative face." A request can also threaten a persons's wish that he or she be desirable and pleasing to others, "positive face."

Negative politeness behaviors are gambits used by the person making the request, gambits aimed at compensating for threats to negative face. These gambits pamper the negative face of the person being requested by apologizing for the interruption, by complimenting the other, by demeaning self, etc. "Sorry ...if it's not too much bother...I know this may seem silly but..." Positive politeness behaviors coddle the positive face of the person being requested by emphasizing his/her solidarity with the requestor, "Say ol' buddy, how about...." (Brown and Levinson 1987).

Politically ascendant peoples, like North Americans, typically make greater use of negative politeness behaviors. Politically subordinate peoples generally make use of relatively more positive politeness behaviors. These associations suggest that politeness behaviors are more than just psychologically significant face-saving stories. They are gambits which reflect and

211

confirm experiences of the social lives of a people. Politeness expressions confer coherence on the familiar, strange, dominant, or subordinate relationships of everyday life.

Politeness expressions confirm the reality of social life. They are not "optional, arbitrary, merely decorative embellishments as we in Western societies are inclined to" think (Myerhoff op. cit.). The use of politeness expressions to manage faces makes relationships real in our experience. As Bateson argues that "the relationship *is* the exchange of messages; the relationship is immanent in messages" (1972: 275). In the case of politeness expressions which create experiences of group coherence the group is the exchange of such messages. Let me say it again with emphasis: The group *is* the exchange of messages.

Politeness behaviors, like all other events of storytellings, bring a community into being by *doing* community in speaking at the same time that they *are about* community. Politeness behaviors actually do the work of bringing people into a specific relationships with one another at the same time that they comment on those relationships.

People create community by *doing* community in their speaking. When peoples, like the Yanomamo as seen in the film <u>The Feast</u>, engage in litany-like ritual dialogues, they are actually doing community. They are staging a long-winded face-pampering gambits of coherence that accomplish social relationships. The participants in such dialogues express wishes, desires, plans, deeds, etc., but as they advance those topics, they also accomplish a bringing together of persons for collaborative action. In such ritual dialogues, it is often the individuals who disagree with one another who labor together to carry off the singsong ritual. There, in that moment, the antagonists are working towards collaboration by collaborating; they are working towards community by doing community (Urban 1986).

Story-told relationships are, even when they respond to external threats, rarely simple, consistent, and homogeneous. More often, they are, as Bakhtin suggests, as "heteroglot" as is the reality of social life. Hence, we should not be surprised to find that face-threatening anomalies sometimes arise from *within* the very stories that people tell to resolve face-threatening anomalies.

Consider, for example, the utterance of a Mexicano (Nahuatl) woman recorded by Hill and Hill (1986: 387): "It is said of the Malinche there, that she has those *earrings*, and those, those those *necklaces*. We say, "icolalex in Malintzin ['the Malinche's necklaces']. She has them, beautiful, she shines, the Malinche there. Beautiful, she is guarding them, those, *her necklaces*, and those *her earrings* that are beautiful." (The utterance was originally spoken in Mexicano except for the italicized words which were spoken in Spanish.) Here the Spanish borrowings are themselves anomalies that threaten the integrity of the image of the Mexicano speaker. The speaker confronts and comments on those Spanish borrowings, which leads the Hills to suggest that the speaker here is using "double-voiced words, uttered with what he (Bakhtin) would call a 'side-long glance' at the Spanish possibility. The entire passage becomes not a simple description of the beautiful spirit of the Malinche, but a translinguistic battlefield upon which two ways of speaking struggle for dominance. This capacity for words to 'emerge' from one category into a new level is, for Bakhtin, a pivotal problem for translinguistics" (Ibid., p. 392).

We can find a similar struggle in anecdotes collected in West Texas (Bauman 1986). These tales may seem to be simple, and homogeneous, but their surface simplicity belies the wrestling that is taking place between the lines. Take, for example, the story of Mr. Trimble and Mr. Means, both elderly and notoriously inept drivers. Mr. Trimble crashes into Mr. Means's car one day when both were in town. Mr. Means apologizes for the accident. Mr. Trimble tries to exhonerate Mr. Means by confessing that the accident was in fact his fault. Mr. Means says, "No, it wasn't your fault, it was my fault. When I knew you was in town, I should have left."

This story is a curious one in that it both reinforces the moral order of the community, with respect to competent driving, and simultaneously subverts it. The body of the tale supports the moral order. But the wry twist in the punch line subverts it by "refusing to take the ideal, normative moral expectations too seriously" (Bauman 1986: 75). In this way the story both supports and undercuts the moral order.

Gossip is a kind of storytelling that similarly reinforces, at the same time that it threatens to undercut, the moral order. The social effect of gossiping pulls people together, but the conscious intent behind the gossip is often the enhancement of one's personal image at the expense of others (Haviland 1977). Gossip can pull people apart. It takes a shrewd gossip to balance off the two effects.

In summary, communities are formed through storytelling. Just as persons create experiences of themselves in and by story-tellings, so communities are formed in experience by the gambits and performances, all of which are stories of sorts, stories which make, break, and re-make experiences of group coherence.

The Story-Forming of Communities: A Comparison of Structuralist, Ethnographic, and Translinguistic Proposals

The translinguist suggests that the experience of community is formed through the actions of storytelling. How does this account of the story-forming of community square with common and prevalent view of community and community formation?

Early in this century, Saussureans adopted the view that a community is a group in which a language is identically distributed. But try as they might, Saussureans could not demonstrate the objective existence of identically distributed language systems. Throughout this century, sociolinguists--and kindred scholars who worked under other labels--have been turning up evidence of variation at every level of grammar and in every linguistic community. As chapter seven demonstrated, structuralists have had a hard time confirming the view that communities are formed by a sharing of grammatical competences.

While structuralist sociolinguists were wrestling with these matters, linguistic anthropologists took up the same issues on their own turf. Chapter eleven presented one common anthropological proposal on the nature of a community: speech communities are groups in which communicative competences are shared. Ochs (1979), for example, implies that while grammars may not be shared within a community, a knowledge of the context of communication is shared, and such shared knowledge of context is what constitutes a community and holds it together. Tannen argues that "the degree to which cultural background is shared is reflected in the degree to which use of contextualization cues is congruent" (1984: 26).

The focus of these anthropological proposals is still shared knowledge, specifically a knowledge of the appropriate contexts for communicating. Communities, they imply, are held together by identically possessed use-knowledges if not by identically possessed form-knowledges.

However, in a recent general and programmatic statement, Gumperz moves beyond this proposal of a community of sharedness, saying that a community ought not be defined in terms of identically distributed rules. Knowing how to use a language, he says, is "quite different from the operation of all-or-none categorical grammatical rules" (1984).

If a community is not a group in which grammatical rules are shared, and if it is not a group in which use-rules are shared, then what is necessarily shared by the members of a community? And if nothing be shared, then what constitutes a community?

Religion and the Concept of Community

Whence the common sense view that communities must be formed by an identical distribution of knowledges? Let me suggest that the great world religions have helped to shape this view. For

214

the past three or four thousand years in state-level societies (Bellah 1958), people have repeatedly been told that their embrace of a single set of beliefs is the primary qualification for membership in a religious community. From antiquity, religious communities are understood to be constituted by an identical sharing of beliefs among members. The religious community is the paradigm community, the model of what a community should be both for the social sciences and for common sense. Hence, the widespread conviction that real communities should be be formed by an identical sharing of beliefs and knowledges among members.

First, sharedness or like-mindedness brought about by an identical distribution of knowledges or behaviors, is not the *sine qua non* of primary human communities like speech comunities. Washabaugh's study (1986) of the deaf people of Providence Island shows that even though the twenty deaf people and the three thousand hearing islanders who live on Providence do not share a language, they do succeed in constructing for each other a single community. Deaf islanders use an indigenous signing system. The hearing speak English Creole. Deaf signers have no access to that Creole; they do not vocalize, lip read, or fingerspell. On the other hand, Creole speakers have only a spotty and variable knowledge of Sign. Yet, the deaf and hearing islanders are equal partners in the island community. Though the hearing and deaf share almost no grammatical competence and a less than complete communicative competence, still they form themselves into a single community.

How do islanders achieve the experience of coherence if not by sharing? The translinguist would answer that the islanders "storytell" themselves into a community by participating in a variety of performance events. They experience themselves as equal partners because they all participate in the same "storytelling" events. John Heritage would say that because of their performances, islanders have come to believe "that their experience are shared and act *as if* their experiences were identical for all practical purposes" (1984: 54).

The storytellings of the hearing and the deaf of Providence Island are subtle aspects of their everyday interaction. Washabaugh says, for example, that the hearing often feign comprehension of deaf signing, and, in so doing, they support the image of deaf persons as communicatively competent islanders. The deaf, for their part, continually return to interaction with the hearing, rather than, say, breaking off into deaf cliques. And that continual return affirms to the hearing their significance as actors in the drama of island life. Thus each contributes to the formation in the other of the experience of coherence.

The objective reality is that the hearing and the deaf of

Providence Island are really quite different from, and significantly out of touch with, each other. But the participation of
both the hearing and the deaf in interaction creates an experience *as if* they were a single coherent community. The experience *as if* coherent *is* the experience of a coherent community.

This experience *as if* coherent is the result of people
speaking into mirrors. Jacques Lacan, the renowned French psy-
choanalyst, described how mirror images can provide the experience of self *as if* unified. Borrowing from Lacan, and emphasizing the role of speaking in the creation of experience, I
suggest that it is by speaking into a mirror, as it were, with
stories and performances, that humans create the experience of
themselves "as if" coherent.

Speaking into a mirror by storytelling requires no shared
knowledge or values, but only, as John Gumperz has recently
argued, "human collectivites held together by shared history and
long-term participation in networks of relationships" (1984:
280). The simple action of participating in storytellings leaves
persons with the sense of sharing, e.g. the ritual dialogues
amongst the Yanomamo (p. 212), and in the interactions of infants
amongst the Kaluli (p. 201). No matter that the Yanomamo ritual
dialogue event is structured so that participants cannot emerge
except as successful collaborators. No matter that Kaluli infants are literally talked for by caregivers, and cannot help but
emerge from interaction as successful participants. Whether
persons in interaction walk freely or are led, the effect of
participating is still the same. Participants come away with a
sense of having collaborated and of being able to collaborate in
the future. And they come away believing that they share the
knowledge and experience of other participants. They cannot help
but approach each next interaction acting *as if* they share in the
life of their community.

Participating in storytelling induces a sense of coherence.
During a storytelling, the memories of participants are led
through the task of making sense of past experiences. Thus, as
Giddens (1984: 46) says, "memory is the medium whereby the past
affects the future." Similarly Varenne (1983: 122) argues that
past actions leave "physical traces" which memory discerns and
"which future action will have to deal with." It is in this
sense that speech communities are "memory-formed" along the lines
suggested by Bellah et al. (1985).

Participation in storytelling performances, not sharing of
beliefs or knowledges, constitutes a community. In fact, participation occurs, often enough, in the absence of sharing. As
Bakhtin says, communities are regularly the sites of communicative struggles rather than of communicative concord. They are
"heteroglot from top to bottom" (1981: 291). The words of each
member are "persuasive discourses" that "struggle with" other

discourses. And the point of the struggle is for members "to liberate themselves from the authority of the other's discourse" (Ibid., p. 348). A community is not, and ought not be idealized as, a unity and a harmony; it is instead a struggle of many voices for power and for liberation from the power of others.

The husband and wife who jab and parry with their words (Rosenburg op. cit.) are confirming their togetherness despite all outward appearances to the contrary. Children, in their squabbling, confirm their togetherness: as Brenneis (1977) has shown, children argue in predictable ways; there is a pattern to their accusations, insults, etc.. The patterns of argument help the children keep track of what the others are doing. With their arguments coordinated, the kids end up experiencing themselves as coordinated competent arguers. In general, struggle and verbal conflict create experiences of coherence.

When women in the West Indies or in Spain are verbally abusing each other in public (Edwards 1978; Mulcahy 1979; Kaprow 1982), they are also confirming their togetherness. They are supporting each other by coordinating distances, by taking turns at hollering, etc.. Contenders leave bouts of conflict stung by words, but confirmed in the perception of their coherence.

In summary, communities are formed by the collaboration of people performing acts of storytelling. Communites are brought into being by deeds of speaking, not by the sharing of mental states.

Languages of Resistance Communities often involve struggling, discordant deeds of speaking, especially when one group of people is dominated and subjected to the language norms of their dominators. In such circumstances, the communicative expressions of the dominated are shot through with expressions of resistance. Frequently--at least in modern societies--such expressions of resistance are marked by a *distancing* of expressions from the language of the dominators, and, simultaneously, by a *recontextualizing* that reshapes expressions to match the experiences of the dominated. *Distancing* and *recontextualizing* are major aspects of a communicative resistance which creates a distinctive experience of group coherence.

Distancing in communicative resistance proceeds in many ways and results in many forms of expression. The rogues, bandits, and outcasts described by Halliday (1976) make use of words that are distanced by inversion. Their lexicon is similar to the mainstream lexicon, only it is stood on its head: *good* is bad and *bad* is good. West Indians distance their Creole languages from metropolitan languages by "recreolization" (LePage and Tabouret-Keller 1985: 200), that is, by adopting linguistic norms that are independent of the norms that are sanctioned by the dominators.

217

The "Dread talk" of West Indian Rastafarians, whose life and style can be glimpsed in the film <u>The Harder They Come,</u> is more intensely resistant because it is **consciously** distanced from mainstream English. Rastafarians consider the pronoun *me* to be subordinating and they refuse to use it. In its place they employ a strongly stressed *I*, and, for the first person plural, *I and I.*

Deaf people like Sarah in Mark Medoff's play <u>Children of a Lesser God</u>, distance their language from the dominant hearing world by clinging to Sign and refusing all expressions which smack of the influence of the language of the hearing. For example, the frequency of a signer's use of "initialized signs," which are signs made with hand shapes drawn from fingerspelling, which is, in turn, based on the alphabet of the hearing world, indicates how strongly a signer is resisting the hearing world. The fewer the initialized signs, the greater the distancing. The greater the distancing, the stronger the resistance.

Deaf jokes about initialized signs abound and serve to reinforce the distancing maneuvers of the signers. Klima and Bellugi report such a joking jab at the sign for Total Communication, which is a system of communication devised by deaf educators to facilitate interaction between the deaf and the hearing. The sign TOTAL COMMUNICATION (below) is made with the right hand shaped according to fingerspelled "T" and the left hand shaped according to the fingerspelled "C":

(a) TOTAL-COMMUNICATION

The total communication of drinking and smoking: (a) TOTAL-COMMUNICATION (single sign); (b) SMOKING and DRINKING, SMOKING and DRINKING (alternating signs).

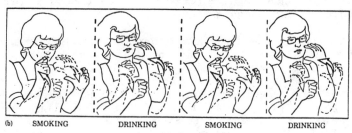

(b)   SMOKING   DRINKING   SMOKING   DRINKING

(Klima & Bellugi 1979)

A visitor to a school for the deaf, so the story goes, asked one of the students why everyone seemed so carefree and happy. the student smiled and signed TOTAL-COMMUNICATION, making the sign as it would normally be made, hands moving alternatively toward and away from him. But as the movement continued, his hands moved gradually closer and closer to the mouth and his head began to tilt from side to side, until the single sign had become transformed into the two highly iconic signs DRINK-ING (alcohol) and SMOKING (marijuana), made alternatively: 'drinking and smoking, drinking and smoking'" (Klima and Bellugi 1979: 323).

Recontextualization, i.e. the use of context-sensitive expressions, goes hand in hand with distancing. This close association between recontextualization and distancing can be appreciated if linguistic resistance is understood to be a kind of anti-structural process (Turner 1969) of rejecting a highly codified, oppressive structure. In rejecting the oppression, the resister also rejects the structures that makes possible decontextualized communication. Hence, when Francis of Assisi in the thirteenth century distanced himself from the hierarchically organized but corrupt Church, and when the Haight-Ashbury youth in the 1960's distanced themselves from the military-industrial establishment, they found it necessary to employ a recontextualized language: Francis had his mystical poetry and Haight-Ashbury had its psychobabble.

In general, whenever one community becomes "focussed," concentrated, well-established and powerful, its expressions tend to become decontextualized. When a subordinate community resists such a powerful unity by distancing itself from it, then that subordinate community's expressions must take leave of the clarity of the dominator's language and turn to recontextualized discourse. Hence, resisting speakers make use of specific intonations, rhythms, and gestures to get their meanings across. They use shrewdly indirect and strategically ambiguous expressions to lay their meaning "between the lines" (Abrahams 1976). Lexical, phonological, and syntactic distinctions may become decreasingly significant in everyday conversation. With just these terms, B. Bernstein (1975) described the speech style of lower class Londoners.

A. Gouldner aptly summarized the role of recontextualization in resistance when he said that "goal of a recontextualization of communication is the recovery of the class character of the

219

speaker" (1976: 44). Recontextualization enables speakers to find themselves in their own experiences. Recontextualized speech is a mirror which reflects back to speakers experiences of their coherence and legitimacy as a group.

Besides verbal expression, musical expression is frequently a vehicle for resistance. And, like verbal resistance, musical resistance exhibits both distancing and recontextualization vis-a-vis the musical expression of the dominators.

Music Creates Coherence

Music is often the "symbolic medium out of which ritual communication is fashioned." With music, "there is a merging of the self with what is sung about resulting in a person's feeling at one with group" (Basso, E. 1985: 254). For these reasons, musical communication ought not be excluded from the consideration of communicative practices that create an experience of coherence.

We can recognize resistance in the musics of Black Americans and of Spanish Gypsies. Both these musical traditions arose from within highly stigmatized and severely oppressed ethnic groups. The performers/creators of these musics were not professionals, but laborers whose musics provided them with dignifying experiences of themselves.

Both musical traditions involve a kind of recontextualization. The Blues that grew up in Black America and the Flamenco music of Spanish Gypsies are both judged in terms of deep feeling, *soul* and *duende*, rather than in terms of technical precision. The improvizational expression of strongly felt sentiments is more important in both traditions than is a well-balanced composition.

Besides recontextualization, both musics also involve distancing. That distancing can be seen operating in the history of both Blues and Flamenco. The growth in popularity of these musics in their respective countries, prompted imitations by mainstream musicians. Blues and Flamenco musicians responded to these imitations by reinventing yet more extreme varieties. For example, Blacks in New Orleans developed a blend of blues and marching band music. The mainstream imitated that music, and so Black musicians developed jazz. The mainstream imitated the jazz, so Black musicians developed bee bop, etc.. Thus Black American music developed by distancing, imitation, and redistancing.

Eating Up the Other

The imitation of these resistance musics by the mainstream seems to be driven by a hunger for the coherence of the dominated Other. Clifford (1981) suggests that the mainstream became particularly cynical and hungry for the Other during the inter-war period. The cynicism of the era led to both Surrealism and to the ethnographic interest in "the primitive." It is as if the primitive Other, being outside of the mainstream, offered a kind of hope for coherence which the mainstream had lost in the twentieth century.

The history of Black and Flamenco musics in the twentieth century illustrates the "relentless appetite" (Fabian 1983: 104) of the mainstream, its hunger for the Other.

Languages of Domination Resistance to domination proceeds by distancing and contextualization. Inversely, domination itself proceeds by *decontextualization*. Again, Gouldner's arguments are apt: "As decontextualization of discourse increased, strengthening the speaker's orientation to his grammar and focussing attention on discourse as embodied in printed objects, there was a corresponding defocalization on those persons to whom it was addressed and of the speaker making the address" (Gouldner 1976: 43). In other words, communicative domination is made possible by low-context speech (Hall 1977) which mirrors back to speakers experiences of themselves as detached from the people and the activities of their days.

Analytic, writerly communication, considered above in chapter eleven, is just such a decontextualized communication. Writerly speech is deliberately planned in the cool of the moment before interaction. It is enformed by a grammatical organization and a lexical precision which facilitates interpretation by anyone. It is "universalistic," in the sense used by Bernstein to describe "elaborated codes," because it is tied to no particular people's experiences.

Such decontextualization of writerly talk facilitates a centripetal imposition of organization and uniformity on a people. As Innis observes regarding the development of the great empires in history, "The supreme merit of monarchy was its intelligibility...With the development of writing, officials in the empire could be kept under close supervision..The spread of a

221

more efficient system of writing...had profound implications for imperial organization" (1972: 41).

Besides the organization that comes of communicative efficiency, writerly communication is a language of domination because it creates uniformity that makes control possible. That is, decontextualized writerly speech establishes norms for talk that detach individuals from people and activities. Thus writerly speech facilitates the detachment of individuals from the social and communicative traditions which distinguish groups and define ethnicity (Kay 1977). For such reasons, Standard languages, i.e. decontextualized, abstractly defined, explicitly rule-governed languages, became the major tools for welding together the heterogeneous citizenry of modern nation states (Fishman 1972). Writerly talk, abetted by dictionaries, grammars, and language-standardizing activities, fashioned the now commonplace experience of words and meanings that float in mental space removed from concrete and traditional social practices. Thus, writerly talk has served as the language of domination by both faciliating organization and by creating a uniformity.

Writerly Domination

Decontextualized, writerly speaking is a vehicle of political domination. It is is also the only sort of discourse through which to pursue truth. As the gnostics of the second century and the Quakers and scientists of the seventeenth century recognized, the search for truth requires a speech that is separated from the distractions of the world and which is totally devoted to representing reality-as-abstracted-by-the-mind. Hence the language of science must be a decontextualized, writerly language.

The fact that writerly discourse is both the language of domination and the language of truth should prompt disturbing questions about truth and power. Such questions will be explored in the next chapter.

Summary In summary, the notion of community that is consistent with the theory of storytelling is different from the linguist's notion of community. In the translinguist's view, community *is* participation in storytelling events. Any sharedness of knowledges and/or behaviors is incidental to the collaborative participation.

On the Evolution of Communication

How did communicative action and community arise amongst humans? Through what evolutionary sequence did human acquire the ability to collaborate in speaking and to tell stories which integrate their collaborative routines? These questions are, as was shown in chapter eight, important, not so much in themselves, but as demonstrations of the plausibility of the theory of community formation through storytelling.

Eric Gans (1979; 1985) offers a plausible account of the emergence of collaborative action in human communication. In this account, he is not attempting to reconstruct the factual details of the original human community, but only suggesting happenings that can account for the complexities of human communication. That emergence, he suggests, occurs with the first truly human uses of *pointing* expressions.

In order to appreciate his argument we should rehearse some fundamental facts about non-human pointing. Behaviors very much like pointings are common amongst non-human species. The male tri-colored blackbird, for example, orchestrates a pointing display in the course of locating a nesting site. While the female is within sight, the male perches at an appropriate spot in low-lying vegetation and then lowers his head and spreads his wings to indicate the nesting site. The female follows suit and then begins nest building (Smith 1977: 117). In similar manner male pygmy chimps, during bouts of copulation, produce hand motions which are like pointings. A male indicates "What he would like the recipient to do. These gestures varied from indicating to the recipient to move his whole body to (indicating) another location in the cage" (Rumbaugh et al. 1978: 144). Again, honey bees perform complex pointings in their waggling dances which indicate the direction and distance of a food source.

Each of these non-human behaviors consists of a "movement toward." Each makes use of directionality. To that degree they are like human pointing expressions which also involve "movement toward." But amongst non-humans, pointing behaviors are more than just indicators. They are also ostensive acts which present behavior to be reproduced.

Non-human pointings do more than inform; they model behavior to be performed. Consider the tri-colored blackbird again. The head down posture of the male points to a nesting spot, but it also "tells" the female to assume a head down position to build the nest. And the female proceeds to assume just that position. Similarly the gestures of the male pygmy chimps point to location and position, but they simultaneously present locations and positions that the female should take up. And in regard to the dance of the honey bees, Smith (1977: 144) argues "the signaling that attracts recruits and gives them the actual information about direction is not a waggle but an actual flight of the communicator back partway towards her site." Behavior like this says more than "Look over there!." It says, "Do what I do as I look over there!"

223

How does your pet dog get you to move in a certain direction? Does he not walk off in that direction, return to you and then repeat the act if necessary? The dog's behavior is like a pointing. But in addition to designating some aspect of the situation, the dog's action models behavior to be produced by the master.

Human indexical acts differ in one major respect from these non-human behaviors. Human pointings indicate features of the situation without simultaneously presenting bits of behavior to be imitated.

Among humans, the action of an index finger as it points to an apple or a chair or a man is a transparent act. It means nothing in itself. It does nothing in itself. Its whole function is to focus the recipient's attention on the apple, the chair, or the man for whatever that may mean.

How, we should wonder, did human pointings become transparent? And what is the significance of this transparency for human social life? These are the questions that Gans aims to answer.

Gans answers these questions by proposing that somewhere and sometime in the youth of the human species a gathering occurred in which an act of pointing became a community-constituting act. This "originary event" occurred when a desired object, say, the spoils of the hunt, was layed in the midst of a group. One individual moved his (or her, for this originary pointer could have been female as well as male) hand to take the desired object, a selfish grab, so to speak. But then, aware of possible reprisals from his fellows, he halted that movement in midstream. Here, half-made, his gesture is stalled for fear of reprisal. And stalled as it is, it is the prototype of a human pointing.

The pointed hand simultaneously represents the selfish man's desire and the group's response to that desire. It includes the group as part of its symbolic content. Thus begins the process, repeated with each next symbolic expression, of creating expressions which simultaneously embody the individual and the community. Such expressions presuppose community and in that way they are community-creating expressions.

The pointed hand is the originary negotiated act. A collaborative adjustment of a communicative movement. The pointing responds to pressures from both the individual who is doing the pointing and from the surrounding community that is witnessing the pointing.

In addition, this originary indexical act accounts for the simultaneous consciousness of self and of other which is characteristic of human communicative practice. The pointing man is aware of himself and of his desires, but he is also aware that others are also desirous and are ready to respond to him aggressively. And as he carries off the communicative act of pointing he rectifies the differences between his own desires and the desires of the others. The successful completion of the pointing leaves him with conviction that his consciousness and those of others in his group have been brought into line and rendered identical.

Gans's description of the originary act of pointing thus accounts for the distinctive transparency of human pointing, and it provides a plausible social circumstance in which there arises collaborative communicative activity and a sense of sharedness.

Summary

The translinguistics outlined by Bakhtin emphasizes the collaborative and bivalent nature of communicative actions. Communicative expressions are collaborative actions in which participants simultaneously affect each other. Conflict and disunity is one result of such action. Experiences of coherence are another.

Storytellings are the specific sorts of speakings which integrate experiences. Storytellings come in variety of forms including narratives, names, pronouns, politeness behaviors, and other experience-creating actions.

Participation in storytelling is the sole criterion for membership in a community. The singlemost significant impact of the storytelling on participants is that it creates in them a sense of identity with others and a feeling that they are coherent persons involved in coherent groups. Thus as a result of participating in events of storytelling, participants believe and act as if they shared beliefs and/or behaviors.

Human communication and human community arose together, probably in an event in which an expression simultaneously presupposed the individual and the community. A pointing finger might well have been just such a symbolically complex expression.

Chapter Fourteen

Anthropologist as Translinguist

A good dose of strangeness is a powerful antidote to complacency and self-satisfaction. If you perform a strange exercise on any afternoon, the following morning will greet you with a bracing awareness of taken-for-granted muscles. Translinguistics has, like strange exercise, provided a bracing disturbance to American anthropology, and has helped to awaken it to some of its taken-for-granted views.

Translinguistics comes to us as a discipline from another era. It is born of a strange theology and it proceeds according to strange literary methods. Its impact on American anthropology has been twofold. First, it has helped to sow seeds of doubt about the absoluteness of traditional ways of doing science; it supports a "blurring" of the distinction between scientific and literary practices (Geertz 1983; Toulmin 1982a). And second, it has reinforced the concern with *communicative practice* that has been cultivated in the ethnography of speaking.

The present chapter will explore the bracing impact of translinguistics with regard to the first issue, taken-for-granted views about science and scientific methods. The second issue, the matter of communication versus language, will be revisited in chapter fifteen.

Science and Anthropology

Science, as Bacon understood it in 1620, and as it has been generally understood since, is a discourse which operates by the systematic detachment of the scientists from all experiences which might bias description. Bacon counseled scientists to flee "idols of the marketplace," "idols of the cave," etc.. He counseled scientific detachment, claiming that such detachment makes possible true scientific descriptions.

The problem with Bacon's proposal is that no communicator ever composes discourse in a condition of detachment. Translinguists tell us that all discourse is collaborative. All discourse is negotiated. Therefore, scientific discourse cannot be what it claims to be. If it should appear to us that scientific discourse is produced by detached speakers, then we must be looking through tinted glasses and seeing what is not really there.

The suggestion that scientific discourse cannot be what it claims to be is disturbing at such a fundamental level that we might be tempted to set the problem aside for someone else or sometime else. However, there may be no better person than an anthropologist and no better time than now to wrestle with this

227

problem. As Wagner (1986: 124) says, "To be confronted with one's meaningful frame of reference in unfamiliar form is, perhaps discomfiting. But it is a better sort of objectivity than the unthinking acceptance of major propositions so that one can be clinically precise about minor ones."

Detached scientific discourse parades as something it is not. The masquerade succeeds because we scientists repress our awareness of the collaborations that stand behind our discourses. Above all we maintain an "unthinking acceptance" of scientific detachment (see Woolgar and Latour 1979).

Let us consider this repression of collaboration as it occurs in anthropological discourse. We can do this by describing the discourse of anthropologists as storytellings of the sort described in the preceding chapter. In this way we will see how we anthropologists collaborate in providing ourselves with identities in a discourse that boasts detachment, autonomy, and freedoom from collaboration.

This project of analyzing the collaboration that undergirds an anthropological discourse that boasts freedom from collaboration is an intensely reflexive project. To carry it off, we will make use of scientific discourse to analyze scientific discourse. As in Escher's "Drawing Hands" (p. 173), we will be using our left hands to analyze the scientific discourse of the right hand. The scientific discourse of the right hand, though, is the very discourse that makes possible our left handed analysis.

The intensely reflexive character of this project might be likened to the penchant of the legendary serpent Ouroboros (below) for swallowing its own tail. We anthropologists will be grabbing our tails with our teeth and chewing a bit. We will be taking advantage of ethnographic methods of description to describe how we ourselves describe, and how our own descriptive communications lead to our self-experiences.

Naming the Anthropologist

The preceding chapter suggested that self-experiences are formed as (1) individuals take on linguistic dimensions of existence, and as (2) they plug those linguistic dimensions of existence into storytold projects. Individuals take on linguistic dimensions of existence by adopting names, pronouns, metaphorical usage, etc. for themselves and for others with whom they relate.

Names, pronouns, and metaphors confer a linguistic reality on individuals. In the same way that phones instantiate abstract phones, and in the same way that morphs betoken abstract morphonemes, so names draw individuals into the realm of language, betokening them and making them linguistically real. Once betokened, individuals take on the coherence of the storytold project in which their names or pronouns appear.

Scientific discourse is a storytelling of this sort. And the scientists are the individuals who experience coherence as a result of naming themselves into the storytold project of science.

In the case of the discourses of linguistic anthropology, scholars have named themselves with specific names. Those names and expressions serve to mark their places in the storytold project of linguistic anthropology. Parts I and II of this book have shown that such names include *linguist, reformer,* and *non-linguist.*

The structuralists are the *linguists* whose name implies a devotion to puzzling out the nature of language systems and to explicating the human mental language faculty. The early Boasians are the *reformers* as well as *linguists.* They were eager to reshape modern life, and they were attracted by the prestige of the science of language. Accordingly they built an edifying discipline of cultural description around a linguistic model. Finally, the ethnographers of speaking are the *non-linguists* whose name dissociates them from the mind-centered, individual-centered project of linguists but it still authorizes their pursuit of communicative interaction.

Each of these names plugs individual anthropologists into the storytold project of anthropological discourse in a different way. But the differences to the side, each of these names is associated with a single metaphor which presupposes an identical experience for all these differently named anthropologists. The metaphor is one of spatial distancing. It is the metaphor of *detachment.*

The association of the differently named anthropologists with the single metaphor of detachment serves to storytell them all into a single and overarching self-experience, the generality of which invites closer scrutiny.

On Detachment

Background The metaphor of detachment finds its way into all modern discourse, not just the discourse of linguistic anthropologists, and not just the discourse of scientists. The metaphor of detachment is a commonplace figure of speech for talk about selves.

Modern commonplace talk with its central metaphor of detachment is explored and explicated most fully in the philosophical discipline of phenomenology and in the social scientific writings that have spun off of phenomenology in the twentieth century (Roche 1973). In that literature of phenomenology, detachment is described as the condition that arises as a result of human self-consciousness.

Individuals are conscious of themselves as moral centers, agents of action, and subjects of feeling. Simultaneously, "the individual orients himself (sic) to another person whom he *believes* to be really there and to be the same kind of entity as himself" (Ibid., p. 299, emphasis added). However, one's knowledge of oneself is direct and immediate whereas one's knowledge of another is indirect, a matter of belief.

The direct knowledge of oneself is, in common parlance, usually described as an unconstructed innate self-consciousness. Asimov's fictional characterization of the human condition as one of alienation and disconnection implies such an unconstructed self-consciousness:

> Every human being lived behind an impenetrable wall of choking mist within which no other but he existed. Occasionally there were the dim signals from deep within the cavern in which another man was located--so that each might grope toward the other. Yet because they did not know one another, and could not understand one another, and dared not trust one another and felt from infancy the terrors and insecurity of that ultimate isolation--there was the hunted fear of man for man.

> Feet, for tens of thousands of years, had clogged and shuffled in the mud--and held down the minds which, for an equal time, had been fit for the companionship of the stars.

> Grimly, man had instinctively sought to circumvent the prison bars of ordinary speech (Asimov 1953: 86).

230

But a good deal of the literature of phenomenology leans in another direction, implying that humans construct their self-consciousness in the course of living life amongst others.

KEEPING IT IN PERSPECTIVE

One can find numerous different accounts of how self-consciousness is constructed in social life. See Norman O. Brown (1959) for a psychoanalytic perspective, Luckmann (1983) for a phenomenologist's account, Jaynes (1976) for an unusual psycho-historical view, Hofstadter (1979) for a suggestion from studies of artificial intelligence, and Henriques et al. (1984) for a post-structuralist view.

Once self-consciousness has been constructed, it becomes the source of the experience of human detachment, that is, the sense of distance from all experience beyond the experience of self-consciousness:

> As a subject, man (sic) distances his world more thoroughly than any other animal (van Baal 1981: 58).

> Man (sic) is and at the same time knows that he is. Through the various forms of his consciousness he can emancipate himself from what is. He can transcend his position in space. This transcendence of the immediately given experience is the source and cause of existential alienation (Weisskopf 1971: 19).

> Detachment is the presupposition for the construction of the most elementary framework of interpretation relating past, present, and future experience...Detachment becomes a crucial dimension of personal identity. Consequently the individual now can create meaning" (Luckmann 1967: 47f).

Detachment, in the views expressed above, is the central feature of the human condition without which meaning would not exist. One must first experience detachment, and only then can one construct a project which makes sense of the human condition.

Scientific discourse presupposes the centrality of detachment in the human condition. Indeed, the project of scientific discourse is a project of making use of detachment so as to develop and share a knowledge which ultimately overcomes detachment. The project of scientific discourse is a project of enabling detached individuals to share a single knowledge and thus escape the self-imprisonment of detachment.

KEEPING IT IN PERSPECTIVE

A translinguist would not deny the existence of self-consciousness. But the translinguist would argue that self-consciousness is, at its root, a physiological process that has been elevated in the discourse of moderns to the status of an essential human mystery.

The physiological process is the brain's self-monitoring. The brain tracks its own activity, and the report which it gives itself is a disembodied spirit-like readout, "a natural consequence of the way the brain controls is own activities" (Taylor 1982: 182). Modern scholars use these readouts of the brain's self-monitorings as foundations for discourses which imply "private, individual domains of hidden thoughts, sensations, and feelings. In addition, the corresponding abstract nouns (consciousness, thought, mind, and experience) have been given a certain 'false concreteness' as the supposed <u>names</u> for the content of basic sensibility" (Toulmin 1982b: 66f). In other words, moderns have woven central human storytold projects around the physiological process of cerebral self-monitoring.

Detachment in the Discourse of Science Scientific discourse begins with the assumptions that the detachment of human consciousness is an essential, almost mystical, human condition. It installs that detachment at the center of its method, making it the precondition for acceptable discourse. As a result, scientists operate in an atmosphere of detachment, detachment of the speaker from the listener and detachment of the knower from the known.

So detached scientists fancy themselves able to stand apart from the world and mirror it with their discourse. But I suggest, following Gergen (1982: 96), that "theories of human activities are more like dance steps than they are mirrors." They are collaborative through and through.

A detachment ancestral to that of modern science was present in the discourses of the Greeks. In Greek rhetorical practice, public speakers would organize their discourses with memory aides rather than by way of the give-and-take of face-to-face interaction. Detaching themselves from their audiences, speakers would spin out their speech by proceeding from one topic to the next (Fabian 1983).

The topics were the memory aides. Meaning literally "places," *topoi* in Greek refers to locations or spaces in territories or buildings. Rhetoricians would typically associate different issues with different locations, and would walk their minds from one location to another as they moved from issue to issue in their speech.

These *topical* mnemonics paved the way for the modern detachment of the knower from the known. That is, the Greek rhetoricians purposely and intentionally transformed what they wanted to say into visualizable locations, places they could remember. Over many centuries scholars have emulated Greek rhetoric and have imitated the Greek practice of associating that which is known with a visualizable location. This practice of casting the known in the guise of visualizable location became a habit of though, a practice so taken for granted that scholars forgot that they were transforming the known in the process. As a result, knowledge, for us moderns, has taken on the verbal trappings of visualizable objects: Theories have *foundations*, and *forms*. Arguments can be *shaky* and need *buttressing* (Lakoff and Johnson 1980: 46). Knowledge covers a certain *territory*, has certain *boundaries* or *frontiers*, and is beset with *detours, blind alleys,* and *pitfalls* (Salmond 1982).

In the course of the evolution of modern scientific discourse, the visualizability of the known has been taken to be a necessary aspect of the known. But the real roots of that visualizability in rhetorical mnemonics were forgotten. Thus modern knowers erect a barrier between themselves and the known. That barrier is the artifice of visualization.

KEEPING IT IN PERSPECTIVE

The modern natural history museum and zoological garden reinforce what rhetoric leads moderns to assume, namely that knowledge consists of spatially alien objects brought before our eyes. In the early years of European expansion, explorers brought back treasures from foreign lands. These alien treasures were displayed in cabinets that lined the walls of galleries. Hence the collections came to be called "cabinets" and later "galleries." In 1683, the first public museum was begun at Oxford University. Featuring the rare and alien objects collected by one Elias Ashmole, the museum was named the Ashmole.

Greek rhetorical practice involved detachment of the speaker from the listener as well as detachment of the knower from the known. That is, Greek rhetoricians detached themselves from the give-and-take of face-to-face interaction and, turning inward, steered their discourse by "inner lights" (see p. 164).

Writing reinforced this detachment. After all, writing is the solipsistic activity of constructing discourse from the inside out. All the topics are inside; all the logic of linking the topics is inside. Even the audience is reconstructed by imagination on the inside, in the writer's consciousness (Ong 1977). And the writer is lord of that whole internal realm, privileged to pick and choose, promote and demote as ever he or she wishes. To write is to experience a power that catapults the writer above and away from the masses, above and away like the ugly duckling-turned-swan soaring over the flock of ducks, above and away like Cinderella-turned-queen. It could only be this ego-enhancing experience of writing that led Sam Shephard, play-write/actor, to confess that writing is better than sex.

The detachment and ego-enhancement that come with writing are not confined only to circumstances where pen is put to paper. Writing became the valued mode of communication in our tradition and, in consequence, the writerly style, previsioned in Greek rhetorical practice, dominates all serious oral discourse. We moderns talk from notes in our heads. True, we feign "fresh talk" from the heart (Goffman 1981a) for we recognize that to openly "read" to each other would be an insult, a brazen act of non-participation. But our "fresh talk" merely hides our "reading." We do not--maybe we cannot--cease "reading" to each other. Our modern way of life, and *a fortiori* our scientific discourse, is built on the detachment of persons as they "read" to one another.

ANCHORMAN, SCHMANKORMAN! DO YOU NEED CUE CARDS FOR EVERYTHING?

Anthropology, like every other modern science, involves the double detachment of the speaker from the hearer and the knower from the known. Anthropological discourse involves a visualization of topics that detaches the knower from the known, and it proceeds with a "reading" that detaches the speaker from the listener. In linguistic anthropology, these double detachments can be specifically identified as a detachment of the observer (the knower) from the observed (the known), and a detachment of the ethnographer (the speaker) from the reader (the hearer).

The Detachment of the Observer from the Observed Anthropological discourse is heir to the detachment that comes of presuming that that which is known must be a visualizable object. In the case of ethnographic writings, such detachments involve a transformation of people into objects.

The practice of anthropological fieldwork almost always involves interaction. It is called *participant* observation because the observers interact with the observed while simultaneously observing them. And being interactive, participant observation is a collaborative activity in which all parties are active.

But the ethnographic discourse in which ethnographic knowledge is framed transforms observed people from active partners in interaction to passive objects. Specifically, in accordance with the tradition of science that transforms the known into a visualizable spatially located object, ethnographic discourse employs discursive devices that render observed people into spatially distant Others. Observed people become aliens, being described as not just residents of a foreign territory, but more importantly, residents of alien categories in a visualizable typology of human diversity--Fabian (1983) argues that typologies, graphs, scales, and maps abet the process of the visualization of the known.

As if such spatial alienation in itself were not sufficient, the spatially and typological distinct Other is regularly interpreted in a temporal framework with the result that observed peoples become temporally alien to the knower as well. By this double alienation, spatial and temporal, the observed people are transformed in ethnographic discourse into a Primitive Other.

Ethnographic discursive practices accomplish this detaching, alienating transformation of people into Primitive Others despite the ethnographer's recollection that he or she was just now rubbing shoulders with those observed people in collaborative interaction, and despite the best intentions of the ethnographer to describe those observed people as vital.

My Words Are Not My Own

The discursive practices of scientific storytelling are not the scientist's own. They do not respond to the scientist's individual wishes and intentions.

Discursive practices are the property of a community of people; they are fashioned collaboratively over a long period of time, and serve to present the project of a community to itself. It is self-delusion to think that one can give voice to one's own intentions independent of a community's storytelling project.

The alienation of the people who are observed and their transformation into Primitive Others is accomplished by the way observers talk to the observed and by the way observers write their ethnographic reports.

Interviewing, as Briggs (1986) has shown, is a speech event which conspires to transform observed people into dominated objects. Interviewers dominate those being interviewed by the simple discursive practice of questioning. Questions require responses and they further require that the speaking floor be returned to the questioner after responses are made (see p. 167). Thus the questioner is always in control. And those being questioned have very little opportunity to shape the the the interviewing event.

The traditional manner of ethnographic reportage furthers the alienation of the observed people. First, ethnographies are most often written in a time and in a place that is removed from the interactions of participant observation. While observers may take notes in the field, they write their ethnographies well after their time of interacting with the observed and usually in a university at considerable spatial distance from the observed. And in producing those ethnographies, the writers systematically transform those field notes into cohesive, narrated, author-centered accounts. The use of the ethnographic-present tense serves to freeze the observed people in a time out of time. And use of the authorly "I" as the ultimate guarantor of truth in the account sets up a frame in which the words of the observed come off, like the speakings of characters in a novel, as words put there by the author (Boon 1982; Clifford 1983).

Thus in both the gathering and reporting of ethnographic knowledge, the observed people are systematically transformed into aliens who occupy other places and other times. The observed are transformed into Primitive Others.

The Detachment of the Writer from the Reader Ethnographic reports, like all writings, involve a detachment of readers from writers along with a subordination which redoubles the ethnographic subordination of the observed peoples.

All readers engage in an act in which they are active but, in a certain sense, powerless. They are active as readers, interpreters, inquisitors, and critics of what they read, but they are powerless to reshape the text itself. A book, after it is read, remains the same book. Readers who persist in reading--readers who make a life of reading--tacitly grow to assent to, and even thirst for, the circumstance of such powerless activity. Thus reading as an activity can become a cultural "model for the new concentration camp, where the camp has been built by the inmates themselves and the inmates are the guards, and they have this pride in this thing that they've built. And as a result they no longer have the capacity to leave the prison they've made or even to see it as a prison" [with apologies to Shawn and Gregory (1981: 93)].

Insofar as the reader of ethnographies accedes to the power of the ethnographer, the reader accepts the ethnographic world in which the observed people have been transformed into a Primitive Other. And lacking the ethnographer's memory of interactional experiences of participant observation, the reader cannot even reconstruct an alternative image to compete with the image of Primitive Other that comes across in a reading.

Translinguistic Experiments in Reconnection

Experiments designed to transform discursive practices are perilous undertakings. They are perilous for reasons stated above and repeated here: The discursive practices of scientific storytelling are not the scientists own. They do not respond to the scientists individual wishes and intentions. Discursive practices are the property of a community of people; they are fashioned collaboratively over a long period of time, and serve to present the project of a community to itself. It is self-delusion to think that one can give voice to one's own intentions independent of a community's storytelling project.

The experiments to be considered here are on the order of proposals of new stories for old. They are proposals of new names for old, new pronouns, new metaphors, new speech situations, and new instruments for old. However, none of these new stories-for-old directly addresses the global project of ethnographic and/or scientific storytelling. It is self-delusion to believe that any individual living in the midst of a cultural project can even identify that project definitively--as if cultural projects were objects with spatial boundaries--though Clifford (1981) and Fabian (op. cit.) have both suggested that the cultural project of ethnographic writing is a cannibalistic feast in which modern

237

society consumes cultural Others. Cultural projects, like lives
themselves, develop and change with each new discourse. Just as
one cannot write a biography until the subject has died, so one
cannot identify a cultural project until the cultural tradition
has ended (see Smart 1976).

We may not be able to define the cultural project of
ethnographic discourse, but we can persist in experimenting with
stories. What follows are some suggestions towards a revision of
ethnographic practice.

Reconnecting the Observer and the Observed   Experiments aimed at
reconnecting the observer and the observed and thereby diminishing the alienation of the observed take aim at revising the
methods of gathering knowledge and the methods of reporting
knowledge.

Briggs (1986) has made a case for ethnographic learning as
an alternative procedure for gathering knowledge of observed peoples. Ethnographic learning is an alternative to interviewing as
a method of observation. In ethnographic learning, the ethnographer takes on the role of student, and in that role, the
ethnographer acquires a knowledge of behavior from teachers who
are themselves the observed people. In this student-teacher
relationship, the teacher dominates, and the ethnographer-student
is subordinate. The teacher controls the floor and directs the
interaction. Thus, in this method of ethnographic learning, the
power relations of the interview are reversed, and, as a result,
the ethnographer gets an opportunity to experience the observed
as active and powerful.

Clifford (1983) has struggled with practices of ethnographic
reporting which reconnect the observed to the observer and which
avoid the creation of the ethnographic Primitive Other. He has
proposed that "polyphonic" ethnographies replace traditional
ethnographies dominated by the author's voice. Drawing on the
Bakhtinian notion of "polyphony," Clifford suggests that the
observed should be represented in ethnographic writings as
speaking for themselves rather than through the authoritative
voices of authors. Like characters in one of Dostoevsky's
novels, the voices of the observed should leap off the page and
out from under the control of the author's pen.

Reconnecting the Writer and the Reader For writer's to be
reconnected with readers two things must happen simultaneously:
first, the authorial power of the writer must be subverted;
second, the writing must become an interactional, participational
event in which "readers" play active roles.

Numerous strategies have been suggested for reducing authorial power in ethnographic writing. Clifford's aforementioned
"polyphonic" style of ethnography diminishes the significance of

the author's voice. Rose (1982) has suggested that ethnographers attach autobiographical discourses to their ethnographic writing so as to underscore the human and fallible nature of the ethnography and to avoid any temptation to hide the least reliable aspects of ethnographic observation.

Another suggestion advanced by Paul Bove (1986) is for scholars to identify themselves by pseudonyms. Pseudonyms, of course, are commonly used by authors, but more often to enhance than to detract from a writer's authority. Here, in this work, I expect that the name "John Doe" detracts from my authorly status implying as it does, a faceless sort of character. Better still might be the practice of anonymous authorship, though experimentation along such lines might confound the classifying practices of librarians.

Towards the objective of transforming writing into a collaborative activity, ethnographers might well follow classical and modern models of collaborative writing. Augustine of Hippo is one classical figure who wrote collaboratively. True, writing and reading in late antiquity were probably more social than they are today--it was Augustine who was awestruck by the sight of his mentor Ambrose reading without moving his lips. Still, Augustine went to unusual lengths in this regard. He ate, played, studied, and, notably, he wrote with a coterie of fast friends. He was, "for all his inward gazes, a man hardly ever alone" (Brown 1967: 202).

Bakhtin was also a collaborative writer. He wrote with a group of scholars in Nevel, Vitebsk, and Leningrad. Some of those scholars, like Voloshinov and Medvedev, remained together through dislocations, and were named authors of books for which Bakhtin was largely responsible. One of the reasons for the passing around of authorship was that the writing was as dialogical as the subject matter. "The actual method of composition may have resembled that found in a Renaissance artist's studio: the master, Bakhtin, would draw the main sections on the canvas, while his disciples did some of the less important painting following his direction" (Clark and Holquist 1984: 150). Voloshinov and Medvedev, however, "were more than mere epigoni and possibly contributed material of their own." On the whole, the collaborative dialogical style of writing employed by Bakhtin and his colleagues is a marvelously consistent complement to the content of their writings.

The theoretical writings of Henriques et al. (1984) serve as a contemporary example of collaborative writing. However theirs is a rare case in a world where scholarship, especially ethnographic scholarship, is usually produced by solo writers.

Experiments also aimed at reconnecting writers and readers include efforts to produce "performance ethnography" by scholars

like Turner and Scheckner (Ruby 1982) together with the ethno-
poetic efforts of scholars like Tedlock (1983) and Rothenburg
(1968). These experiments all proceed by giving the audience a
vital role to play in the ethnography event. Performers and
audience together recreate the experience of observers and the
observed in interaction. Participatory, rather than just descriptive, performance ethnographies reproduce ineffable social
realities. They provide, for both the performers and the audience, an opportunity to experience another world of interaction
by recreating that world.

The form of performed ethnographies drastically revises the
relationship of readers to writers which prevails in traditional
ethnographies. Writers and readers are both active and equally
powerful contributors to the event. Most importantly, performed
ethnography replaces with a communally negotiated discourse the
discourse that is produced in isolation. Thus it is consistent
with the collaborative nature of human speech and with what
Schrag (1980: 105) considers to be the social nature of human
reason: "The performance of reason is as much the work of the
community as it is of any particular self."

Science and Truth, the Whole Truth

The ethnographic discourses that result from the experimentation suggested above will look far different from classical
ethnographies, e.g. (Firth 1936; Malinowski 1922; Wilson 1951) or
from the prototypes of linguistic ethnography, e.g. (Gossen 1974;
Witherspoon 1977; Calame-Griaule 1965). But the test of the new
ethnographies will be the same test to which the classical and
prototypical ethnographies were put, namely, truth. Are the
ethnographic reports true? We can do whatever we want to ethnographies, but if they are not true, or more precisely coursing
toward the truth, then they are not science.

Truth in science is the cleaver of discourses. It is the
knife that pares away and disgards disconfirmed and falsified
accounts to leave behind the lean red meat of science. As the
cleaver of discourse, truth itself deserves some discussion here.

On Philosophical Pragmatism

There exists a rich literature on the foundation of truth in
practice which I find attractive enough to mention (see Schrag
1980), but too much a digression to pursue at length. According
to this tradition the most desirable style of human activity is a
habitual, unconsciously produced, automatic style. "Civilization," according to Whitehead (1929), "advances by extending the
number of operations which we can perform without thinking about
them. Operations of thought are like cavalry charges in a bat-

tle---they are strictly limited in number, they require fresh horses, and must only be made at decisive moments."

Thought arises, according to C.S. Peirce (1877), only when habitual activity is frustrated in one way or another. When habitual activity goes awry, conscious thought comes to the rescue, but it does so with the ultimate aim of returning action to its habitual condition. Truth is that condition of thought such that it can direct action appropriately. And upon directing action appropriately, truth can preside at its own return to slumber.

Truth, understood as the correspondence of a description to experience, is rightly touted as the criterion to be followed in attaching value to scientific discourse. But unfortunately, too regularly only part of scientific discourses have been evaluated in the light of experience, the content but not the form. Scientific discourses are wrongly assumed to be pure content, and only the correspondence of that content to experience needs to be weighed. However, scientific discourse involves a specific style of interacting, and that style needs to be weighed and assayed.

Manners of discoursing, styles of interacting, modes of communicating have an impact on what is said. Such, in very general terms, is the finding of both ethnographic linguistics and translinguistics. Manners of discoursing are not like clear windows which present accurate pictures of the world outside. They bend and shape the content of talk, and therefore, the style of scientific discourse needs to be considered in any assessment of the truth of scientific discourse.

The style of unreconstructed scientific discourse is inegalitarian. It is a style that enhances the power of speakers, detaching them from contact with both the known about which they talk and the audience to whom they talk.

It is just this inegalitarian style of science which prompted Foucault (1980) to indict science as a discourse of power which creates rather than reveals truth. And it is just this inegalitarian style of communicating that invites the outrage of subjugated speakers, especially feminist scientists: "The entire range of tools of science is penetrated by the principle of domination." Thus penetrated, science is said to be the story-telling which creates the overarching project of Western culture: "To be in control of things, people, phenomena, information, and institutions, is an essence of our Western industrial class culture" (Bleier 1984: 196, 202).

Assessing the truth of scientific discourse must mean assessing its form as well as its content. Feminist scientists have

241

offered specific suggestions for transforming the style of scientific discourse into a truthful style. Three of those feminist suggestions are especially applicable to ethnographic practice: constant critical self-reflection, a willingness to tolerate diversity, and a willingness to listen and hear.

Constant critical self-reflection means "recognizing the degree to which investment of ego and pride in one's previously stated beliefs and theories may corrupt the scientific approach" (Bleier 1984: 204). Every kind of science involves a danger of ego-involvement (Feyerabend 1975). But ethnographic discourse is filled to overflowing with possibilities for such truth-skewing investment of pride in oneself and in one's own cultural project. Hence, ethnographers must be especially self-reflexive in their work (Ruby 1982).

A willingness to tolerate diversity implies a dialogical rather than a monological science. The most highly reputed sciences are paradigms organized around undisputed axioms shared by communities of scholars. But a dialogical science is one in which scholars continue to talk despite the absence of shared beliefs in fundamental axioms. The American anthropological tradition, according to Strathern (1987), is already dialogical in this sense. However, anthropologists need to learn to evaluate the diversity and conflict of their scholarly discourses as an asset rather than a default of scientific rigor or disciplined thought.

Finally, doing science well requires listening: "to listen and hear, to be aware and perceptive, to understand and appreciate process and interaction. It is 'letting the material speak to you'" (Bleier, op. cit., p. 206). In ethnographic research, "the material" literally speaks. But ethnographers, though they have listened, have generally not heard well. Flushed with confidence in their own cultural projects and in their own scientific discourses, ethnographers have traditionally been quick to demythologize, demystify, decontextualize, and analyze the words of the people they observe. But they have rarely taken the trouble to hear those words. We will know that we have approached the goal of truly scientific ethnographic discourse when we ethnographers find ourselves really hearing the words of a Navaho or a Dogon sage. We will be operating as true scientists when we listen to them as peers rather than as parents to children or as scientists to microbes. We will be operating as scientists when we find ways of believing them when they talk to us in what we now call mythical language.

242

Chapter Fifteen

A Translinguistic History of Western Linguistics

Taking tail in teeth in the fashion of Ouroboros, let us consider the history of language descriptions. Let us embark on the task of writing a critical history of that curious sort of discursive practice called "doing linguistics."

My goal is to develop a critical appreciation of contemporary language studies by describing linguistic discourses of the past. The method will be the method advocated by Bakhtin for translinguistics: for each era of language study, we will determine who is talking to whom, making a special effort to raise to light those voices in the discourse which have been systematically hidden, all so that we might arrive at a general understanding of the project of language study in our tradition.

A Story of Linguistics

In order to understand the goal and methods of this chapter it is important to realize that what we call linguistics is, in essence, an activity of storytelling. It is a special kind of storytelling, being a dialogical display. Linguistics is, we might say, a hyperextended conversation-like performance that spans centuries and continents. It is a conversation focussed on a definite topic and with explicit rules for participation.

Who talks to whom in this hyperextended conversation is not so obvious as it may seem at first glance. Bakhtin advises us that voices are often masked and reclothed; their identity is often hidden. In line with Bakhtin's admonition, we should prepare ourselves to find that linguistic discourses will only *seem* to be presented by curious professors to students and other curious professors. Appearances, in this case, may be deceptively simple; the voices involved may be multiple, heterogeneous, and invested with power to different degrees.

Furthermore, we should expect that, as in so many other storytellings, the medium of the linguistic story is its message. What linguists say is not usually so important as how they say it. Specifically, the rhetorical deeds of linguists are far more influential than the contents of their speakings. And, as Bakhtin has noted, most of the time those deeds have favored the centripetal imposition of an experience of individual autonomy and group unity: "linguistics, stylistics and the philosophy of language--as forces in the service of the great centralizing tendencies in European verbal-ideological life--have sought first and foremost for unity in diversity" (1981: 274).

Bakhtin is telling us that the form of most Western linguistic discourse operates at an unconsicous level to create ideas

243

and behaviors which are consistent with the needs of nation-states. Bakhtin is not saying that linguists are puppets of kings. He wouldn't claim that Boas and Chomsky dance to tunes played by presidents? Far from it. However contents and intentions to the side, the medium and form of linguistic writings, including Chomsky's and Boas's, have regularly served the needs of the state.

The form of linguistic discourse is the open-sesame to the deeply unconscious politics of linguistics. Simply put, form establishes coherence, and coherence perpetuates presuppositions. Let me offer a workaday example. Suppose my neighbor Alphonse were to ask me, "Have you stopped beating your kids yet?" I would hope I would refuse the presupposition of the question by interrupting the form of the conversation and short-circuiting the discourse. If I were to try answering the question by trotting out evidence that I am not beating my kids, the form of my talk would maintain the coherence of the conversation and would, despite the content of my protests, constitute an affirmation of the presupposition of the question.

The discourse on language in the West, being a conversation of a sort, proceeds in a similar fashion. Uninterrupted form establishes coherence, and coherence perpetuates presuppositions. The most significant presupposition in this discourse has been the presupposition of objectified language, the assumption that a language is an entity, an acquirable commodity, a non-historical abstract thing. This assumption is encoded in the very grammar of linguistic discourse: is it not the case that "a language" is a noun phrase?

The presupposition of objectified language has too rarely been fingered as suspicious (see Voloshinov 1973). The scholars who engage each other in the hyperextended conversation of linguistics often disagree with one another over political issues. And the contents of their turns at talk frequently reveal their anti-establishment intentions. However, they rarely question the presupposition of the simple noun phrase "a language" (see Harris 1980). Rather than interrupting the coherence of the conversation, they contribute to it, and, unwittingly, they reinforce the hegemony of language which is made possible by the presupposition that a language is a thing.

The purpose of the present chapter is, first, to explore the manner in which different phases of the hyperextended conversation of linguistics have contributed to the coherence of the conversation, and have perpetuated the politically significant presupposition of "a language." And second, I will demonstrate the variable but incorrigible association between the objectification of language and the needs of state.

Before we launch into this critical history of language '

studies, a double admonition is in order. First, in doing a critical history of language study we must operate with sympathy. We must listen sympathetically to the writings of philologists and linguists of other eras for every age has its distinctive assumptions, and the assumptions of one age ought not be judged by the assumptions of another. The Romans had a clear sense of tradition, but their notion of tradition is not equivalent to our notion of tradition. For the Romans, tradition was a sacred way, the fulfillment of their glorious past, the end-all and be-all of their lives. For us, tradition is much less often a source of principles and programs for the shaping of our future. Hence, for us to discuss the Roman concept of tradition as if it were identical to our own would involve a terrible misunderstanding. The potential for similar misunderstandings surrounds every step that we take along the way as we develop this critical history of Western language studies.

Besides the dangers of mistaking assumptions of other eras, we can fail in sympathy by seeing either too grand a connection between past discourses and our own, or by seeing too little a connection. To discern too grand a connection is to do what Butterfield (1959) called a "Whig history." "Whig histories" interpret past discourses as if they were precursors of present discourses. Chomsky (1966) has been accused of writing just such a Whig history of modern language theory because he was too ready to characterize certain linguists of the 18th and 19th centuries as proto-generative linguists. To discern too little a connection implies that history is an unconnected series of abrupt and unconnected leaps. Michel Foucault (1970) has been accused of writing such a disconnected history of the human sciences which stresses the incomparability of the "climates of opinion" in the sixteenth, eighteenth, and twentieth centuries. A sympathetic reading in any intellectual history must find a middle way between the Scylla of continuity and the Charybdis of discontinuity.

Second, critical discernment is a necessary quality of the history of the discourses of linguists. Such discernment is especially important in appreciating modern texts. Readers tend to be too deeply habituated to the assumptions of contemporary writings and consequently too little able to discern the masked voices of those texts. This problem is the age-old anthropological problem of ethnocentrism, which ethnographers have always had to combat with unflagging self-criticism.

A History of Language Studies

The Ancient Greeks "In the course of the fifth century, Greek society became language conscious in a way and to a degree hitherto unprecedented, and as a direct result of the requirement imposed by the institution of the democratic city state" (Harris 1980: 116). These Greeks found themselves in a situation where decisions were being arrived at by way of debate amongst equals. In such a situation, their rhetorical capabilities became all important. The art of persuasion became the all-in-all, and the cultivation of that art was the objective toward which all speech description tended.

The Sophists, being cynics who had lost all faith in the gods and all confidence in the celebration of the ancient myths, carried this rhetorical art to its extreme, even to the point of supposing that "technical expertise and astuteness must always win, regardless of truth and justice" (Ibid.).

Plato spoke up against this subordination of truth-saying to persuasion. He, no less than the Sophists, had lost faith in the gods, and was seeking a new ground on which to erect Greek democracy. But he suspected that the vaunting of persuasive rhetoric would only replace democracy with demagoguery.

As Plato saw it, the ground for the democratic state was not the power of the word to convince, but the capability of words to be true. Powerful rhetoric only creates heroes. But truth founds an egalitarian society because truth is accessible to all persons.

Plato argued his line by saying that words stand for larger than life realities. The meanings of words had to be larger than life, in some sense, because they were replacing the gods at the foundation of their complex society. They had to instill as much faith and trust as the gods once did. So Plato argued that the meanings of words were objectified essences--as if cow-ness could exist independently of individual cows--which were located in the heavenly realm of ideal forms.

Aristotle differed with Plato regarding the nature of meanings. He proposed a psychological account: "Spoken words are the signs of mental experience." Meanings such as "cow-ness" exist in the intellect as concepts. They are general meanings because the mind--the powers of which had in the past been under-estimated--not only reflects experience but also sorts and classifies that experience in the same way for all humans. According to the Aristotelian theory, the meanings of words are essences extracted by the intellect from perceptions and then stored in the mind. Words stand for noetic essences.

If theories could have shapes, then the shape of Aristotle's theory would be triangular (as shown on the next page). Words at A stand for concepts at B which are correlated with objects at C. The words (A) do not mean the objects (C); their meanings are concepts (B). Words (A) are only indirectly linked to objects (C).

According to this triangular theory, words are mere flesh.

Meanings are souls that enliven that flesh. Being flesh, words are without worth in themselves. Meanings, the souls of words, give words their worth. Meanings, concepts, noetic essences, are the larger than life realities that can replace that gods at the center of Greek life.

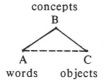

Aristotle's theory, like Plato's, arose as part of a political solution to the very practical problem of how people were going to be governed. The implication of Aristotle's suggestion was that their governance should be guided, not by the gods, but by reason. And he developed his semantic theory of language to show what reason was and how it was available to every language user.

In the somewhat later era of imperial Greece (c. 300 B.C. - 100 B.C.) conditions differed from those in Athenian democracy. But language and discourse continued to play a central and grounding role in social life. The dominant political concern of the empire was to insure the organization of social life which was by then spread thin and wide. And social life could be best organized by creating some linguistic uniformity throughout the diverse imperial territories.

Not that the Greeks had a mind to replace the languages of their minions with Greek. They did not (E. Glyn Lewis 1977). They simply desired to teach their subjects the Greek language so as to insure political harmony.

Greek grammars of this period borrowed from the Aristotelian view that a language consists of words with distinctive conceptual meanings. The grammarian's job was to isolate the words in discourse and to compare them according to their logical relations. Nouns were distinguished from verbs because of the differences in logical function of the two sets, and, in a later period, pronouns, adverbs, and prepositions were isolated.

Through this method, cases were distinguished. Nouns and verbs were divided into transitive and intransitive, active and passive. And so it happened that grammars began to take on their now familiar appearance.

The Ancient Romans The Romans borrowed heavily from this Greek tradition of language study. But the Romans had their own political conditions which gave a distinctive twist to Roman linguistics. Latin grammars began to appear in the Roman imperial period: "When citizenship had been extended in Italy to the point where native speakers of Latin were in a minority...the promotion of Latin became part of a political policy aimed at the unification of the pennisula under Roman rule" (Harris Ibid., p. 123). The major objectives for these Roman grammars was to insure that the Roman tradition continued to be respected.

Latin grammars were, like the grammars of imperial Greece, pedagogical and prescriptive. And like those Greek grammars, the Latin grammars described word classes. But the Romans added their own distinctive twist to grammatical studies. They emphasized the need for precise imitation of past models and the development of impeccable Latin rhetoric.

As the Romans saw it, classical Roman models of rhetoric formed the core of the Roman tradition. The Greeks may have been concerned with the analysis of the conceptual underpinnings of their language. But the Romans used grammatical analysis as a platform for appreciating rhetoric. Grammars were devices which taught rhetoric and which therefore sustained the core of the Roman tradition.

Both the Greeks and the Romans supposed that the social order pivoted on discourse. For the Greeks, it pivoted on the truth of discourse. For the Romans it pivoted on the style of discourse. The model Greek citizen was a person who was enlightened by grammatical studies. The model Roman citizen was a "highly serious man (who) imitates and that keeps his ordinary self within the bounds of decorum..." (Babbitt 1919: 28).

The Christians of Late Antiquity In its later stages as a Christian society (c. 313-510), Rome depended on language in two ways. First, the Christian Romans continued to cultivate traditional rhetorical skills. Second, they promoted a theological commitment to discourse. This theological commitment shared a good deal with the older Hebrew view of the word as world-creating event, e.g. "In the beginning is the Word..."

Augustine of Hippo was the foremost scholar of this era. His work marries secular and theological scholarship and brings forth a fresh speculative linguistics. Discourse plays a large part in Augustine's argument because he was at once a Roman and a Christian, and both these traditions pivot on discourse.

Augustine was the quintessential Roman scholar who cultivated his skills through imitation of classical models. Being so committed to Latin scholarship, he was torn apart by the inescapable fact that the pillars of his cultural life were crumbling--Alaric sacked Rome in 410 before the completion of The City of God. So he sought a new and indestructible ground for social life which would both explain the collapse of the Roman tradition and promise a new tradition of social life that would never

248

collapse. He located that new and indestructible ground in divine grace.

An appeal to divine grace may strike us as simplistic and magical. But Augustine's theory of the new society is anything but simplistic, and it is magical only in part. Divine grace, Augustine argued, works its way in and through normal cultural processes. A community's traditional styles of communicating constrain the thought of the people of that community. Communicative habits mold human minds: "Men are different from each other precisely because their wills are made different by the sum total of unique past experience" (Brown 1967: 174).

Communicative traditions, for their part, evolve according to laws and patterns that are beyond individual human control. Individuals have very little control over the directions taken by their traditions or even over the content of their tradition at any moment in time. The only choice which individuals can make is to participate or not participate in the social life of a community. In making the choice to participate, individuals take on the tradition and contribute to its development in time.

Christians, as members of a heavenly community, realize their membership in the same way as any other, by participating in the social life of the community. Having done so, they automatically share in, though not by dint of individual will, the tradition of that heavenly community.

Traditions, even great traditions like Rome, eventually collapse. And individuals, aside from their choices of participating or not participating, cannot stand in the way of that inevitable collapse. The heavenly city, however, is the one and only tradition which is guaranteed not to collapse. Its guarantee is divine grace which steers it around all the pitfalls in cultural evolution.

Augustine's linguistics was a composite of semantic analysis and rhetoric which was tailored to correspond to his theory of social life. Communicative practices are crucial aspects of a cultural tradition. To participate in communicative activities is to participate in the life of a community. Indeed--and here Augustine's Roman classicism shows through--participation in communicative practice is the necessary and sufficient condition for community life. For Augustine, participating in communicative activities meant, especially, participating in the liturgical rituals of Christian life.

The purpose of linguistic analysis in Augustine's view was to lay bare the roots of a community. The linguistic analysis of the practices of the elect was a sacred activity for it revealed the manner in which the Spirit steers the community of the elect. On this account linguistic analysis could only be authentic if

249

it, like the tradition in which it arises, is led by the "Inner Spirit." Linguistics here is a sacred activity which has the potential of revealing the invisible hand of God working amongst humans.

In summary, during the 800 years between Aristotle and the fall of Rome, linguists carved out a significant place in the world for language studies. Linguistics was born and grew to a strapping size during this period. Its birth and development were driven by a need to explain social change and to anchor political authority in some firm ground that could not be eroded by that change.

Different political orders located different firm grounds. For the Greeks, that ground was conceptual universals. For the Romans it was their distinctive rhetorical tradition. For the Christians of Late Antiquity it was God's hand at the helm of the social and communicative practices of a community.

One school of linguistic thought replaces another school. And we might be tempted to call such replacements developments or advances in linguistic theory. But a different viewpoint on the history of linguistics suggests that each such school of thought is part of each community's way of establishing its own political hegemony. Each era finds distinct threats to its political order, and each searches for a political foundation which can resist those threats.

From the time of the Greek republic to the present the political foundations of societies have rested in one way or another on the identification and nurturing of an object called "a language." Early on scholars may have been conscious of the significance of "a language" as a political lever. However, as time went on and as the conversation continued, the political significance of "a language" was muted. Momentarily we will see that Nebrija was well aware of the political importance of documenting the Spanish language, but, a couple centuries later, the Quakers could think that their language revisions were motivated by purely religious objectives, and, more centuries later, the Palevi regime in Iran could think that its strigent literacy campaign was motivated by purely educational objectives. In other words, the association between "a language" and the good of the state has been, through the centuries, a firm association, but, with time, an increasingly unspoken association. No less strong for being unspoken, however, the association of "a language" and the good of the state has meant that to discuss "a language" in any way whatsoever is to bolster the power of the state.

The Middle Ages The early Middle Ages was an era in which the Augustinian theory of language and social life was elaborated. The great linguistic problem of the Middle Ages was how to discern God's truth through the shadowy glass of words. The scholastic philosophers sought to penetrate that glass and discern, by the application of syllogistic logic to discourses, the structure of reality. Debates centered on the manner in which words signify. So abundant were studies of the typologies of modes of signifying (*de modis significandi*) that the grammarians of the era were often referred to as "modistae."

By the fourteenth century the theological underpinnings of twelfth century Europe were crumbling. And the fifteenth century brought economic and political changes that ushered in a new era of social life. Predictably, this was also a new era of language studies.

Early Modern Europe   The nation-state, as it emerged in the modern era, brought with it a focus on shared languages. The nation-state required the unification of diverse people under a single central authority, and the authentification of that new unit as uniquely magnificent and specially destined for greatness. The judicious manipulation of discourses on languages by those in power proved successful in accomplishing both these objectives.

The designation of a vernacular language as the standard for the nation-state was the surest way of melding diverse peoples into a unit. The task was easier said than done, however. In every instance of newly formed nation-states, the speech of the subjects varied dramatically. Therefore in order to establish unity, the speakers of non-standard varieties had to be taught the standard. Again, as in earlier eras, language teaching became a central objective for language study.

Grammars were used in this era to teach and to authenticate languages. These grammars were designed to turn dirt-languages into jewel-languages. Don Elio Antonio de Nebrija in the very first grammar of any modern European language, 1492, makes his intentions very clear:

My illustrious Queen, whenever I ponder over the past that writing has preserved for us I return forever to the same conclusion: language has for ever been the mate of empire and always shall remain its comrade. Together language and empire start and together they grow and flower, and together they decline...Castilian went through its infancy at the time of the Judges, it waxed in strength under Alphonse the Wise who gathered laws and histories and who had many Arabic and Latin works translated...This language followed our soldiers who went abroad to rule; it spread to Aragon, to Navara, and hence to Italy, wherever, my lady, you sent your armies. The scattered bits and pieces of Spain were thus gathered and joined into one single Kingdom...So far this Castilian language has been left by us loose and unruly, and in just a few centuries this language has changed beyond recognition because comparing what we speak today with the language of five hundred years ago, we notice a difference and diversity that could not be greater if these were two alien tongues. To avoid these vary variegated changes I have decided to turn the Castilian language from a loose possession of the people into an artifact so that whatever shall henceforth be said or written in this language, shall be of standard coinage, of a coinage that can outlast the times...Greek and Latin have been governed by art and thus have kept their uniformity throughout two thousand years. Unless the like be done for our language, in vain your majesty's chroniclers shall praise your deeds, your labour will not outlast more than a few years, and we shall continue to feed on Castilian translations of foreign tales about our kings.

The purpose of Nebrija's enterprise should be underscored. His goal is to describe the language of Castile and so permit a full flowering of the Spanish state. His grammar is intended to be the catalyst for his people's greatness. And, as that greatness is achieved, his grammar will serve as the vehicle through which citizens can be brought together under the rule of the state.

In France, grammars served the same purpose of precipitating unity of out the diversity of peoples within the territory of France. "The Academy (dating from 1635) existed prior to and independent of, the French nationality. Indeed, French nationality was but a by-product of the work of the Academy" (Fishman 1972). Though France, like Spain, had long since established itself as a state with a central government and defined territories, it was still an emerging nation. That is, it was building unity out of ethnic diversity. Vernacular grammars served as well as any military measure to accomplish that goal.

Sixteenth century grammars were aimed at creating linguistic unity, not just reflecting it. A grammar was a tool of conquest. But why, one wonders, would any "foreigner" ever go to the trouble of learning the language of the king? Where exactly did a grammar get its attractiveness?

The answer to this question is a tale worth telling. In brief, grammatical prescriptions of standard languages were widely adopted because they were so intimately linked to the printed word. But let me elaborate this short account for greater clarity.

Communicating through writing or printing is dramatically

different from communicating face to face. Writing is not simply another way of speaking. It is a distinct act, different in form and function from speaking. And in order to acquire competence in reading and writing a person must be schooled in the novelties of the written word. Learning to read is not at all the small step which is implied by the suggestion that written words represent spoken words. Learning to write and read is an arduous task, a task which involves learning wholly new ways of communicating.

However, despite all the difficulties of learning to read, the masses wanted to read. Indeed, the message of Protestantism was that they *had* to read; they had to read the Bible if they wanted to be saved. The citizenry of the new states was readied for literacy by a theology which said that salvation depended on reading the Word. Thus, the people were thirsty for literacy.

As far as the nation-state was concerned, the new-found desire to read was a fortunate and felicitious desire. The thirst for literacy worked to the benefit of the new nation-states in two subtle ways. First, the state saw to it that books were printed in their vernacular-become-Standard language. Hence, as citizens became literate, they simultaneously became versed in the Standard language, and they proceeded to betoken themselves through that Standard, storytelling themselves into coherence through it. Second, the practice of literacy encouraged a kind of "universalist" mentality of the very sort which states needed in order to seal the seams between the diverse peoples within their borders. Literacy encourages a decontextualization from concrete experience (Goody 1986: 12). It encourages the use of an elaborated code of speaking and a universalistic mode of interpreting both of which rely little on context and experience. In this way, the practices of literacy encourage readers and writer to overlook and eventually set aside the "ethnic" experiences which differentiate them and to focus on the abstractions which might unify them.

In earlier eras, before the world was politically reorganized with the birth the nation-states, literacy was viewed with ambivalence. Both the Church and the state regarded it as a danger as much as a benefit (Burke 1987). But, starting in the sixteenth century, that ambivalence gave way to a whole-hearted embrace of literacy by the state.

Along with the religious pressures for literacy described above, encouragements to acquire literacy and a universalist mentality came in the concrete forms of prescriptive grammar and the monolingual dictionary. Prescriptive grammars were devices for teaching literacy. Hence these grammars assisted in teaching state languages and in cutting the ties of a people to their traditional ways of speaking.

Dictionaries and dictionary writing reinforced this language teaching. The monolingual dictionary, which makes its first appearance in the works of scholars in the sixteenth century, served to standardize spellings and usage. And to that degree it was an "Academy" in a book. But on a more abstract plane, dictionaries subtly inclined people to believe that their language was little more than an ensemble of words which had no significant tie to tradition or culture. Dictionaries presuppose the notion that words and meanings are the building blocks of a language. But they suggest too that words and meanings are abstraction, like numbers, which are independent of histories and cultural ways.

A dictionary deals with word meanings as if they formed a closed, ahistorical system. "By the systematic use of words to define other words in the same language, in such a way that no words are eventually left undefined, the monolingual dictionary demonstrated that meaning could be regarded as inherent in language. No appeal to what lies outside is needed. The semantic value of words are seen to arise from their relations with other words and can be expressed in terms of them" (Harris 1980: 140). A closed system of meanings is a system divorced from experience and from history. Thus the dictionary, like the prescriptive grammar, encourages a universalistic mentality by weakening the ties of speakers to their concrete historical traditions.

The political significance of the dictionary should be as familiar to us as the name Webster which so frequently appears on the covers of authoritative English dictionaries. Noah Webster was a scholar who lived during the time of the rupture between the American colonies and England. And in the tradition of the founding fathers (e.g. Madison, Jay, etc.) going back to English philosophy (e.g. Hume), Webster felt that the new nation of the United States needed a single and independent language of its own. Accordingly, like Franklin before him, he sought to introduce spellings into American printing practices which would distinguish American English from British English, e.g. *labor* for *labour*, *theater* for *theatre*, but also *soop* for *soup* and *det* for *debt*, etc.. However with time, and especially with the influx of non-English speaking immigrants, Webster found it desirable to take advantage of widely shared conventions for spelling and to give this new nation's language some historical depth. Such desiderata led him to temper his earlier proposals on spelling. The British spellings of *soup*, *debt*, etc. were preserved so that the common parentage of the new American language and the older British version might be apparent (Weinstein 1982). The Webster dictionary and its spellings, just similar enough to British English to enjoy its authority, just different enough to enjoy independence, was used by educators to shape the sentiments of a newly emerging American people.

Seventeenth century scholarship only reinforced sixteenth

century ahistorical approaches to languages. Seventeenth century philosophers spurned alchemy and the Augustinian linguistic thought that went with it. They embraced the scientific method which had been gaining momentum since the time of Galileo. In regard to language, Locke proposed that all words are arbitrarily related to the objects they represent and are arrived at by conventions among persons who share similar experiences. Thus words can differ from people to people. But what does not differ from people to people is the logic of manipulating words. Locke explained that while experience and the words which represent experience may vary, the form of human knowledge is invariant. All humans are endowed with an identical reasoning faculty. As Locke saw it, speech is constructed from deep level mental structures and provides, for whoever troubles to look, clues to the mysteries of the operation of the human mind.

Locke and Descartes

Locke's philosophy contrasts in many respects with those of rationalists like Descartes. However, linguists have generally misinterpreted Locke's opposition to the notion of "innate ideas" (e.g. Sampson 1979), and have used that misinterpretation as the grounds for claiming that Locke and Descartes embraced polar opposite theories of human language. In contrast to this common view, I suggest that Locke and the Cartesian rationalists were in substantial agreement on many principles of language theory (Aarsleff 1976). Both these philosophers were laboring at the same task of making the world safe for science by propounding and elaborating the notion of an autonomous agentive human mind such as can be understood through the analysis of language.

Seventeenth and eighteenth century understandings of speech differ in a number of respects from the views of grammarians like Nebrija in the sixteenth century. But interestingly, they continued to offer substantial support to nationalism, even as the older linguistics did, by belittling the significance of history and tradition in the constituion of language and thought. The older grammarians accomplished this goal devoting their efforts to god (outside of time) or to future national glory; the rationalists accomplished this goal by stressing logic and the scientific method.

The Eighteenth and Nineteenth Centuries   In France, England, and America, scholars in the late eighteenth and nineteenth centuries carried Locke's conclusions one step further. By considering this move, we can appreciate the manner in which an ideology is extended and deepened in the service of an increasingly well entrenched political order.

255

Locke's rationalist account of the capabilities of the individual mind paved the way for the philosophical glorification of individual behavior. According to disciples of Rousseau, behavior arises spontaneously from within and is free of the trammels of tradition. This is yet another denial of the significance of history, and like the Lockean-Cartesian accounts which preceded, it heroized "the endeavor of the intellect to emancipate itself from perception and set up an independent power" (Babbitt 1919: 137).

Rousseauists emphasized the individual as the locus of this independent power. They played up the individual's "spontaneous play of impulse and temperament." And they systematically de-emphasized all authority external to the individual. "Every attempt, whether humanistic or religious, to set up some such centre, to oppose a unifying and centralizing principle to expansive impulse, seems to him (the Rousseauist) arbitrary and aritificial" (Ibid., p. 54).

The message here is that the human mind creates rational objects, like languages, which are inherently free of history and which function best when kept free of the constraints of history.

Counterpoise: The OED

If the eighteenth and nineteenth centuries were so whole heartedly devoted to denying the historicity of languages, how does one explain the appearance of the Oxford English Dictionary, the greatest document on the history of a language ever compiled?

In the realm of the perverse-but-true, I suggest that the most convincing denials of history have been histories. Unilineal accounts of cultural evolution, for example, seem to be histories, but they regularly subordinate the significance of the interactions of particular persons in their times and places to the significance of general mechanisms which, as laws of cultural evolution, are really non-historical regularities that only happen to play themselves out in time (Collingwood 1946). Such accounts *seem* to be focussed on concrete events through time, but they are more probably devoted to the task of legitimating some current "ideal" conditions. For example, nineteenth century cultural evolutionary accounts used historical illustration to legitimate the political ascendancy of "the civilized world."

The OED, despite all its talk of history, similarly subordinates the significance of the interactions of particular persons to the regularities of the literary evolution of English. The OED is not an illustrated history of English so much as device which happens to use historical illustration to grant authority to the contemporary elite forms of written English.

On the one hand, French scholarship celebrated the rationality of *ahistorical* languages of the mind. On the other hand, post-revolutionary French writings about languages pressed for the elimination of *historical* languages, and this latter gambit, no less than the former, was enabled by a process of linguistic objectification. A French "culte castrateur" gutted patois varieties of political significance by transforming them into objects of science, primitive throwbacks to the feudal era, languages to be collected and shelved in a museum for the edification of rusticophiles, lovers of the primitive. (Certeau 1975). Here linguistic study disempowered as effectively as it has elsewhere empowered. Certeau says, "Ethnology (and linguistics) appear at the moment when a culture can no longer defend itself" (Certeau 1980: 54).

Modern writings on language involve objectifications which both nominate and eliminate. The description of a language as an ahistorical object of the mind, a spontaneous creation by individuals, nominates one sort of a language as a ground and an authority. And the rationalist account of the adherence of such a language to the universal logic of the mind nominates it as a unifier of humans. Nominated as an authoritative unifier, an objectified mental language is a candidate for service to the state. However, the objectification of languages also eliminates, as when languages are rendered impotent by philologists who write of them as if they were museum pieces, artefacts of other times and other peoples, and therefore essentially irrelevant to modern life.

German Language and Culture   The French accounts of languages as historical objects favored the elimination of patois varieties and the promotion of French national unity. In a curious reversal, German accounts of languages as historical objects, written at roughly the same time, favored the emergence of German as a national language and promoted the unification of the German state. The lesson of this reversal is that the impact of writings that objectify languages is relative to the socio-political conditions of the society in which those writings are consumed.

At the time of these writings about German as a historical language, the German political situation was different from that of her neighbors to the west. Specifically, the German states were independent of one another. And a strong movement was afoot to weld them together into a federation.

The distinctive German language was used as the pretext for establishing that federation. Promotors of a unified German nation-state argued, in effect, that a people with one language and one culture ought to have a single state. National unity legitimates political unity.

It is not accidental that the anthropological notion "culture" was born in this period of German history when unification occupied the thoughts of German scholars as well as German statesmen. Scholarly attention was turned to the matter of cultural integrity and national character. And along with culture, language occupied center stage in almost all these disquisitions on the distinctiveness of the German culture. Early on, Johann Herder described "the language of a nation as the repository of all that has happened to that nation throughout history." And fifty years later W. von Humboldt said that "language is an external manifestation of the spirit of nations. Language is their spirit and their spirit is their language."

Curiously this German "linguistic determinism," as it is commonly referred to, springs out of Enlightenment thought. Condillac, for example, had argued in the eighteenth century, that language is a primary experience without which conception cannot arise. Johann Herder extended Condillac's view, arguing that language must precede thought both in the individual and in society. "Language is not only an instrument; it is also a treasure house and a form of thinking. It is a treasure house because the experience and knowledge of generations are accumulated in language, and it is a form of thinking because experiences are transmitted through language to the next generation in the process of upbringing."

A language as a whole and integral system is a treasure. With this principle, Herder criticized French and British analytic philosophers of his time, arguing that whenever language is subjected to analysis which reduces the whole to its parts, the treasure house and the life that it bears is lost. Like Humpty Dumpty, once language is broken into pieces, it cannot be put back together again.

The most startling feature of this hypothesis of linguistic determinism is that it arose out of a mainstream philosophical conception of language, yet its conclusions regarding the relationship of language to thought are directly contrary to those of the main line French and British philosophers. Whereas French and British thought *undercut* the relationship of language and history, the German scholars *underlined* that relationship. Whereas the former tradition concluded that words and phrases are insignificant realities which merely represent the more significant and universal aspects of thought, the latter concluded that words and phrases are the significant realities which channel thought and by which thoughts are shaped.

This extraordinary contrast in philosophies of language can be accounted for in terms of the different political situation in which they appeared. In France and England the already formed states had to build cultural unity out of diversity. Hence, the theories of language which arose in those nations emphasize the independence of language and history. In Germany, however, the culturally and linguistically unified German people found themselves fractured into independent states and in need of political unification. Hence, the German tradition emphasized the dependence of language and history, that dependence being the fact which legitimates political unification.

The correlation of different descriptions of language and different socio-political situations in Europe at the turn of the eighteenth century is dramatic, but not unexpected. Ever since Plato, descriptions of communicative behavior have covaried with political situations. The Romans supposed that continuity with the past made sense of social life, and accordingly they understood grammatical description to be a device for continuing a tradition. For Augustine and the Middle Age scholars, continuity with the past was critical, but so too was the invisible hand of the Spirit in human affairs. Hence grammatical description became a prescription and a description of God's work. In the sixteenth century, communication became the vehicle of nation-building, and so languages, as described in grammars and dictionaries, were unleashed from history. In the seventeenth and eighteenth centuries Europeans disencumbered themselves of the mystical foundations of both social life and knowledge, and the nature of language description shifted again as they searched for the rational roots of society. Finally German scholars in the nineteenth century faced the task of political unification in Germany, and in the course of their efforts they described languages as intimately tied to histories. They retied a knot that had just barely been undone.

Conclusion

Western writings on languages are held together by discourse forms which perpetuate politically significant presuppositions. The single most significant presupposition of linguistic writings is that a language is an object which can be possessed like property and assayed like gold. As an object, a language is the guarantor of the citizenship which is sought after and cherished by residents of nation-states.

"Objectified language" is a primary politically significant presupposition in Western discourses on languages. It paves the way for other presuppositions such as the linkage of language and mind, and the celebration of the individual as the the center of thought, action, and authority. The bulk of modern Western politics owes its existence to discourse enformed by such presuppositions.

In their contents, modern linguistic writings stand sometimes on one side of a political fence, sometimes on the other. Often they straddle fences. But, contents to the side, the form of such writings are in accord: language is an object; language reveals the mind; the individual mind is the quintessence of

259

human nature. In these presuppositions, modern linguistics fits hand-in-glove with political liberalism and so underwrites the institutionalizations of political liberalism in the modern era (Ryan 1983). These presuppositions in the hyperextended conversation of linguists mute, hide, and thus devalue "past associations" and, in turn, elevate "the naked individual." Dewey thumbnails the history of this devaluation and elevation in this way: "The obnoxious state was closely bound up in fact and in tradition with other associations, ecclesiastic... economic, etc. The easiest way out was to go back to the naked individual, to sweep away all associations as foreign to his nature and rights save as they proceeded from his own voluntary choice and were guaranteed by his own private ends" (Dewey 1954: 88). We moderns have, through our linguistic talk, contributed to this process of sweeping past associations away. We have done so talking in such a way as to presuppose a world in which all authority is internal and individual.

Structuralist linguistic theories, in particular, dovetail with this liberalist move to depreciate past associations and to relocate all authority within the skins of individuals. Structuralisms help to establish a climate of opinion in which we accept and even embrace such a relocation of authority. Structuralists speak into a mirror with their linguistic talk, and the persons whom they see reflected back are most often persons who find "the center of the earth" within.

The translinguist, expects that hegemony is a function of discourse forms. And so the translinguist leads the way to a new kind of anthropological discourse, one which recognizes that a struggle for reform must begin by interrupting the hyperextended conversation through which language has been linked to power, and by questioning the presupposed notion "a language." The upshot of this translinguistic criticism is the recognition that what has come down to us as linguistic anthropology must, if it is to be faithful to the Boasian vision, somehow refuse to be a *linguistic* anthropology. It must become a "non-linguistic" anthropology (p. 229), an anthropology which refuses to talk about what is conventionally called a language.

Chapter Sixteen

Summary and Resources

This survey of the writings of linguistics and anthropology has been disjointed, not by accident, but by intention. Linguistics and anthropology should be the noisy storytelling of scholars, educators, rulers, and the ruled, all struggling to advance different objectives and different methods. We have focussed our attention here on the structuralists who strive to explicate the universal language faculty, on the ethnographers who celebrate language differences, and on the translinguists who describe communicative practice.

The noisiness of this story should not be surprising. Bakhtin argued that every discourse, every conversation, every story is a struggle of competing voices. True, contending scholars sometimes try to apply a cosmetic of one sort or another in order to hide the struggle, e.g. many texts whitewash their fields portraying differing viewpoints as complementary perspectives. But just beneath the whitewash of uniformity all scholarly fields, including linguistics and anthropology, are full of disagreement and conflict.

The purpose of this final chapter is not to try to tie all the loose ends together. Such an effort would run contrary to Bakhtin's principle above. Rather the purpose is to review the principle points of disagreement. Along with this review, this final chapter will cite some major bibliographical resources which can facilitate further research on all fronts. As a summary of what has preceded, this final chapter is retrospective. As a bibliographical resource for further reading, this chapter is prospective.

Structuralisms

The nineteenth century had pinned its hopes for humanity on a rationality that it could see, e.g. magnificent bridges, breath-taking buildings, and well-planned cities, all of which implied a "denial of suffering, doubt, and negation" (Berman 1982: 245). But the World War revealed the emptiness of those hopes. In recovering, the twentieth century has pinned its hopes on a rationality that it *cannot* see, the rationality of mental faculties. And structuralists have sought to explicate that invisible rationality through linguistic analysis. Little wonder that the twentieth century has carried on a love affair with language.

Since mid-century, generative linguists have been laboring as pioneers along the trail towards this invisible rationality. Presently, the generative linguistic program is being advanced on a number of fronts all of which border on longstanding interests of anthropologists. Fromkin and Rodman (1978) and Newmeyer (1980) along with journals like Language, Lingua, Linguistics, and Studies in Language cover the general territory of generative linguistics. For further reading in the phonological issues discussed in chapter four, see S. Andersen (1985), Kenstowicz and Kisseberth (1979), and Sommerstein (1977). Further reading in syntax, discussed above in chapter five, see Radford (1981) and Chomsky (1986). Current research on the frontiers of both phonology and syntax can be found in journals like Linguistic Inquiry and Natural Language and Linguistic Theory.

Current research in the typological studies discussed in chapter six is represented in Shopen (1985) and in Comrie (1981). Researches on Sign languages of the deaf are regularly reported in Sign Language Studies, and investigations of Creole languages are reported in the Journal of Pidgin and Creole Language Studies. Tartter (1986) reviews the extraordinary language processes involved in Creole and Sign languages together with a variety of kindred issues. Major collections of essays on Creole language studies include (Hymes 1968), Valdman (1977), Valdman and Highfield (1980).

General criticisms of the generative linguistic perspective are to be found in Sampson (1980) and Harris (1981). These volumes will make it clear that generative linguistics has not been a Camelot discipline. It is not without criticism and dissent.

General sociolinguistic studies (see chapter seven) are summarized in Downes (1984). Further research is described in the proceedings of the Georgetown Roundtable Conferences on Languages and Linguistics and in the proceedings of the NWAVE conferences, both of which are published by the Georgetown University Press. Practical sociolinguistic research is published by the Center for Applied Linguistics.

Current research on language acquisition (see chapter eight) can be found in Slobin (1985). Language origins issues appear in Harnad and Steklis (1976), and specific research on ape-language experiments (see chapters two and eight) are discussed by Luce and Wilder (1983) and Ristau and Robbins (1982). See also Premack's (1986) recent defence of ape-language studies.

Boasian Ethnography

Structuralists form the mainstream of twentieth century scholarship in pursuit of invisible rationality. Boasian ethnographers have generally floated along with this mainstream but always with ambivalence. Like the European structuralists, they assumed the centrality of language and they trusted in the methods of science to describe languages. However, the tragic beginning of the twentieth century had taught them that to place all trust in anything modern is to misplace trust. Consequently they were suspicious of claims about the absoluteness and objectivity of science and of the universality of linguistic, psychological, or cultural organization.

Like many literary, sculptural, and pictorial artists of the interwar period, Boasian ethnographers sought a new foundation for human hope. They looked not to the material rationality of the nineteenth century, nor to the invisible rationality of the structuralists, but to possibilities for sane and balanced human life among primitive peoples. Their expectation was that lessons in human living were there for the learning, there, that is, amongst the primitive peoples who were fast being crushed by the juggernaut of modern society.

The trust of the Boasians in the promise of cultural diversity and linguistic relativity was complete. All their other loyalties were provisional. The methods of science were trustworthy only so long as science both justified and facilitated research among culturally and linguistically diverse peoples. Trust in language as the center and pivot of cultural life was equally provisional. If either the methods of science or the developments in linguistics were to lead them away from the pursuit of cultural and linguistic diversity, then, at that point, science and linguistics would have exhausted their utility. Boasians reserved unqualified trust only in human diversity and in the principle of linguistic relativity. Consider, for example, Whorf's use of scientific linguistics to analyze culturally different world views. His proposals raised doubts about the absoluteness--how could it be otherwise?--of the modern scientific world view. Those doubts were, in effect, doubts about the very methods that made his analysis possible. This apparent self-negation in the work of Whorf illustrates the Boasian subordination of science itself to the objective of pursuing cultural diversity, which is the sole promise of hope for twentieth century humans.

And when, in the seventies, linguistics, under the influence of Noam Chomsky, became a discipline that virtually stood for universality, innateness, and underlying uniformity, ethnographers of speaking pulled up stakes, left the topic of language and languages, and began exploring communicative practice for what it might reveal about human potentiality. Here again, the continuers of the Boasian tradition of ethnography showed themselves fair weather friends to all principles and all assumptions save the principle of human diversity. This steadfast commitment of ethnographers to describing human diversity is a sign of an abiding cynicism about the potentiality of all things modern, including language, science, and society, and of an ultimate trust that sanity and balance can be found outside of modernity.

263

The volumes edited by Hoijer (1954) and Hymes (1964) present research that pursued the directions established by Sapir and Whorf (see chapter nine). Volumes edited by Tyler (1969) and Casson (1981) together with Casson (1983) present research of ethnoscientists. Keesing (1972) and Tyler (1978) provide a rational for a shift away from structural studies of vocabulary systems and towards studies of communicative practice. Bauman and Sherzer (1974) and Shopen (1979a; 1979b) illustrate the researches of ethnographers of speaking (see chapter eleven). The journal Language in Society is a major outlet for publications in this area. Research on all issues pertaining to language and culture also appears in general anthropology journals like American Anthropologist, American Ethnologist, and Journal of Anthropological Research.

Special topics in the ethnography of speaking have generated a considerable literature of their own. For discussions of the role of speech in education, see Heath (1983). For more on the relationship of literacy to communicative practice, see Cicourel (1985).

Translinguistics

Boas's program for ethnography was ambivalent, devotedly scientific and linguistic, but willing, in the end, to lay even these aside in order to facilitate the pursuit of human diversity. Bakhtin's program for translinguistics was not ambivalent in the least. Both science and linguistics came under his attack. And he relied on neither in designating his promise for humanity and his objective for translinguistic study.

The source of his promise for modern humanity was his theology, kenotic Christianity. And that kenotic Christianity told him that the interaction of unique human individuals is both the objective of human living and the source of sanity in human life. Specifically, the noisy, laughing, struggling, talk of people in interaction is itself the best of human living. Translinguistics, a conversation about the conversations that occur in human interaction, is the activity which makes apparent that fullness and potentiality of human interaction.

Bakhtin's translinguistics, with its focus on heterogeneous communicative practice and with its tradition of criticizing the sacred cows of modernity, is breathing new life into the work of American ethnography and especially into the ethnography of speaking. Besides providing principles for the description of communicative practice, it is stimulating new self-critical approaches to ethnographic description. Thus translinguistics is a two edged sword: it builds an understanding of communicative practice as it cuts away obstacles to further understanding.

For more on translinguistics as described in chapter twelve, see Clark and Holquist (1984) and Morson (1986). The issues treated in chapters thirteen and fourteen are elaborated in a variety of resources, though few are labeled translinguistics (Crick 1976; Crick 1982; Parkin 1982; Fardon 1985; Marcus and Cushman 1982; Clifford and Marcus 1986). For research on storytelling, discourse analysis, and the reflexive perspective see journals like Discourse and Multilingua. For more on the history of linguistics see the journal Historiographica Linguistica, and for specific discussions of language and politics, see Sampson (1979), Newmeyer (1987), and the journal Language Problems and Language Planning.

REFERENCES CITED

Aarsleff, Hans

1976 An outline of language origins theory since the Renaissance. *Origins and Evolution of Language and Speech*, ed. S. Harnad and H . Steklis. Annals of the New York Academy of Science 280: 4-13.

Aberle, David

1968 The influence of linguistics on early culture and personality theory. *Theory in Anthropology*, eds. R. Manners and D. Kaplan. Chicago: Aldine.

Abrahams, Roger

1976 *Talking Black*. Rowley, MA: Newbury House.

Abrahams, Roger and Bauman, Richard

1971 Sense and nonsense in St. Vincent: speech behavior and decorum in a Caribbean community. *American Anthropologist* 73 (3): 262-272.

Adams, Richard

1972 *Watership Down*. New York: Avon Books.

Albert, Ethel

1972 Culture patterning of speech behavior in Burundi. *Direction in Sociolinguistics: The Ethnography of Communication*, ed. J. Gumperz and D. Hymes. New York: Holt, Rinehart & Winston.

Alleyne, Mervyne

1980 *Comparative Afro-American*. Ann Arbor: Karoma.

Andersen, Stephen

1985 *Phonology in the Twentieth Century: Theories of Rules and Theories of Representations*. Chicago: University of Chicago Press.

Argyle, M. and Cook, M.

1976 *Gaze and Mutual Gaze*. New York: Cambridge University Press.

Asimov, Isaac

    1953 *The Second Foundation.* New York: Avon.

Baal, Jan van

    1981 *Man's Quest for Partnership: The Anthropological Foundations of Ethics and Religion.* Assen, The Netherlands: Van Gorcum.

Babbitt, Irving

    1977 [1919] *Rousseau and Romanticism.* Austin: University of Texas Press.

Bakhtin, M.M.

    1981 *The Dialogic Imagination.* Austin: University of Texas.

Basso, Ellen

    1985 *A Musical View of the Universe.* Philadelphia: University of Pennsylvania Press.

Basso, Keith

    1979 *Portraits of the "Whiteman": Linguistic Play and Cultural Symbols among the Western Apache.* New York: Cambridge University Press.

Bateson, Gregory

    1972 *Steps to an Ecology of Mind.* New York: Ballantine.

Bauman, Richard

    1981 "Any man who keeps more'n one hound'll lie to you": Dog trading and storytelling in Canton, Texas. *Other Neighborly Names: Social Process and Cultural Image in Texas Folklore,* eds. R. Abrahams and R. Bauman. Austin: University of Texas Press.

Bauman, Richard

    1983 *Let Your Words Be Few: Symbolism of Speaking and Silence among 17th Century Quakers.* New York: Cambridge University Press.

Bauman, Richard

    1986 *Story, Performance, and Event: Contextual Studies of Oral Narrative.* New York: Cambridge University Press.

268

Bauman, Richard and Sherzer, Joel, eds.

1974 *Explorations in the Ethnography of Speaking.* New York: Cambridge University Press.

Bean, Susan

1980 Ethnology and the study of proper names. *Anthropological Linguistics* 22(7): 305-316.

Becker, Alton

1982 The poetics of a Javanese poem. *Spoken and Written Language: Exploring Orality and Literacy,* ed. D. Tannen. Norwood, NJ: Ablex.

Becker, Carl

1959 [1932] *The Heavenly City of Eighteenth Century Philosophers.* New Haven: Yale University Press.

Bellah, Robert

1958 Religious evolution. *Readings in Comparative Religions,* eds. W. Lessa and E. Vogt. New York: Harper and Row.

Bellah, Robert et al.

1985 *Habits of the Heart.* Berkeley: University of California Press.

Benedict, Ruth

1934 *Patterns of Culture.* New York: Houghton Mifflin.

Berger, Peter

1976 *Pyramids of Sacrifice.* Garden City, NY: Doubleday.

Berlin, Brent and Kay, Paul

1969 *Basic Color Terms: Their Universality and Evolution.* Berkeley: University of California Press.

Berman, Marshall

1982 *All That is Solid Melts into Air: The Experience of Modernity.* New York: Simon and Schuster.

Berman, Morris

1981 *The Reenchantment of the World.* Ithaca: Cornell University Press.

Bernstein, Basil

1975 *Class, Codes and Control: Theoretical Studies Towards a Sociology of Language.* New York: Schocken.

Bettelheim, Bruno

1975 *Uses of Enchantment: The Meaning and Importance of Fairy Tales.* New York: Vintage.

Bickerton, Derek

1971 Inherent variability and the variable rule. *Foundations of Language* 7: 457-92.

Bickerton, Derek

1981 *Roots of Language.* Ann Arbor: Karoma Press.

Bird, Charles and Shopen, Timothy

1979 Maninka. *Languages and Their Speakers,* ed. Timothy Shopen. Cambridge: Winthrop Press.

Bishop, Michael

1979 *Transfigurations.* New York: Berkley Corporation.

Bleier, Ruth

1984 *Science and Gender: A Critique of Biology and its Theories of Women.* New York: Pergamon.

Boas, Franz

1911 *Introduction to the Handbook of the American Indian Languages.* Washington: Georgetown University Press. (reprint)

Bohannan, Paul and Glazer, Mark

1973 *High Points in Anthropology,* eds. P. Bohannan and M. Glazer. New York: Alfred Knopf.

Bookchin, Murray

1982 *The Ecology of Freedom.* Palo Alto: Cheshire.

Boon, James

  1982 *Other Tribes, Other Scribes.* New York: Cambridge.

Bove, Paul

  1986 *Intellectuals in Power: A Geneology of Critical Humanism.* Columbia University Press.

Brenneis, Donald and Lein, Laura

  1977 "You fruithead:" A sociolinguistic approach to children's dispute settlement. *Child Discourses,* eds. S. Ervin-Tripp and C. Mitchell-Kernan. New York: Academic Press.

Brown, Cecil

  1984 *Language and Living Things: Uniformities in Folk Classification and Naming.* New Brunswick, NJ: Rutgers University Press.

Brown, Norman O.

  1959 *Life against Death: The Psychoanalytic Meaning of History.* New York: Vintage.

Brown, Penelope and Levinson, Stephen

  1978 Universals in language usage: politeness phenomena. *Questions and Politeness: Strategies in Social Interaction,* ed. Esther Goody. (reprinted as *Politeness: Some Universals in Language Usage,* 1987). New York: Cambridge University Press.

Brown, Peter

  1967 *Augustine of Hippo.* Berkeley: University of California Press.

Brown, Peter

  1983 The saint as exemplar in late antiquity. *Representations* 1(2): 1-25.

Brown, Roger

  1973 *A First Language.* Cambridge: Harvard University Press.

Brown, Roger and Lenneberg, Eric

  1954 A study in languge and cognition. *Journal of Abnormal*

271

Social Psychology. 49: 454-462.

Bruner, Edward

> 1986 Experience and its expressions. *Anthropology Experience,* eds. E. Bruner and V. Turner. Urbana, IL: University of Illinois Press.

Burke, Peter

> 1987 The uses of literacy in early modern Italy. *The Social History of Language,* eds. Peter Burke and Roy Porter. New York: Cambridge.

Butterfield, Herbert

> 1959 [1937] *The Whig Interpretation of History.* London: Bell and Sons.

Calame-Griaule, Genvieve

> 1985 *Words and the Dogon World.* Philadelphia: Ishi Press.

Campbell, Joseph

> 1959 *The Masks of God: Primitive Mythology.* New York: Penguin.

Capra, Fritjof

> 1983 *The Turning Point: Science, Society, and the Rising Culture.* New York: Bantam.

Carroll, John B. and Casagrande, Joseph B.

> 1958 The function of language classifications in behavior. *Communication and Culture: Readings in the Codes of Human Interaction,* ed. Alfred G. Smith. New York: Holt, Rinehart and Winston.

Cassirer, Ernst

> 1945 Structuralism in modern linguistics. *Word* 1: 97-120.

Casson, Ronald, ed.

> 1981 *Language, Culture, and Cognition.* New York: Macmillan.

Casson, Ronald

> 1983 Schemata in cognitive anthropology. *Annual Review of Anthropology* 12: 429-462.

Certeau, Michel de

1975 *Une Politique de La Langue: La Revolution Francaise et Les Patois.* Paris: Editions Gallimard.

Certeau, Michel de

1980 (1974) *La Culture Au Pluriel.* Paris: Christian Bourgois Editeur.

Chardin, Teilhard de

1959 *The Phenomenon of Man.* New York: Harper and Row.

Chomsky, Noam

1957 *Syntactic Structures.* The Hague: Mouton.

Chomsky, Noam

1965 *Aspects of the Theory of Syntax.* Cambridge: MIT Press.

Chomsky, Noam

1966 *Cartesian Linguistics.* Cambridge: MIT Press.

Chomsky, Noam

1977 *Language and Responsibility.* New York: Pantheon.

Chomsky, Noam

1980a On binding. *Linguistic Inquiry* 11: 1-45.

Chomsky, Noam

1980b *Rules and Representations.* New York: Columbia University Press.

Chomsky, Noam

1986 *Knowledge of Language: Its Nature, Origin, and Use.* New York: Praeger.

Cicourel, Aaron

1985 Text and discourse. *Annual Review of Anthropology* 14: 159-185.

Clark, Katerina and Holquist, Michael

1984 *Mikhail Bakhtin.* Cambridge: Belknap.

References

Clifford, James

    1981 On ethnographic surrealism. *Comparative Studies in Society,* 23 (4): 539-564.

Clifford, James

    1983 On ethnographic authority. *Representations* 1(2): 118-146.

Clifford, James and Marcus, George, eds.

    1986 *Writing Culture: The Poetics and Politics of Ethnography.* Berkeley: University of California Press.

Collingwood, R.G.

    1946 *The Idea of History.* New York: Oxford University.

Comrie, Bernard

    1981 *Language Universals and Language Typology: Syntax and Morphology.* Olford: B. Blackwell.

Coward, Rosalind and Ellis, John

    1977 *Language and Materialism: Developments in Semiology and in the Theory of the Subject.* Boston: RKP.

Cox, Harvey

    1965 *The Secular City: Secularization and Urbanization in Theological Perspective.* New York: Macmillan.

Crapanzano, Vincent

    1979 The self, the third, and desire. *Psychosocial Theories of the Self,* ed. Benjamin Lee. New York: Plenum.

Crick, Malcolm

    1976 *Explorations in Language and Meaning: Towards a Semantic Anthropology.* London: Malaby.

Crick, Malcolm

    1982 Anthropology of Knowledge. *Annual Review of Anthropology* 11: 287-313.

Crocker, Jon C.

    1985 *Vital Souls: Bororo Cosmology, Natural Symbols and*

274

Shamanism. Tucson: University of Arizona Press.

Curtiss, Susan

    1977 *Genie: A Psycholinguistic Study of a Modern-Day "Wild Child."* New York: Academic Press.

Cutting, James and Eimas, Peter

    1975 Phonetic feature analyzers and the processing of speech in infants. *The Role of Speech in Language,* eds. J. Kavanaugh and J. Cutting. Cambridge: MIT.

Dewey, John

    1954 *Logic, The Theory of Inquiry.* New York: Macmillan.

Dillard, J.L.

    1972 *Black English: Its History and Usage in the United States.* New York: Random House.

Dore, John and McDermott, R.P.

    1982 Linguistic indeterminacy and social context. *Language* 58 (2): 374-398.

Downes, William

    1984 *Language and Society.* New York: Fontana.

Drummond, Lee

    1981 The serpent's children: semiotics of cultural genesis in Arawak and Trobriand myths. *American Ethnologist* 8: 633-660.

Dumont, Louis

    1965 The modern conception of the individual. *Contributions to Indian Sociology* 8: 13-61.

Durkheim, Emile

    1895 *The Rules of Sociological Method.* New York: The Free Press.

Eckman, Fred

    1976 On the explanation of some typological facts about raising. Bloomington, IN: Indiana University Linguistics Club.

References

Edwards, Walter

    1978 Tantalisin' and busin' in Guyana. *Anthropological Linguistics* 20: 194-213.

Elgin, Duane

    1981 *Voluntary Action.* New York: Morrow.

Erickson, Frederick

    1984 Rhetoric, anecdote, and rhapsody: coherence strategies in a conversation among Black American adolescents. *Coherence in Spoken and Written Discourse,* ed. D. Tannen. Norwood, NJ: Ablex.

Erickson, Frederick and Shulz, J.

    1982 *The Counselor as Gatekeeper: Social Interaction in Interviews.* New York: Academic Press.

Errington, Frederick

    1984 *Manners and Meaning in Western Sumatra: The Social Context of Consciousness.* New Haven: Yale University Press.

Fabian, Johannes

    1983 *Time and the Other: How Anthropology Makes its Object.* New York: Columbia University Press.

Farb, Peter

    1974 *Word Play: What Happens When People Talk.* New York: Bantam.

Fardon, Richard, ed.

    1985 *Power and Knowledge: Anthropological and Sociological Approaches.* Edinburgh: Scottish Academic Press.

Feldman, Heidi, Goldin-Meadow, Susan, and Gleitman, Lila

    1978 Beyond Herodotus: the creation of language by linguistically deprived children. *Action, Gesture, and Symbol: The Emergence of Language,* ed. A. Lock. New York: Academic Press.

276

References

Ferguson, Marilyn

1980 *The Aquarian Conspiracy: Personal and Social Transformation in the 1980's.* New York: St. Martin's Press.

Feyerabend, Paul

1975 *Against Method: An Outline of an Anarchistic Theory of Knowledge.* London: NLB.

Firth, Raymond

1957 (1936) *We, The Tikopia: Kinship in Primitive Polynesia.* Boston: Beacon.

Fisher, John

1964 Social influence in the choice of a linguistic variant. *Language in Culture and Society: A Reader in Linguistics and Anthropology,* ed. Dell Hymes. New York: Harper.

Fishman, Joshua

1972 *Language and Nationalism: Two Integrative Essays.* Rowley, MA: Newbury House.

Fortune, Reo

1932 *The Sorcers of Dobu: The Social Anthropology of the Dobu Islanders of the Western Pacific.* New York: Dutton.

Foucault, Michel

1970 *The Order of Things: The Archeology of the Human Sciences.* New York: Vintage.

Foucault, Michel

1980 *Power/Knowledge: Selected Interview and Other Writings, 1972-1977.* New York: Pantheon.

Frake, Charles

1964 How to ask for a drink in Subanun. *Language and Social Context,* ed. Pier Paolo Giglioli. New York: Penguin.

Friedrich, Paul

1979 *Language, Culture and the Imagination.* Stanford:

Stanford University Press.

Friedrich, Paul

1987 *The Language Parallax: Linguistic Relativism and Poetic Indeterminacy.* Austin: University of Texas Press.

Fromkin, Victoria and Rodman, Hyman

1974 *An Introduction to Language.* New York: Holt, Rinehart and Winston.

Gans, Eric

1979 *The Origin of Language: A Formal Theory of Representation.* Berkeley: University of California Press.

Gans, Eric

1985 *The End of Culture: Towards a Generative Anthropology.* Berkeley: University of California Press.

Garfinkel, Harold

1967 *Studies in Ethnomethodology.* Englewood Cliffs, NJ: Prentice Hall.

Geertz, Clifford

1973 Person, time, and conduct in Bali. *The Interpretation of Cultures.* New York: Basic Books.

Geertz, Clifford

1983 *Local Knowledge: Further Essays in Interpretive Anthropology.* New York: Basic Books.

Gergen, Kenneth

1982 *Toward Transformation in Social Knowledge.* New York: Springer Verlag.

Gergen, Kenneth and Gergen, Mary

1983 Narratives of the self. *Studies in Social Identity,* eds. T.R. Sarbin and K.E. Scheibe. New York: Praeger.

Giddens, Anthony

1984 *The Constitution of Society: Outline of the Theory of Structuration.* Berkeley: University of California Press.

Gilman, David

    1987 *Agression and Community.* Yale University Press.

Ginzburg, Carlo

    1980 *The Cheese and The Worms: The Cosmos of a Sixteenth Century Miller.* New York: Penguin.

Goffman, Erving

    1957 *The Presentation of Self in Everyday Life.* Garden City, NJ: Doubleday.

Goffman, Erving

    1967 *Interaction Ritual.* Garden City, NJ: Doubleday.

Goffman, Erving

    1974 *Frame Analysis.* New York: Harper and Row.

Goffman, Erving

    1981a *Forms of Talk.* Philadelphia: University of Pennsylvania Press.

Goffman, Erving

    1981b Felicity's condition. *American Journal of Sociology* 89(1): 1-53.

Goody, Jack

    1986 *The Logic of Writing and the Organization of Society.* New York: Cambridge University Press.

Gossen, Gary

    1974 *Chamulas in the World of the Sun: Time and Space in a Maya Oral Tradition.* Cambridge: Harvard University Press.

Gouldner, Alvin

    1976 *The Dialectic of Ideology and Technology: The Origin, Grammar, and Function of Ideology.* New York: Seabury.

Goulet, John

    1975 *Oh's Profit.* New York: Morrow.

Greenberg, Joseph

1966 Language universals. *Current Trends in Linguistics* 3: 61-112.

Greenblatt, Stephen

1980 *Renaissance Self-Fashioning.* Chicago: University of Chicago Press.

Grice, H.P.

1968 Utterer's-meaning, sentence-meaning, and word-meaning. *Foundations of Language* 4: 1-18.

Gumperz, John

1968 Types of linguistic communities. *Readings in The Sociology of Language,* ed. Joshua Fishman. The Hague: Mouton.

Gumperz, John

1982 *Discourse Strategies.* New York: Cambridge University Press.

Gumperz, John

1984 Communicative competence revisited. *Meaning, Form, and Use in Context: Linguistic Applications,* ed. D. Schiffrin. Washington: Georgetown University Press.

Habermas, Jurgen

1970 Toward a theory of communicative competence. *Recent Sociology, No. 2: Patterns of Communicative Behavior,* ed. Hans Dreitzel. New York: Macmillan.

Hall, Edward

1977 *Beyond Culture.* Garden City, NY: Doubleday.

Halliday, M.A.K.

1973 *Explorations in the Functions of Language.* London: Edward Arnold.

Halliday, M.A.K.

1976 Anti-languages. *American Anthropologist* 78: 570-584.

Haraway, Donna

1986 Primatology Is Poltics by Other Means. *Feminist Approaches to Science,* ed. Ruth Bleier. New York: Pergamon.

Harnad, S. and Steklis, H., eds.

1976 Origins and Evolution of Language and Speech. *Annals of the New York Academy of Sciences,* vol. 280.

Harrington, Michael

1983 *The Politics at God's Funeral: The Spiritual Crisis of Western Civilization.* New York: Penguin.

Harris, Roy

1980 *The Language Makers.* London: Duckworth.

Hatch, Elvin

1973 *Theories of Man and Culture.* New York: Columbia University Press.

Hauerwas, Stanley

1977 *A Community of Character.* South Bend, IN: Notre Dame University Press.

Haviland, John

1977 *Gossip, Reputation, and Knowledge in Zinacantan.* Chicago: University of Chicago Press.

Heath, Shirley Brice

1983 *Ways with Words: Language, Life, and Work in Community and Classrooms.* New York: Cambridge University Press.

Henriques, Julian et al.

1984 *Changing the Subject: Psychology, Social Regulation and Subjectivity.* New York: Methuen.

Henson, Hilary

1974 *British Social Anthropologists and Language.* New York: Oxford University Press.

Heritage, John

1984 *Garfinkel and Ethnomethodology.* New York: Cambridge University Press.

Herzfeld, Michael

1985 *The Poetics of Manhood.* Princeton: Princeton University Press.

Hewes, Gordon

1973 Primate communication and the gestural origin of language. *Current Anthropology* 14: 5-24.

Hill, Jane and Hill, Kenneth

1986 *Speaking Mexicano: Dynamics of Syncretic Language in Central Mexico.* Tucson: University of Arizona Press.

Hockett, Charles

1985 Distinguished lecture: F. *American Anthropologist* 87 (2): 263-281.

Hockett, Charles and Ascher, R.

1964 The Human Revolution. *Current Anthropology* 5: 135-147.

Hofstadter, Douglas

1979 *Godel, Escher, Bach: An Eternal Golden Braid.* New York: Basic Books.

Hoijer, Harry

1954 *Language in Culture.* Chicago: University of Chicago Press.

Howes, David

1980 The well-springs of action: an enquiry into 'human nature.' *Journal of the Anthropological Society of Oxford* 11: 15-30.

Huey, Edmund

1916 *The History and Pedagogy of Reading.* New York: Macmillan.

Hymes, Dell

1971 On linguistic theory, communicative competence, and the education of disadvantaged children. *Anthropological*

282

Perspectives on Education, eds. M. Wax et al. New York: Basic Books.

Hymes, Dell, ed.

1964 *Language in Culture and Society.* New York: Harper and Row.

Hymes, Dell, ed.

1968 *Pidginization and Creolization of Languages.* New York: Cambridge University Press.

Illich, Ivan

1977 *Toward a History of Human Needs.* New York: Bantam Books.

Illich, Ivan

1980 Vernacular values. *The Schumacher Lectures,* ed. Satish Kumar. New York: Harper Colophon.

Innis, Harold

1972 *Empire and Communication.* Toronto: University of Toronto Press.

Jakobson, Roman

1960 Linguistics and poetics. *Style in Language,* ed. T. Sebeok. Cambridge: MIT.

Jakobson, Roman

1970 *Main Trends in the Science of Language.* New York: Harper and Row.

Jaynes, Julian

1976 *The Origin of Consciousness in the Breakdown of the Bicameral Mind.* Boston: Houghton Mifflin.

Katz, J. and Postal, P.

1964 *An Integrated Theory of Linguistic Description.* Cambridge: MIT.

Kay, Paul

1977 Language evolution and speech style. *Sociocultural Dimensions of Language Change,* eds. Ben Blount and M.

Sanches. New York: Academic Press.

Kaye, Kenneth

1982 *The Mental and Social Life of Babies: How Parents Create Persons.* Chicago: University of Chicago Press.

Keenan, Edward and Ochs, Elinor

1979 Becoming a competent speaker of Malagasy. *Languages and their Speakers,* ed. T. Shopen. Cambridge: Winthrop.

Keesing, Roger

1972 Paradigms lost: the new ethnography and the new linguistics. *Southwest Journal of Anthropology* 28: 299-332.

Kendon, Adam

1981 Some functions of the face in a kissing round. *Nonverbal Communication, Interaction, and Gesture: Selections from Semiotica,* ed. A. Kendon. The Hague: Mouton.

Kenstowicz, Michael and Kisseberth, Charles

1979 *Generative Phonology: Description and Theory.* New York: Academic Press.

Klima, Edward and Bellugi, Ursula

1979 *Signs of Language.* Cambridge: Harvard University Press.

Koerner, E.F.K.

1972 *Ferdinand de Saussure: Origin and Development of his Linguistic Thought in Western Studies of Language.* Vieweg: Braun-Shweig.

Kripke, Saul

1972 Naming and necessity. *Semantics of Natural Language,* eds. D. Davidson and G. Harman. New York: Humanities.

Kroeber, Alfred L.

1909 Classificatory systems of relationship. *Journal of the Royal Anthropological Institute of Great Britain and Ireland* 39: 77-84.

Kuhn, Thomas

1962 *The Structure of Scientic Revolutions.* Chicago: University of Chicago Press.

Labov, William

1969 Contraction, deletion and the inherent variability of the English copula. *Language* 45: 715-62.

Labov, William

1970 *The Study of Nonstandard English.* New York: National Council of Teachers of English.

Labov, William

1972a *Sociolinguistic Patterns.* Philadelphia: University of Pennsylvania Press.

Labov, William

1972b *Quantitative Study of Sound Change in Progress,* two volumes. Philadelphia: U.S. Regional Survey.

Lakoff, George and Johnson, Mark

1980 *Metaphors We Live By.* Chicago: University of Chicago Press.

Lakoff, George

1987 *Women, Fire, and Dangerous Things: What Categories Reveal about the Mind.* Chicago: University of Chicago Press.

Lasch, Christopher

1979 *The Culture of Narcissism: American Life in an Age of Diminishing Expectations.* New York: W.W. Norton.

Lasch, Christopher

1987 Soul of a new age. *Omnni* 10 (1): 78 ff.

Latour, B. and Woolgar, B.

1979 *Laboratory Life: The Social Construction of Scientific Facts.* Beverly Hills: Sage.

285

Lee, Dorothy

1959 *Freedom and Culture.* New York: Spectrum.

Leenhardt, Maurice

1979 [1947] *Do Kamo: Person and Myth in the Melanesian World.* Chicago: University of Chicago Press.

Lehmann, Winfred

1978 The great underlying ground plans. *Syntactic Typology: Studies in the Phenomenology of Languge.* Austin: University of Texas Press.

LePage, Robert and Tabouret-Keller, Andree

1985 *Acts of Identity: Creole-based Approaches to Language and Ethnicity.* New York: Cambridge University Press.

Levinson, Stephen

1983 *Pragmatics.* New York: Cambridge University Press.

Lewis, E. Glyn

1977 Bilingualism and bilingual education: the ancient world to the renaissance. *Frontiers of Bilingual Education,* ed. B. Spolsky and R. Cooper. Rowley, MA: Newbury House.

Lieberman, Philip

1975 *On the Origins of Language.* New York: Macmillan.

Lieberman, Philip

1984 *The Biology and Evolution of Language.* Cambridge: Harvard University Press.

Lightfoot, David

1982 *The Language Lottery: Toward a Biology of Grammars.* Cambridge: MIT.

Lounsbury, Floyd

1968 One hundred years of anthropological linguistics. *One Hundred Years of Anthropology,* ed. J.O. Brew. New York: Cambridge University Press.

Luce, Judith de and Wilder, H., eds.

1983 *Language in Primates: Perspectives and Implications.*
New York: Springer-Verlag.

Luckmann, Thomas

1967 *The Invisible Religion: The Problem of Religion in Modern Society.* New York: Macmillan.

Luckmann, Thomas

1983 Remarks on personal identity: inner, social, and historical time. *Identity: Personal and Sociocultural,* ed. Anita Jacobson-Widding. Atlantic Highlands, NJ: Humanities.

Malinowski, Bronislaw

1961 [1922] *Argonauts of the Western Pacific.* New York: Dutton.

Manual, Frank and Manual, Fritzie

1979 *Utopian Thought in the Western World.* Cambridge: Harvard University Press.

Marcus, George and Cushman, Dick

1982 Ethnographies as texts. *Annual Review of Anthropology* 11: 25-70.

Marcus, George and Fischer, Michael

1986 *Anthropology as Cultural Critique.* Chicago: University of Chicago Press.

Marler, Peter

1975 On the origin of speech from animal sounds. *The Role of Speech in Language,* ed. J. Kavanaugh and J. Cutting. Cambridge: MIT.

McNeil, David

1984 Language viewed as action. *Culture, Communication and Cognition: Vygotskean Perspectives,* ed. J. Wertsch. New York: Cambridge University Press.

Meeker, Michael

1979 *Literature and Violence in North Arabia.* New York:

Cambridge University Press.

Myerhoff, Barbara

1982 Life history among the elderly: performance, visibility, and re-membering. *A Crack in the Mirror: Reflexive Perspectives in Anthropology,* ed. Jay Ruby. Philadelphia: University of Pennsylvania Press.

Montague, Ashley

1976 Toolmaking, hunting, and the origin of language. *Origins and Evolution of Language and Speech,* ed. S. Harnad and H. Steklis. Annals of the New York Academy of Sciences 280: 266-74.

Morson, Gary, ed.

1986 *Bakhtin: Dialogues on His Work.* Chicago: University of Chicago Press.

Mulcahy, F. David

1979 Studies in social ecology: conflict and verbal abuse. *Maledicta* 3: 87-100.

Newmeyer, Frederick

1980 *Linguistic Theory in America: The First Quarter-Century of Transformational Generative Grammar.* New York: Academic Press.

Newmeyer, Frederick

1987 *The Politics of Linguistics.* Chicago: University of Chicago Press.

Newport, Elissa

1982 Task specificity in language learning? *Language Acquisition: The State of the Art,* eds. E. Wanner and L. Gleitman. New York: Cambridge University Pres.

Nisbet, Robert

1969 *Social Change and History: Aspects of the Western Theory of Development.* New York: Oxford University Press.

Ochs, Elinor

1973 A sliding sense of obligatoriness: the poly-structure

of Malagasy oratory. *Language in Society* 2: 225-243.

Ochs, Elinor

  1979 Introduction: what child languge can contribute to pragmatics. *Developmental Pragmatics,* ed. E. Ochs and B. Schieffelin. New York: Academic Press.

Ochs, Elinor and Schieffelin, Bambi

  1984 Language acquisition and socialization: three developmental stories and their implications. *Culture Theory: Essays on Mind, Self, and Emotion,* eds. R. LeVine and R. Shweder. New York: Cambridge University Press.

Ong, Walter

  1967 *The Presence of the Word.* New Haven: Yale University Press.

Ong, Walter

  1977 *Interfaces of the Word: Studies in the Evolution of Consciousness and Culture.* Ithaca: Cornell University Press.

Pagels, Elaine

  1979 *The Gnostic Gospels.* New York: Vintage.

Parkin, David, ed.

  1982 *Semantic Anthropology.* New York: Academic Press.

Pattison, Robert

  1982 *On Literacy: The Politics of the World from Homer to the Age of Rock.* New York: Oxford University Press.

Pearce, W.B. and Cronen, V.E.

  1980 *Communication, Action and Meaning.* New York: Praeger.

Peck, Scott

  1987 *The Different Drum: Community Making and Peace.* New York: Simon and Schuster.

Peirce, Charles Sanders

  1877 How to make ideas clear. *Popular Science Monthly.*

Pirsig, Robert

　　1974 *Zen and the Art of Motorcycle Maintenance.* New York:
　　Bantam.

Popper, Karl

　　1963 *Conjectures and Refutations: The Growth of Scientific
　　Knowledge.* New York: Harper and Row.

Premack, David

　　1986 *Gavagai.* Cambridge: MIT Press.

Radford, A.

　　1981 *Transformational Syntax.* New York: Cambridge
　　University Press.

Reddy, Michael

　　1979 The conduit metaphor: a case of frame conflict in our
　　language about language. *Metaphor and Theory,* ed. A.
　　Ortony. New York: Cambridge University Press.

Riesman, David

　　1949 *The Lonely Crowd: A Study of the Changing American
　　Character.* New Haven: Yale University Press.

Rifkin, Jeremy

　　1979 *The Emerging Order: God the the Age of Scarcity.* New
　　York: Ballantine.

Ristau, Carolyn and Robbins, Donald

　　1982 Language in the great apes. *Advanced Studies in Animal
　　Behavior* 2: 141-255.

Roche, Maurice

　　1973 *Phenomenology, Language, and the Social Sciences.*
　　Boston: Routledge and Kegan Paul.

Rochester, S. and Martin, J.R.

　　1979 *Crazy Talk: A Study of the Discourse of Schizophrenic
　　Speakers.* New York: Plenum.

Romaine, Suzanne

1982 What is a speech community? *Sociolinguistic Variation in Speech Communities,* ed. S. Romaine. London: Arnold.

Rorty, Richard

1979 *Philosophy and the Mirror of Nature.* Princeton: Princeton University Press.

Rose, Dan

1982 Occasions and forms of anthropological experience. *A Crack in the Mirror: Reflexive Perspectives in Anthropology,* ed. J. Ruby. Philadelphia: University of Pennsylvania Press.

Rosenburg, Marc

1981 The case of the apple turnover. *Nonverbal Communication, Interaction, and Gesture: Selections from Semiotica,* ed. A. Kendon. The Hague: Mouton.

Roszak, Theodore

1979 *Person/Planet: The Creative Disintegration of Industrial Society.* [Garden City, NY: Doubleday.

Rothenberg, Jerome, ed.

1968 *Technicians of the Sacred.* Garden City, NY: Doubleday.

Ruby, Jay, ed.

1982 *A Crack in the Mirror: Reflexive Perspectives in Anthropology.* Philadelphia: University of Pennsylvania Press.

Rumbaugh, Duane, Savage-Rumbaugh, E.S., and Gill, T.

1978 Language skills, cognition and the chimpanzee. *Sign Language and Language Acquisition in Man and Ape,* ed. F.C.C. Peng. Boulder, CO: Westview.

Ryan, Michael

1983 Deconstruction and social theory: the case of liberalism. *Displacement: Derrida and After,* ed. Mark Krupnick. Bloomington, IN: Indiana University Press.

Salmond, Anne

1982 Theoretical landscapes: on a crosscultural conception of knowledge: *Semantic Anthropology,* ed. D. Parkin. New York: Academic Press.

Sampson, Geoffrey

1979 *Liberty and Language.* New York: Oxford University Press.

Sampson, Geoffrey

1980 *Schools of Linguistics.* Stanford, CA: Stanford University Press.

Sapir, Edward

1921 *Language.* New York: Harcourt, Brace and World.

Sapir, Edward

1949 *Selected Writings of Edward Sapir in Language, Culture and Personality,* ed. David Mandelbaum. Berkeley: University of California Press.

Sarles, Harvey

1978 *After Metaphysics.* Lisse: Peter de Ridder.

Saussure, Ferdinand

1959 *Course in General Linguistics,* trans. Wade Baskin. New York: McGraw-Hill.

Saussure, Ferdinand

1974 *Notes Inedits sur Linguistique Generale.* Wiesbaden: Harrassowitz.

Saville-Troike, Muriel

1982 *The Ethnography of Communication: An Introduction.* Oxford: Blackwell.

Schaff, Adam

1973 *Language and Cognition.* New York: McGraw Hill.

Schegloff, Emmanuel

1982 Discourse as an interactional achievement: some uses of 'uh huh' and other things that come between sentences. *Analyzing Discourse: Text and Talk,* ed. D. Tannen. Washington: Georgetown University Press.

Schrag, Calvin

1980 *Radical Reflection and the Origin of the Human Sciences.* West Lafayette, IN: Purdue University Press.

Searle, John

1969 *Speech Acts: An Essay in the Philosophy of Language.* New York: Cambridge University Press.

Searle, John

1974 Chomsky's revolution in linguistics. *On Noam Chomsky: Critical Essays,* ed. G. Harman. Garden City, NJ: Doubleday.

Selye, Hans

1956 *The Stress of Life.* New York: McGraw-Hill.

Shawn, Wallace and Gregory, Andre

1981 *My Dinner with Andre.* New York: Grove.

Shopen, Timothy, ed.

1979a *Languages and Their Speakers.* Cambridge: Winthrop.

Shopen, Timothy, ed.

1979b *Languages and the Status.* Cambridge: Winthrop.

Shopen, Timothy, ed.

1985 *Language Typology and Syntactic Description.* New York: Cambridge University Press.

Silverman, David and Torode, Brian

1980 *The Material Word: Some Theories of Language and Its Limits.* Boston: Routledge and Kegan Paul.

Silverstein, Michael

1976 Shifters, linguistic categories and cultural description. *Meaning in Anthropology,* ed K. Basso and H. Selby. Albuquerque, NM: University of New Mexico Press.

293

Silverstein, Michael

1979 Language structure and linguistic ideology. *The Elements: A Parasession of Linguistic Units and Levels,* ed. P. Clyne, W. Hanks and C. Hofbauer. Chicago: Chicago Linguistics Society.

Simak, Clifford

1952 *City.* Garden City, NJ: Doubleday.

Slater, Philip

1974 *Earthwalk.* Garden City, NY: Doubleday.

Slobin, Dan

1985 *The Cross Linguistic Study of Language Acquisition,* two volumes. Hillsdale, NJ: L. Erlbaum.

Smart, Ninian

1976 *The Phenomenon of Religion.* New York: Macmillan.

Smith, John

1977 *The Behavior of Communicating: An Ethological Approach.* Cambridge: Harvard University Press.

Sommerstein, Alan

1977 *Modern Phonology.* London: Edward Arnold.

Stocking, George

1976 Ideas and institutions in American anthropology: toward a history of the interwar period. *Selected Papers from the American Anthropologist: 1921-1945,* ed. George Stocking. Washington: American Anthropological Association.

Stokoe, William

1961 *Sign Language Structure: An Outline of the Visual Communication Systems of the American Deaf.* Buffalo: University of Buffalo, Occasional Papers, No.8.

Strathern, Marilyn

1985 Knowing power and being equivocal: three Melanesian contexts. *Power and Knowledge: Anthropological and*

Sociological Approaches, ed. R. Fardon. Edinburgh: Scottish Academic Press.

Strathern, Marilyn

1987 The awkward relationship: the case of feminism and anthropology. *Signs* 12 (2): 276-292.

Taylor, David

1982 *Mind.* New York: Simon and Schuster.

Tannen, Deborah

1984 *Conversational Style.* Norwood, NJ: Ablex.

Tartter, Vivien

✓ 1986 *Language Processes.* New York: Holt, Rinehart and Winston.

Tedlock, Dennis

✓ 1983 *The Spoken Word and the Work of Interpretation.* Philadelphia: University of Pennsylvania Press.

Terrace, Herbert

1979 *Nim.* New York: A. Knopf.

Thompson, William I.

1972 *At the Edge of History: Speculations on the Transformation of Culture.* New York: Harper Colophon.

Tinder, Glenn

1980 *Community: Reflections on a Tragic Ideal.* Baton Rouge: Louisiana State University Press.

Toulmin, Stephen

1982a The construal of reality. *The Politics of Interpretation,* ed. W.J.T. Mitchell. Chicago: University of Chicago Press.

Toulmin, Stephen

1982b The genealogy of "consciousness." *Explaining Human Behavior: Consciousness, Human Action, and Social Structure,* ed. Paul Secord. Beverly Hills: Sage.

Trudgill, Peter

1983 *Sociolinguistics.* New York: Penguin.

Turner, Victor

1969 *The Ritual Process: Structure and Anti-Structure.*
Ithaca: Cornell University Press.

Tyler, Stephen

1969 *Cognitive Anthropology.* New York: Holt, Rinehart and
Winston.

Tyler, Stephen

1978 *The Said and the Unsaid: Mind, Meaning, and Culture.*
New York: Academic Press.

Unamuno, Miguel de

1954 [1921] *The Tragic Sense of Life.* New York: Dover.

✓ Urban, Greg

1986 Ceremonial dialogues in South America. *American
Anthropologist* 88 (2): 371-386.

✓ Valdman, Albert, ed.

1977 *Pidgin and Creole Linguistics.* Bloomington: University
of Indiana Press.

✓ Valdman, Albert and Highfield, Arnold, eds.

1980 *Theoretical Orientations in Creole Studies.* New York:
Academic Press.

Valentine, Charles

1972 Black Studies and Anthropology: Scholarly and Political
Interests in Afro-American Culture. (McCaleb Module)
Reading, MA: Addison-Wesley.

Varenne, Herve

1976 Is Dedham American? The diagnosis of things American.
Anthropological Quarterly 231-245.

Varenne, Herve

1983 *American School Language: Culturally Patterned
Conflicts in a Suburban High School.* New York:

Irvington.

Varenne, Herve

1984 Collective representations in American anthropological conversations: individual and culture. *Current Anthropology* 25 (3): 281-299.

Voloshinov, V.N.

1973 *Marxism and the Philosophy of Language.* New York: Seminar Press.

Wagner, Roy

1986 *Symbols that Stand for Themselves.* Chicago: University of Chicago Press.

Wallace, A.F.C.

1961 *Culture and Personality.* New York: Random House.

Washabaugh, William

1977 Constraining variation in decreolization. *Language* 53 (2): 329-352.

Washabaugh, William

1986 *Five Fingers for Survival.* Ann Arbor, MI: Karoma.

Weinstein, Brian

1982 Noah Webster and the diffusion of linguistic innovations for political purposes. *International Journal of the Sociology of Language* 38: 85-108.

Weisskopf, Walter

1971 *Alienation and Economics.* New York: Dutton.

White, Hayden

1980 The value of narrativity in the representation of reality. *On Narrative,* ed. W.J.T. Mitchell. Chicago: University of Chicago Press.

Whitehead, Alfred N.

1929 *The Aims of Education.* New York: Mentor.

Whitney, William D.

    1971 *Selected Writings of W.D. Whitney,* ed. M. Silverstein. Cambridge: MIT.

Whorf, Benjamin L.

    1956 *Language, Thought and Reality: Selected Writings of B.L. Whorf,* ed. John Carroll. Cambridge: MIT.

Wicker, Brian

    1975 *The Story-Shaped World.* London: Athlone Press.

Wilshire, Bruce

    1982 *Role Playing and Identity: The Limits of Theatre as Metaphor.* Bloomington, IN: Indiana University Press.

Wilson, Monica

    1951 *Good Company: A Study of Nyakyusa Age Villages.* Boston: Beacon.

Witherspoon, Gary

    1977 *Language and Art in the Navaho Universe.* Ann Arbor: University of Michigan Pres.

Wittgenstein, Ludwig

    1961 [1921] *Tractatus Logico-Philosphicus,* trans. D.F. Pears, and B.F. McGuiness. Boston: Routledge and Kegan Paul.

Wollheim, Richard

    1984 *The Thread of Life.* Cambridge: Harvard University Press.

Zimmerman, D. and West, C.

    1975 Sex roles, interruptions and silences in conversation. *Language and Sex: Difference and Dominance,* eds. B. Thorne and N. Henley.

301

305